D0893666

Virginia Woolf
and the Great War

Roger Fry, *German General Staff*.
Courtesy of Annabel Cole.

Virginia Woolf
and the Great War

Karen L. Levenback

Syracuse University Press

The paper used in this publication meets the minimum requirements of
American National Standard for Information Sciences—Permanence
of Paper for Printed Library Materials, ANSI Z39.48-1984. ♾™

Library of Congress Cataloging-in-Publication Data

Levenback, Karen L., 1951–
Virginia Woolf and the Great War / Karen L. Levenback.—1st ed..
p. cm.
Includes bibliographical references (p.   ) and index.
ISBN 0-8156-0546-3 (alk. paper)
1. Woolf, Virginia, 1882–1941—Political and social views.
2. Literature and history—England—History—20th century.
3. World War, 1914–1918—England—Literature and the war.
4. War strories, English—History and criticism. I. Title.
PR6045.072Z778 1998
823'.912—dc21   98-27678

To my Michael

Then suddenly, like a chasm in a smooth road, the war came.

—Virginia Woolf, "The Leaning Tower"

Karen L. Levenback teaches at George Washington University. She has written articles for *Woolf Studies Annual*, *English Literature in Transition*, *Virginia Woolf Miscellany*, *Modern Age*, and *The Milton Quarterly*.

CONTENTS

ACKNOWLEDGMENTS

I T IS CUSTOMARY to begin by thanking those who are still around to acknowledge such appreciation. Yet I prefer to begin by remembering with gratitude those who have died since I began the manuscript for Syracuse University Press, and whose encouragement meant a great deal. None died in war. But three, Penny Painter, Stephen Weinrib, and Laura Bigman, died in the war against disease. I also remember the kind assistance and permissions offered by the late Quentin Bell (and his wife, Anne Olivier Bell); the style and good works of Lola Szladits at the Berg Collection; and the collegiality and friendship of Sonya Rudikoff.

This book could never have been done without Michael J. Neufeld, whose historical expertise and knowledge are exceeded only by his love, boundless good nature, and support. I also owe a special debt of gratitude to Estelle Weinrib for her faith both in me and in this project.

Of my many colleagues and friends in the International Virginia Woolf Society, Mark Hussey, who read chapters of the manuscript with a keen eye, scrupulous attention to detail, and unwavering enthusiasm, has been sustaining. I also thank Alex Zwerdling, whose wit, work, and words were a source of inspiration; J. J. Wilson and Lucio Ruotolo, who always found the time to write letters; Judith Johnston for her comments on chapter 2; Helen Wussow for her understanding of manuscript notation; Roger Poole for encouraging the project and inspiring me to begin; Jane Emery and Joanne Trautmann Banks for their generous responses to my questions; and, Mitchell Leaska for lending me a copy of *Pointz Hall*, when it could not even be found at the Library of Congress. I also thank John Fuegi for sharing with me the Gestapo Arrest List for England, which includes the names of Virginia and Leonard Woolf, and Stuart Clarke, who sent me a duplicate of the *Orlando* typescript when I lost confidence in the mails. My thanks goes as well to Diane Gillespie and Wayne Chapman for their help along the way.

Of my friends, colleagues, and family outside the Woolf community, I am grateful to Tod Levenback, who financed the computer upon which the manuscript was written; to Ken Weinrib for offering his legal expertise; to Albert Auster for so willingly getting me a copy of a rare manuscript when I needed it the most; to Miriam Dow for her friendship; to George A. Panichas, who made the Great War live in my imagination and who saw me through my earliest work in this area; to Connie Kibler, Chris Sten, and Lucinda Kilby in the Department of English, George Washington University, who helped to ease the way.

My sincere appreciation goes to Cecil Woolf for so willingly answering my questions and for giving me permission to quote from his letters in the book; to Mrs. Annabel Cole for so graciously giving me permission to use the photograph of Roger Fry's *German General Staff;* to Marilyn Hunt at the Yale Center for British Art for sending me a photograph of Duncan Grant's *In Memorium: Rupert Brooke;* and to Carolyn Russo, Hugh Talman, and Mark Avino for their photographic expertise. I also thank Richard Cork for his long-distance communication.

I am in the debt of librarians and curators who have offered invaluable assistance (or timely loans of microfilm or photocopies) at the Berg Collection, the New York Public Library; Princeton University; Indiana University; the Hoover Institution; Georgetown University; George Washington University; the Library of Congress; the University of Sussex; the British Library; the Imperial War Museum; the National Air and Space Museum, Smithsonian Institution; and the Takoma Park Public Library. I owe special thanks to Bruce Martin and Evelyn Timberlake (at the Library of Congress); Philip Milato and Steve Crook (at the Berg Collection); Rebecca Brown (at the Takoma Park Public Library); Catherine Moriarty (at the Imperial War Museum); Jeremy Crow (at the Society of Authors); Sally Brown (at the British Library); and Elizabeth Inglis (at the University of Sussex).

I thank the readers and editors at Syracuse University Press for their helpful suggestions and good will, especially Cynthia Maude-Gembler, for her unfailing encouragement, and John Fruehwirth, for his patience. Thanks also to Amy Rashap for her time and effort.

And, of course, I gratefully acknowledge the Society of Authors as the literary representative of the Estate of Virginia Woolf for permission to quote from her published works; the Henry W. and Albert Berg Collection, New York Public Library, Astor, Lenox and Tilden Foundation for permitting the use of unpublished and published materials in this book; the British Library for permitting the use of the "Mrs. Dalloway manuscript" (MSS 51044-51046, 3 vols.); Harcourt Brace & Company for permitting the use of words from *The Diary of Virginia Woolf,* 1; *Mrs. Dalloway; To the Lighthouse;* and *The Years.* Earlier versions of this work have appeared in *Woolf Studies Annual* 2 (1996); *Selected Papers from the Fourth Annual Conference on Virginia Woolf* (1995); the *Virginia Woolf Miscellany* (issues 33, 37, and 42); and *Virginia Woolf and War* (Syracuse University Press, 1991).

Finally, this book may never have been written if my late grandfather, Meyer Levenback, had not survived in the Argonne Forest during the Great War and if my parents, Gloria and Jerry Levenback, lacked serendipity in arranging my birth on Armistice Day. And, most certainly, it would never have been written without the constant companionship of Mister P, his successor Newt, and kindred spirits Birch and Kepler.

Karen L. Levenback
Takoma Park, Maryland
June 1998

ABBREVIATIONS

References in the text to the following works, not explained in the endnotes, are to the editions indicated below.

3G Virginia Woolf. *Three Guineas*. 1938. San Diego: Harcourt Brace Jovanovich, 1966.

A to Z Mark Hussey. *Virginia Woolf A to Z: A Comprehensive Reference for Students, Teachers and Common Readers to Her Life, Work and Critical Reception*. New York: Facts on File, 1995.

BA Virginia Woolf. *Between the Acts*. 1941. San Diego: Harcourt, Brace Jovanovich, 1969.

BgA Leonard Woolf. *Beginning Again: An Autobiography of the Years 1911 to 1918*. New York: Harcourt Brace Jovanovich, 1964.

BPP Sigmund Freud. *Beyond the Pleasure Principle*. Trans. James Strachey. 1919. New York: W. W. Norton, 1961.

CA Søren Kierkegaard. *The Concept of Anxiety. A Simple Psychologically Orienting Deliberation on the Dogmatic Issue of Hereditary Sin*. 1844 Ed. and trans. by Reidar Thomte. Princeton: Princeton Univ. Press, 1980.

CI Søren Kierkegaard. *The Concept of Irony, with Continual Reference to Socrates*. Trans. Howard V. Hong and Edna H. Hong. Princeton, N.J.: Princeton Univ. Press, 1989.

CW Michel de Montaigne. *Complete Works*. Trans. Donald M. Frame. 1948. Stanford, Calif.: Stanford Univ. Press, 1989.

Collected Essays Virginia Woolf. *Collected Essays*. 4 vols. Ed. Leonard Woolf. New York: Harcourt, Brace and World, 1967.

Diary Virginia Woolf. *The Diary of Virginia Woolf*. Ed. Anne Olivier Bell. 5 vols. San Diego: Harcourt Brace Jovanovich, 1977–84.

Downhill   Leonard Woolf. *Downhill All the Way: An Autobiography of the Years 1919 to 1939*. New York: Harcourt Brace Jovanovich, 1967.

Essays   Virginia Woolf. *The Essays of Virginia Woolf*. Ed. Andrew McNeillie. San Diego: Harcourt Brace Jovanovich, 1986 (vol. 1, 1904–12); 1987 (vol. 2, 1912–18); 1988 (vol. 3, 1919–24).

Journey   Leonard Woolf. *The Journey Not the Arrival Matters: An Autobiography of the Years 1939 to 1969*. New York.: Harcourt Brace Jovanovich, 1969.

JR   Virginia Woolf. *Jacob's Room*. 1922. San Diego: Harcourt Brace Jovanovich, 1950.

Kp   B. J. Kirkpatrick. *A Bibliography of Virginia Woolf*. 3d ed. Oxford, England: Clarendon, 1980.

Letters   Virginia Woolf. *The Letters of Virginia Woolf*. Ed. Nigel Nicolson and Joanne Trautman. 6 vols. New York: Harcourt Brace Jovanovich, 1975–80.

Lighthouse   Mitchell Leaska. *Virginia Woolf's Lighthouse: A Study in Critical Method*. New York: Columbia Univ. Press, 1970.

MrsD   Virginia Woolf. *Mrs. Dalloway*. 1925. San Diego: Harcourt Brace Jovanovich, 1953.

RF   Virginia Woolf. *Roger Fry: A Biography*. 1940. New York: Harcourt Brace Jovanovich, 1968.

Room   Virginia Woolf. *A Room of One's Own*. 1929. San Diego: Harcourt Brace Jovanovich, 1957.

Spotts   Frederic Spotts, ed. *Letters of Leonard Woolf*. San Diego: Harcourt Brace Jovanovich, 1989.

Times   *Times of London*

TL   Virginia Woolf. *To the Lighthouse*. 1927. San Diego: Harcourt Brace Jovanovich, 1955.

TLS   *Times Literary Supplement*

VW   Quentin Bell. *Virginia Woolf: A Biography*. New York.: Harcourt Brace Jovanovich, 1972.

"War and Death."   Sigmund Freud. "Reflections upon War Death" 1915. Trans. E Colburn Maynes. *Character and Culture*: 107–33.

Years   Virginia Woolf. *The Years*. 1937. San Diego: Harcourt Brace Jovanovich, 1965.

Reference in the text to the "Berg Collection, NYPL" is to the Henry W. and Albert A. Berg Collection, New York Public Library, Astor Lenox and Tilden Foundations. References in the text to Roger Poole, *The Unknown Virginia Woolf* are to the 3rd edition.

Virginia Woolf
and the Great War

INTRODUCTION

IT IS EASY ENOUGH to forget that Virginia Woolf *lived* through the Great War. But she did. Recalled by her husband as "the least political animal . . . since Aristotle invented the definition" (L. Woolf, *Downhill,* 27), she was subsequently represented by her nephew as having shown little interest in this war or any other (Q. Bell, *Virginia Woolf* 2, 23). This figuration gained popular acceptance not only because Woolf was thought "mad" or because she was a woman but also because she had been a civilian, and, as Lord Northcliffe said in *At the War* (1917), the war was "a regular business" run by the military and civilians were intruders or outsiders (37). Northcliffe, a newspaper mogul and (in 1918) director of propaganda in foreign nations, had visited the front lines in civilian garb, and speaking from this personal experience, had acknowledged (in a footnote) "the great part played by women in the effective running of the war" (29n), particularly those who did "manly" occupations as part of the war effort. Yet, Virginia Woolf had neither these experiences nor occupations.

Subsequently, without a historical framework, when Woolf and her writings were evoked, the word *war* was used as a metaphor—or, seemingly taking a cue from the narrowly interpreted (and widely misinterpreted) *Three Guineas* (1938)—defined solely in terms of a feminist peace polemic. In *Women and War* Jean Bethke Elshtain calls *Three Guineas* a "classic tract" about the war between the sexes (235), and studies involving Woolf and the real world regard her as an "instinctive pacifist" (Zwerdling 272) and war as signifying that "commensurability between man and nature" is an "illusion" (Hussey, *Singing,* 113). But to Virginia Woolf, whatever the associations or connotations, after 1914 war was not a figure of speech. She saw its experience, on the front or at home, as its history—yet increasingly its constructions had replaced individual memory and become its reality.

Not surprisingly, in the seventies, during the resurrection of interest in the Great War, Virginia Woolf and her contribution were roundly ignored. She had, after all, seen the war from the streets of London and in the village of Asheham—not from the Somme or in Flanders fields. "The Generation of 1914," to apply the title of Robert Wohl's study, included, significantly, only combatants, as did Eric Leed's *No Man's Land*. Paul Fussell's *The Great War and Modern Memory*, a germinal cultural text suggesting the mythic dimensions of the experience on the western front, found little worth remembering of Woolf's work after *Jacob's Room* (1922), whose significance was reduced to involve only a young man destined to "play his part in an unthought-of kind of amateur theater, where he will be destroyed" (230). Excluded from such representations of the war were not only Virginia Woolf, her husband, and their friends in and around Bloomsbury but also the civilian population. This oversight went unnoticed, even though it was generally agreed that "[t]he distinction of combatants and bystanders is enormously important in the theory of war" (Walzer 30), and has only become part of the discourse as such categorical differences have become increasingly blurred. Studies such as Sandra Gilbert and Susan Gubar's three-volume *No Man's Land; Behind the Lines* (Higonnet and Jenson, eds.); *Arms and the Woman* (Cooper et al, eds.); Claire Tylee's *The Great War and Women's Consciousness;* Dorothy Goldman's edited volume *Women and World War I;* and, to some extent, Samuel Hynes's *A War Imagined* signal movement in that direction. Yet, although George Mosse's *Fallen Soldiers* and Morris Eksteins's *Rites of Spring* involve memory and constructions of the war, and Martin Gilbert's recent book, *The First World War,* is subtitled "A Complete History," they ignore Virginia Woolf and her contribution.

Mark Hussey's collection *Virginia Woolf and War* (1991) augments interpretations and appreciation of Woolf both because it identifies her as a "theorist of war" and because it "recognizes the centrality of war in her life's work" (Hussey, "Living," 3). The volume's unanimity in subject, whatever the approach, suggests an antiwar message as informed as that of any combatant. Each of the essays published in the volume (including my own, which is an early version of chapter 1), disputes the notion that Virginia Woolf had been an impassive bystander whose interest in the war was "negligible," thus suggesting the need to reexamine not only our appraisal of Woolf's achievement but also the ways in which we measure it. Her novels, even those traditionally believed to be nonpolitical (like *The Waves* [1931]) or to have no connection to war (like *The Voyage Out* [1915]), are deconstructed and reconstructed to evidence Woolf's sense of the "fiction, reality, and myth" of war, the collection's subtitle. Thereafter, references to war in both her personal and formal writings became significant markers in the study of women's consciousness of war. More recently, studies of war and gender take Woolf to account, like *Gendering War Talk* (1993), a volume that includes Sarah Ruddick's "Notes Toward a Feminist Peace Politics," an essay that begins where Woolf herself ends: by recognizing that the chasm dividing civilians and combatants is an illusion.

Yet, neither these views nor the profoundly important *The Body in Pain* (Scarry) has had a significant impact on the wider genre of war writings and theory, an ironic and at the same time tragic oversight given the increasingly blurred line between civilians and combatants. Alarmingly, we see this most recently in the reinvention of the nuclear threat in India and Pakistan, and before that in Bosnia, Rwanda, and Zaire (the Democratic Republic of the Congo); in "civilian bombing, wars of national liberation, civil wars, and genocide" (cited in Cooke and Woollacott, "Introduction," *Gendering War Talk*, ix); and, repeatedly, in acts of terrorism. Even if Woolf's "version of th[e] feminist/antimilitarist weave" is acknowledged (Ruddick, 109), most historians (even literary historians like Hynes and certainly military historians like John Keegan) continue to privilege a masculinist combatant standard when it comes to the experience of war and its narratives. This practice, evidenced in Keegan's *A History of Warfare* and discussed in the excellent *Blood Rites* (Ehrenreich), is apparent not only in the selection of combatant texts for literary anthologies like *The Norton Book of Modern War* (Paul Fussell, ed.) but also in the works analyzed in critical texts like Evelyn Cobley's *Representing War,* all of which are written by or about combatants (albeit, as with Cobley, to demonstrate the subversive intention of these narratives). The assumption that all things related to war can be accounted for in books that, like those mentioned above, disregard or give lip service to the civilian population remains in effect, even as the historian Jay Winter continues to expand the parameters of Great War history to include civilians.[1] Although the boundaries of Woolf studies have widened to in-

---

1. Jay (also J. W.) Winter has made a great contribution to our understanding of the history of the home front during the Great War and is currently editing "The Legacy of the Great War" series for Berg Publishers (Oxford, England). However, the only volume in the series to acknowledge Virginia Woolf's contribution (Sharon Ouditt, *Fighting Forces,* 1994) ignores all sources published on the topic after 1986 (including Mark Hussey, ed., *Virginia Woolf and War* 1991). Two volumes not in the series (Allyson Booth, *Postcards from the Trenches* [1996], and Suzanne Raitt and Trudi Tate, eds., *Women's Fiction and the Great War* [1997]) were, regrettably, not published in time to be included in this study.

clude historicist treatments, such as Kathy Phillips's *Virginia Woolf against Empire* (1994) and Michael Tratner's *Modernism and Mass Politics* (1995), Woolf remains a conditional figure in war literature and of negligible importance in the history of the Great War.

Woolf's life and work have not been seen to have been directly affected by her experience of the Great War, even by those who have a biographical interest in Woolf. Notwithstanding the recent contribution made in *Virginia Woolf* (1997) by Hermione Lee,[2] a significant amount of the autobiographical material today available in her published letters, memoirs, and diaries (as well as in unpublished materials) has been reduced, simplified, and deprived of a context that gives them meaning and value both in the study of war and in the study of her war polemic. At the same time, this reduction empties Woolf of full credit for what Alex Zwerdling calls her "great range and extraordinary powers of transformation" (2), even as these powers extend beyond the vision of some combatants, and past the actual fighting. Certainly we can find evidence of the limiting effect of combat in the poetry of Ivor Gurney, who went mad—or in Siegfried Sassoon, who did not.

In fact, any effort to assess Woolf's writings or her life without a sense of her experience of the Great War is as incomplete as it would be in a study of Robert Graves, for example, who was a combatant, or D. H. Lawrence, who, like the Woolfs, remained a civilian. Roger Poole, whose phenomenological *The Unknown Virginia Woolf* is now in its fourth edition, makes the case that her novels speak "of the obsessive themes of the period of life to which it refers or in which it was conceived" but offers no special place to the Great War, even though he is sensitive to its importance (see his "'We all'"). And, although Panthea Reid, the author of a recent biography of Virginia Woolf (*Art and Affection,* 1996), aims to break the time-honored practice of shaping evidence to follow theory by penetrating the "periphery" of Woolf's life ("On Writing"), she does not guarantee a reorientation along the lines I follow here. The common assumption is that Woolf's "pacifism" rests on her experience of what Quentin Bell calls "skirmishes" in the nursery and childhood fistfights with her brother Thoby (see Bell, *VW* I, 23, 43)—and the prewar "Dreadnought Hoax," which remains, quite literally, a footnote in military history (see Massie 489–90n). Important studies, including Jane Marcus's defense of historicism, "The Asylums of Antaeus," use

2. Hermione Lee's impressive biography was published just as I completed the final manuscript of this study. Reading it would undoubtedy have enriched my findings.

Woolf to suggest that "history and literature deserve equal narrative force in a cultural text" (134). Still others (such as the groundbreaking works of Lynne Hanley and Pat Barker) blur the boundaries between biography, history, and literature altogether. And, because there are such obvious benefits to this approach, there is also a possibility that the absence of boundaries will deprive us of both the pleasure of and insight from tracing the sometimes circuitous, but always purposeful, route taken by Virginia Woolf in coming to terms with her own experience of the war.

My focus in this book, then, is on the *development* of what I see as Woolf's war-consciousness, that is, her progressive vision of how representations of the Great War in the popular press and official histories affected the people she describes in her personal, nonfictional, and fictional writings. Significantly, in "The Leaning Tower," based on a speech she delivered to the Workers Educational Association in 1940, she chooses "chasm" to represent not the Great War, but its constructions. She observes that in the nineteenth century, wars were seen as "remote," the division between combatants and "private people" absolute: "Then, suddenly, like a chasm in a smooth road, the [Great] war came" (164, 167). Her characterization is based on the seemingly seamless history of the prewar world and suggests the unlikelihood of significant change. Anticipating the loss of distinction between civilians and combatants, Woolf looks back to the nineteenth century to identify modes of representation that shaped perceptions of the war. In fact, the language she uses ("hedges," for example, and "gulf") suggests that what we read about war in authorized sources may take us further from recognizing the real threat of modern war and encourage us to retain a nineteenth-century illusion of (civilian) immunity. Yet, this way of representing the division between civilians and combatants is inadequate to explain the dynamics of "writing war" (to use Hanley's phrase) as Woolf comes to see it. Significantly, in "The Leaning Tower" even the poet has entered into the business of war and the chasm between the "artist and politics" (the title of a 1932 article) has been deconstructed: no one enjoys immunity from war. This may explain why Woolf was puzzled by the fact that the leaning-tower poets, a special category of artist to her mind, had not been touched by antiwar war poets like Wilfred Owen, that they retained belief in an illusion of immunity built of their class and education. Yet the Woolfs' friends and colleagues in and around Bloomsbury (Vera Brittain, for example, and Rebecca West, Rose Macaulay, and Beatrice Webb), like the Woolfs themselves (see Chapman and Manson), had played a part in the effort to keep the war and its experience alive in popular consciousness. Importantly, the leaning-tower poets were not alone in ignoring the lesson of Owen; like educated men, Woolf observes in *Three Guineas,* many working men "are of opinion that Wilfred Owen was wrong" (8).

Woolf's depiction of the relationship between popular consciousness and constructions of the Great War is examined in this book. "Popular consciousness" here refers to the merging of what is read with what is remembered, thought, felt, and done; and "constructions" refers to representations of what is directly observed, as in a journalist's report, to name one tangible example, or a memoir, or its fictional counterpart, the novel. That Woolf herself represents the correspondence between them paradoxically growing with the fading of memory (or what Husserl calls "retentions" [59]) suggests that checks on "official" versions of history were breaking down, an observation that Woolf found as personally disturbing as it was creatively challenging.

Where explaining such correspondences in this study requires a psychological base, I rely on Freud (who, like Woolf, was a civilian during the war). Where they need a historico-cultural base, Montaigne (whom Woolf read during and after the war) adds insight, as well as Kierkegaard, Husserl, Buber, Bergson, Barthes, and Foucault, each of whom has made constructions of memory, history, and consciousness his life's study. By invoking "realities," the "real world," and, more often, "reality" (sometimes ironically, sometimes as a shorthand term for the phenomenological world of direct, that is, "lived experience" [Husserl 116]), I am referring to those things that exist independent of consciousness, though they are open to direct perception—and indirect communication. Woolf's sense of this chasm in particular undoubtedly moved her to find in fictional combatant characters a vehicle to express her nuanced vision of the war, sometimes when juxtaposed with their civilian counterparts.

In the context of war, the word "civilian" refers to an outsider to military service, someone who presumably stands on the safer side of what Jay Winter calls the "unbridgeable existential divide in the experience of war" (*Great War,* 305). Political scientist Michael Walzer recognizes that there is a lack of sympathy for civilians in military philosophy, which generally regards civilians as "useless mouths" (160)—or worse. The singularly influential Carl von Clausewitz, for example, is nominally deferential to "civilian authority," but never envisaged that "civilized war" would significantly involve civilians.

Clearly, Virginia Woolf was neither a military historian of the Great War nor a military strategist. Yet, her continued interest in the condition of civilians who became combatants and combatants who returned to civilian life points to her sense that the chasm dividing the population owed as much to representations of the war as to class or gender. In fact, in the major novels included in this study (*Jacob's Room, Mrs. Dalloway, To the Lighthouse, The Years,* and *Between the Acts*), Woolf demonstrates a progressive awareness of the ways in which the situations of soldiers and civilians are linked by the very realities of war that are ignored both by history and theory.

At the same time, her sense of this transgression is tested by her understanding of how official language finally deprives the word "war" of its horror. An important connection among the novels is seen as their narratives focus on the ways characters, or narrators themselves, respond when the language of war is so deprived of its emotional underpinnings that war itself cannot be described. So, in *Between the Acts,* by the time Giles Oliver is ready to express his outrage at the prevalence of an illusion of immunity from the next war, he cannot find the words.

> Giles nicked his chair into position with a jerk. Thus only could he show his irritation, his rage with old fogies who sat and looked at views over coffee and cream when the whole of Europe—over there—was bristling like. . . .
> He had no command of metaphor. Only the ineffective word "hedgehog" illustrated his vision of Europe, bristling with guns, poised with planes. (53)

The intention here is ironical: war is seen as metaphorical. In the context of direct experience, in Woolf's essay "Thoughts on Peace in an Air Raid" (1940), for example, such literary language disappears and there are no hedgehogs. The experience, like the language is direct and the danger is real.

> All the searchlights are erect. They point at a spot exactly above this roof. At any moment a bomb may fall on this very room. One, two, three, four, five, six . . . the seconds pass. The bomb does not fall. But during those seconds of suspense all thinking stopped. All feeling save one dull dread, ceased. (176)

What marks these passages, and links them with others in Woolf's work, is her sense of how the language of war has been deprived of the terror and horror it should inspire, so much so that war itself inspires only a "dull dread." The important words here are "all," "feeling," and "ceased."

The important idea in regard to writing war refers to what we remember: "Directly that fear passes, the mind reaches out and instinctively revives itself by trying to create. Since the room is dark it can create only from memory" (176). This way of representing the chasms created between individual memories and constructions of the war is central to understanding the evolution of Woolf's own war-consciousness. It involves transgressive representations and an ongoing process of reorientation, one that becomes more pressing as World War II gets under way. No such reorientation seems to occur to the combatant characters who survive the war and return to England, whatever their class and gender: Septimus Warren Smith and North Pargiter both remain outsiders to the civilian world and its constructions of the war. The opportunity to explore such marginalization in her nonfiction and especially in her fiction is certainly one reason that the Great War remains a constant presence in her writing. What I hope to show in this book is that it was also a constant presence in her life.

Myths of war, illusions of immunity, and realities of survival are recalled, remembered, and observed by Virginia Woolf and can be seen in her work from 1914 to 1941. Memory of the war in *Jacob's Room, Mrs. Dalloway, To the Lighthouse, The Years,* and *Between the Acts* is represented by distinct civilian voices that sometimes serve as surrogates for the author in their narrative functions. As she was writing *The Years,* which may be seen as her most ironic history of the war on the streets (what she called a "novel of fact"), she noted, "A complete reversal to pre-war days" (*Diary* 4, 304). But only after Woolf wrote *Three Guineas,* her ironic answer to war, did she admit, whatever the preparations and expectations, 1939 was not 1914 all over again: "Gradually the sense of siege being normal replaced the fear—the individual fear" (*Diary* 5, 243). Representation had replaced memory; and memory, reality. What I have tried to suggest in this book is how the representations of the Great War had an impact on the memory of Woolf and her fellow survivors, or discouraged it—and, how the herd instinct won after all.

1

Myths of War, Illusions of Immunity, Realities of Survival

> What matters is that lives do not serve as models; only
> stories do that. . . . We can only retell and live by stories we
> have read or heard. . . . Whatever their form or medium,
> these stories have formed us all.
>
> — Carolyn Heilbrun, *Writing a Woman's Life*

> Received war stories may lull our critical faculties to sleep.
>
> — Jean Bethke Elshtain, *Women and War*

1

HAVING REMAINED on the the home front during the Great War, Virginia Woolf was asked by Bruce Richmond, editor of the *Times Literary Supplement,* to review a number of books, some implicitly or explicitly involving experiences of and in the Great War. Woolf had last written for the *TLS* in 1913 and Richmond must have been hard put for reviewers, particularly in 1916, the year conscription began. For her part, Woolf had published her first novel, *The Voyage Out,* in 1915 and welcomed the work. Yet, notwithstanding her frequent mention of the war in her letters and diary, she made little reference either to her one article involving the war ("Heard on the Downs: The Genesis of Myth" in 1916) or to her seven reviews of war-related volumes. In this corpus of published work, however, particularly in "War in the Village" (written during the last year of the Great War) and "The War from the Street" (published two months after the signing of the armistice on 11 November 1918 and five months before the signing of the Treaty of Versailles that officially ended the war), we can trace Woolf's struggle to find a voice that would illuminate both the reality of civilian isolation from the war and the illusion of immunity this isolation engendered, themes which Woolf develops in her postwar fiction, nonfiction, and personal writings.

Virginia Woolf was a civilian, a noncombatant during the Great War. What history called the "real" experience of war was not afforded her; unlike Wilfred Owen, she did not see "God through mud" and unlike her friend Rupert Brooke, who died in Greece before experiencing the war from the front, she was temperamentally, sexually, and, like her husband Leonard, physically unsuited for such an experience. Moreover, she was unwilling to take the leap of faith that inspired "patriotic sentiment" (which she found "revolting" [*Letters* 2, 57]) and that in turn led so many to join the military, and others to join what Lord Northcliffe called "the army behind the army" (9), the British Red Cross Society, for example. Virginia Woolf lived through the war on the streets of London (largely at Hogarth House) and in Asheham House, near the village of Firle; and, from time to time, in 1914–15, at a rest facility in Twickenham or confined to bed at home. What we see in her wartime writings, particularly those after the death of Rupert Brooke in April 1915, is a movement toward understanding that the sense of immunity from effects of the war—shared by much of the civilian population—was an illusion.

That the death of Rupert Brooke marked a change in Woolf's vision of the war has been generally overlooked, in part because of her reluctance to come to terms with the fact of war and the possibility of personal death owing to it. The irony of this disbelief, expressed indirectly and from an elevated vantage, sometimes by members of her circle of friends, was not lost on Woolf, notwithstanding her temperamental aversion to the fact of war in general and to this war, her first, in particular. The day before the declaration of war her response was mild bemusement and curiosity at the atmosphere; several months later, she assumed a self-conscious affectation of false modesty and claimed to have "foretold the murder of the Archduke" (*Letters* 2, 54). On 3 August 1914, when she wrote from Asheham to her sister, Vanessa Bell, Woolf had kept the tone light, asking for a loan because "if war breaks out, we shall probably be in difficulties for ready money." At the same time, she thought the atmosphere reminiscent of "Napoleonic times": "We are just (4. P.M.) off to Lewes to get a paper. There were none at breakfast this morning, but the postman brought rumours that 2 of our warships were sunk—however, when we did get papers we found that peace still exists—save for a stop press message that England has joined in. It is rather like Napoleonic times I daresay, and being a Bank holiday of course makes us more remote from life than ever" (*Letters* 2, 50).[1]

1. Interestingly, according to Lee Kennett, "It was a dictum of Napoleonic warfare—still quoted in 1914—that when the enemy's capital came under bombardment, the war

Her sense of remove from life may, in part, explain her comment to her friend (and Rupert Brooke's former lover) Ka Cox nine days later that "I never felt anything like the general insecurity," yet it does not suggest a dispassionate disregard of the war, as Quentin Bell, Andrew McNeillie, and others assert,[2] but a sense of disbelief, one that seemed offset with something like expectation, as she both received and sought out information about the war:

> We left Asheham a week ago, and it was practically under martial law. There were soldiers marching up and down the line, and men digging trenches and it was said that Asheham barn was to be used as a hospital. All the people expected an invasion—Then we went through London—and oh Lord! what a lot of talk there was! Roger [Fry], of course, had private information from the Admiralty, and had been seeing the German Ambassadress, and Clive [Bell] was having tea with Ottoline [Morrell], and they talked and talked, and said it was the end of civilisation, and the rest of our lives was worthless. I do wish you would write and tell us what you hear—They say there must be a great battle, and here, where we are 15 miles from the North Sea, they expect to be in the midst of it, but then so they did at Seaford. (*Letters* 2, 51)

Even in the last few lines there is an implicit sense of immunity: what will happen happens to and involves "them," notwithstanding "our" proximity and her own access to second- (or third-) hand news from the admiralty. Moreover, despite the immediate popular animation the declaration of war aroused, Woolf would see that "business goes on as usual" and would lament as pacifist articles finally began to appear in the papers "how little one believes what anyone says now [about the war]" (*Diary* 1, 65; *Letters* 2, 178).

---

was considered over" (43). There were frequent comparisons in the press between current events in August and Napoleonic times. On 1 August 1914, for example, three days before the beginning of the Great War and the anniversary of Lord Nelson's victory over Napoleon at the Battle of the Nile, the *Times* commemorates "A Great Naval Anniversary" (9) and invokes Nelson in an article on "England's Duty" in a column called "The War Day by Day" (6).

2. Not surprisingly, besides Quentin Bell (particularly in his *Virginia Woolf: A Biography*) and Andrew McNeillie (particularly his commentary in *Essays* 2), one must add Nigel Nicolson and Joanne Trautmann [Banks] (editors of the *Letters,* particularly the commentary in vol. 2) and Anne Olivier Bell (editor of the *Diary,* particularly in vol. 1) to the group that believes Woolf's interest in the war was "negligible." Although this point of view has been more and more called into question (as I suggest in the introduction to this book) even in *Bloomsbury Recalled* (1995), Quentin Bell remains more or less convinced of his position, which, like Leonard's, involves a definition of politics at variance with that of Virginia Woolf and rather begs the question (see Appendix, "A Room of One's Own and Three Guineas": 212–20).

Until April 1915, however, Woolf's consciousness of the war seems linked to the facts of life during its progress, sometimes directly, as in the possible shortage of ready cash, or indirectly, as in her observation of "patriotic sentiment." The facts of life and experience or perception of these, as demonstrated by both Mark Hussey and Alex Zwerdling, were Woolf's measure of reality, or, to use Kierkegaard's term, "actuality."[3] The war was not a reality unless there were human costs, and until April 1915 there seemed few enough of those—a bit of rationing and the emergence of what Woolf called the "base emotion" of patriotism (*Diary* 1, 5) made for some unease, but these inconveniences also allowed Woolf to question the war's reality, our "view of reality" being, in Woolf's words, "the world we know" ("Notes on an Elizabethan Play," 54). In other words, to quote Mark Hussey, reality was seen as something that had its "rootedness in lived experience" (*Singing*, 97). In spite of aeroplanes and zeppelins flying overhead, Woolf wrote on 1 February 1915 that "it always seems utterly impossible that one should be hurt" (*Diary* 1, 32). This sense of civilian immunity may have been in part Woolf's response to the promulgation of rote patriotism; with it, however, she "could feel . . . the entire absence of emotion," not only in herself but also in "everyone else" (*Diary* 1, 5). This was a reality effected by the leap of faith newspapers encouraged.

---

3. Alex Zwerdling, in his fine and important *Virginia Woolf and the Real World*, identifies "the real world" as "the whole range of external forces that may be said to influence our behavior: family ideals, societal expectations, institutional demands, significant historical events or movements that affect our lives." Zwerdling also notes that "[t]he phrase 'the real world' is often used ironically, both to suggest some hostility to its rules and to record an awareness that our attempts to ignore them are futile" (4). As I said in my review of the book, "The real world, in Zwerdling's hands, provides the context for revealing Woolf's sensitivity to both the pull of past traditions and the push of present contingencies that militate against their continuance" (170–71). In *The Singing of the Real World*, Mark Hussey draws on Harvena Richter's comment that Woolf's "examination of her own encounter with lived experience was transmuted into the novel's form" and centers his study on the "circularity" of Woolf's vision. "Virginia Woolf's art," he writes, "tells us not about an external, objective Reality, but about our *experience* of the world" (xiii).

Louise Levesque-Lopman's feminist "reconsideration" of phenomenological sociology in *Claiming Reality*, aims at coming to terms with the need for a more inclusive paradigm so as to make the invisible visible. Kierkegaard—and indeed Woolf herself—anticipate this reconsideration. In *The Concept of Irony*, it is "actuality" that admits irony as a bridge between phenomena in the outside world and absolute subjectivity (242). Yet, according to Kierkegaard, "the point is that, having embraced the ordinary use of language, one comes to see that the various meanings the word has acquired in the course of time can still all be included here" (245).

The war for the civilian and would-be combatant had been, in fact, fictionalized through what John Terraine calls "the tyranny of the Northcliffe Press" (10) and mythologized in a history that was, in Woolf's words, "all morality and battles" (*Diary* 2, 115), leaving the population at home in a state of what Paul Fussell calls "civilian incomprehension" (*Great War,* 87). Woolf seemed to suspect, particularly in the early years of the war, that the government and the press were engaged in a conspiracy aimed at hoodwinking the unthinking or searching young, such as Rupert Brooke, her friend, and Cecil and Philip Woolf, her brothers-in-law, into becoming players in the drama of war, an effect seen in almost every novel written in the postwar period—in Jacob Flanders, in Septimus Smith, in Andrew Ramsay, in Percival, in North Pargiter, and even (not to cut too fine a point) in Giles Oliver. Whether they go "to save an England which consisted almost entirely of Shakespeare's plays and Miss Isabel Pole in a green dress walking in a square" (*MrsD,* 130) or become part of the "Royal Regiment of Rat-catchers" (*Years,* 285), they go—to return, like Septimus Smith, "shell-shocked," or not to return, like Jacob Flanders and Andrew Ramsay. She was referring to the "damned newspapers" when she called the war "this preposterous masculine fiction" in 1916 (*Letters* 2, 76); it was the newspapers that eschewed the reality of war and made it appear nonthreatening to those at the home front.

Woolf might be represented as having enjoyed a privileged position, sometimes being (in her words) "in touch with one [like Herbert Fisher, or Maynard Keynes, or even Philip Morrell] who was in the very centre of the very centre, sitting in a little room at Downing St. where, as he said . . . the fate of armies does more or less hang upon what two or three elderly gentlemen decide" (*Diary* 1, 204), words she would use again in *Jacob's Room.* But she was aware that, to use Rupert Brooke's words, she was receiving "third-hand muffled . . . news from the Real World," which made both rumors and newspaper reports suspect.[4]

Rupert Brooke's death seems the pivotal event that moved the war into the real world for Virginia Woolf by becoming closely tied to what Hussey calls "temporality," which, he argues, is closely allied to a kind of "religion" (*Singing,* xx) or spirituality. Yet, it seems to me that in the years between the wars, spirituality was conflated with the accretions of war memory and the

4 Brooke in a letter to Virginia Woolf in 1912, wrote that he had heard of her rumored breakdown "in the thirdhand muffled manner I get my news from the Real World" (*Letters of Rupert Brooke,* 364). The relationship between Brooke and Woolf and some of its implications are examined in my "Virginia Woolf and Rupert Brooke: Poised Between Olympus and the 'Real World.'"

ongoing institutional (public) memorialization of combatant death. At no time had the temporal reality of death been more in evidence than in the Great War and nowhere was Woolf's consciousness of her helplessness in the face of it more frustrating. Having been childhood friends, Woolf and Brooke grew together owing to their common literary bent and the diagnoses of their common literary "disease" of "hypersensitivit[y] and introspection," both having been under the care of Dr. Maurice Craig.[5] The diagnosis had not prevented Brooke from being accepted in September 1914 as an officer in the British Naval Division (which was an infantry unit drawn from naval volunteers[6]); he died, presumably of blood poisoning, on 23 April 1915, while awaiting action in the Gallipoli.[7] Although it is not known exactly when in that year Woolf learned of his death (Woolf was under the constant care of nurses in March, April, May, and into June), it is clear that in the last two years of the war she turned her sharp powers of observation to evidence of both the civilian sense of immunity and its source, seeking the truth that the reality of death obscured.

In the aftermath of his death, mourners were divided into those who knew Rupert Brooke and those who saw how his death could be exploited. The obituary written by his friend and patron Edward Marsh and printed anonymously in the *Times* on 26 April begins with elegant simplicity: "He died before he had fulfilled his own hopes or ours; but either we believe in waste altogether or not at all. And if any seeming waste is not waste, there is none in a young life full of promise and joyfully laid down" (quoted in Lehmann, 150). The death of Rupert Brooke was most timely, his popular deification having already begun with the *Times* account of Dean Inge's Easter sermon at St. Paul's, which had included lines from one of Brooke's "War Sonnets" ("Dean Inge" 5 April 1915, 8). Three weeks later, Winston Churchill, First Lord of the Admiralty, offered his own elegiac myth, calling Brooke one of "England's noblest sons" and lamenting the loss of his "clas-

5. See Hassall, 313, 332–33; Trombley, 183–208; Levenback, "Virginia Woolf and Rupert Brooke," 6.

6. This is not to be confused with the navy, which, as it turns out, was the least risky of the armed forces. Based on the statistical findings—that during the Great War there were 23,000 deaths in the Royal Navy as compared with 677,515 deaths in the British armies—Colin McIntyre's claim that "it was clearly much safer to be part of the war at sea than serving in the trenches" seems reasonable (39).

7. William Laskowski, in an effort to correct the myths and countermyths that Brooke's death engendered, explains that Brooke fell ill after visiting Egypt, en route to Gallipoli. The cause of his death was undoubtedly cumulative, as he had suffered from sunstroke and dysentery, but the fatal blow was probably an insect bite (29).

sical symmetry of mind and body," a description realized in the photograph included in Brooke's posthumously published *1914 and Other Poems,* which was, in the words of Robert Wohl, "highly stylized" and "heavily touched up." His friends, Wohl continues, "considered it obscene" (quoted in Lehmann, 151; *Generation,* 91).

No one objected to the distorted and manipulated vision of Rupert Brooke more than Virginia Woolf, though she largely confined her detractions to those who, like her, were appalled by it. Her public review of Edward Marsh's *The Collected Poems of Rupert Brooke: With a Memoir* ("Rupert Brooke"), like Brooke's public glorification of the war (something that contributed to the myths and countermyths his death inspired [see Laskowski]), was muted in contrast to her private view of it, just as Brooke's published writings masked his own complex and sometimes conflicting emotions. In a letter to Ka Cox, Woolf called the biography "repulsive," and criticized Marsh for having "contrived to make the [Brooke] letters as superficial and affected as his own account of Rupert" (*Letters* 2, 267–68). To Brooke's mother, she was less forthcoming, and while acknowledging the limitations of Marsh's "impression," mitigated her criticism by writing that "no memoir could possibly be good enough." In spite of their infrequent visits, she continued, "I always felt that I knew him as one knows one's own family" (*Letters* 2, 271).

There is no record of when Woolf learned that Brooke had died; Leonard apparently received a phone call with the news (Spotts, 411), but there is no mention of it in Virginia Woolf's writings. There is also no record of her last meeting with Brooke in London, shortly before the Hood Battalion, Royal Naval Division (recruited by Churchill and regarded by him with proprietary interest [Field, 117]) was sent to Turkey, though Leonard comments on the meeting in his own autobiography (*BgA,* 19–20). In 1917, reminiscent of a death notice for Rupert Brooke that was found in the *Times* under "killed in action," a one-line entry in her diary covers the bizarre passage of a single shell at the front that killed one of Leonard's brothers and wounded another: "On Sunday we heard of Cecil's death, & Philip's wounds" (*Diary* 1, 83).[8] In her 1918 letter to Mrs. Brooke, she wrote that she had not seen Rupert since before his trip to America in 1913, neglecting to mention their having tea together with Leonard, two months before Brooke died. And in

8. The death notice for Rupert Brooke was published in the *Times* on 26 April 1915: "BROOKE: On the 23rd April, from septicaemia, while on active service at the Dardanelles, Sublieutenant Rupert Chawner Brooke. Hood Battalion Royal Naval Division. Fellow of King's College, Cambridge. Aged 27. . . ." (1).

her journal entry for 22 January 1919, three days before her thirty-seventh birthday, Woolf poses the question "How many friends *have* I got?" (emphasis added, *Diary* 1, 234–35). Suggesting that there may have been a pattern of repression occasioned by news of death in the war, the name "Rupert Brooke" is included among the more than thirty offered in answer.

Perhaps the lived experience of the war at the front—or, for that matter, at sea or in the air—that she and other civilians knew only through receiving thirdhand muffled news of "what journalists call 'historic days,'" an expression she uses in "The War from the Street" (3), led to denial as a way of coping, a distancing that allowed Woolf herself to resist the reality of death owing to the war. Unlike the traumatizing effect of personal deaths (her mother, Julia Duckworth Stephen; Stella Duckworth, her half-sister; her father, Leslie Stephen; Thoby, her elder brother) in her youth, deaths in the war would leave Woolf in denial, as the incredibly reduced entries in her journal seem also to suggest, and lead her to efface her personal feelings for a studied impersonality. This posture, which she believed necessary to literary control, also allowed Woolf to demonstrate, through indirection and irony, that the civilian reality was based in illusions, chief among them an illusion of immunity.

What the war would teach her is that her experience of reality needed to be tied to her experience of the war, that individual authenticity was to be achieved by a kind of commerce between the civilian experience of the war and that of those on the front. She was finally able to do this in her fiction— after the war was over—in part by effecting a narrative distance that was at the same time real and ironical. What Woolf sought was to come to terms with the reality of the war that existed apart from her and to which she was not privy. What she came to see progressively in the war years proper was that the civilian experience of the war was no less real for being inherently ironic and that the facts of life thereafter would be measured against the experience of the war whether on the front or on the streets or in the village. In 1920, Woolf wrote that "our generation is daily scourged by the bloody war" (*Diary* 2, 51); six years later, she would write in "The Cinema" that "the war sprung its chasm at the feet of . . . innocence and ignorance" (269). In the postwar years Woolf would come to terms with the experience of the war that, she said, "destroyed illusion and put truth in its place" (*Room*, 15).

"War in the Village," an essay written by Virginia Woolf as a *TLS* review of Maurice Hewlett's fifty-nine-page poem *The Village Wife's Lament,* is largely a study in and of incomprehension of war in general, though it is the experience of the Great War in particular to which the poem refers. Though Woolf sees the village wife through the prism of Hewlett's elevated and educated elocution, her own vision of the village wife is more down to earth.

The poem, according to Hewlett, assumes a coincidence of "conviction" in himself and the village wife and, reflecting his own incomprehension of the war (which, not unlike Rupert Brooke, he owes to the bellicosity of the Germans), he peers into the mind of a simple "Village Wife [who] knows nothing of the Germans, and [whose] reproaches strike at the heart of Mankind" (Hewlett, 61); that is, at "human nature" (62). Woolf suggests that though Hewlett's heart may very well be in the right place, the task was too much for him. "He has succeeded, beyond doubt," she said, "in writing a terse, moving, and very sincere poem; but that it is the lament of a village woman for her shepherd husband killed in France, and for the baby whose death followed upon his death, we are not so sure" ("War in the Village," 291).

What Woolf sees and what her review suggests is that "'the unending war,'" fought for centuries between man and woman struggling against nature, has been replaced with a man-made war that cuts at the roots of belief in a natural order and the "security" it afforded. What Woolf sees is that the village wife, accustomed to struggle against the elements, has witnessed a transformation in the *natural* adversarial relation and finds herself "at the mercy of a force so remote that, though it has power to take her husband from her, she can hardly figure to herself what the nature of it is" (292–93). This, Woolf suggests, is a most natural incomprehension. It is the grassroots rage at this incomprehension, what Woolf calls "coarseness," that Hewlett does not re-create. It is inarticulate emotion that Woolf seeks; instead, Hewlett offers arguments and ratiocination that are applied and transferred to the simple village wife, which are not natural to her. What Woolf finds lacking is not appreciation of the irony, but of the particular reality, "something vehement, full throated, carrying down in its rush sticks and stones and fragments of human nature pell-mell" (293). Woolf is suggesting not something that narrows the gap between comprehension and incomprehension, but something that recognizes it, that, as she says in "An Essay in Criticism," "stands close up" to "life, truth, reality, whatever you like" and lets it pass close by (258), something that takes to account the natural indignation, the grief, the separate realities that the "unreal" war brought about.

Woolf's vision of the village wife's distance from war is proximate, and Woolf seeks to understand her in real and concrete rather than in elevated and abstract terms, an approach Woolf herself used in 1916 in the *TLS* article "Heard on the Downs: The Genesis of Myth," in which abstract imaging and mythologizing is contrasted with "more prosaic" views. Unlike this article, however, in which Woolf examines explanations of reminders of the war with myth, "War in the Village" examines the shattering of myth with the reality of war, the ultimate reality, loss of life. Where in "War in the Village," Woolf examines belief struggling with the seeming unreality of war, in general, to the civilian and the loss of belief in the face of the Great War, "Heard on the Downs: The Genesis of Myth" examines the "many phantoms hovering on the borderland of belief and scepticism," that is, the struggle to use myth to distance oneself from evidence of war and the natural inclination to believe oneself immune from any reality other than that of nature, as if you are a spectator "of some Titanic drama": "[Y]ou turn sharply to see who it is that gallops behind you. But there is no one. The phantom horseman dashes by with a thunder of hoofs, and suddenly his ride is over and the sound lapses, and you only hear the grasshoppers and the larks in the sky" ("Heard," 40).

An irony implicit in "Heard on the Downs" involves not only the fact of using myth to obscure the reality of the war but also the fact that both "well-known," presumably cosmopolitan, "visitors" to the South Downs and the simple rural population use distinct myths to cope with reminders of the war's reality; the first, elevated metaphors, and the other, an embodied domestic allusion. The article begins as the sounds of war from across the channel, like the tinkling of glasses in "Time Passes," are described in epic or mythological terms, by "[t]wo well-known writers" (possibly Leonard Woolf and Lytton Strachey), and in the domestic and "[m]ore prosaic" terms that Woolf would use again in *Jacob's Room*. This ironic juxtaposition of different approaches to civilian incomprehension shows the worldly-wise Oxbridge types obscuring the "sound of the guns in France, as they heard it from the South Downs" by "liken[ing] it to 'the hammer stroke of Fate'" and "'the pulse of Destiny,'" and the rurals finding the "sinister sound" to be "like the beating of gigantic carpets by gigantic women" (40).

Common to each is the dwarfing of a civilian, in the first by an elevated avoidance and in the second by a domestication of what is seen to be at the same time mythic and exclusively unknowable: "It is none of our business to supply reasons; only to notice queer signs, draw conclusions, and shake our heads" (40), for "to offer a reason for such sublime transactions would be almost to cast a doubt upon them" (41). Not without a certain wonder at the tenacity of such faith, Woolf could only exploit these variations on the theme of civilian incomprehension of the war. The resultant sense of civilian immunity, which she would develop in Mrs. McNab and Mrs. Bast in

"Time Passes", is linked here to the need to "gratif[y] [their] sense of [their] own importance" by being acknowledged in and by history coupled, ironically, with the capacity for deep conviction in the face of the war: "[W]e are by no means downcast, and merely turn our minds to the next riddle, with a deeper conviction than before that we live in a world full of mysteries" (41–42). But between the publication of this article (1916) and the review (1918), any illusion of immunity was becoming harder to maintain, even for the village population.

The shift in emphasis and direction of the 1916 article and the (Septmber) 1918 review suggests a growth in Woolf's consciousness of the war. It suggests a keener ability to see beyond the "preposterous masculine fiction" created by the *Times,* to read between the lines of "those damned newspapers" with their jingoistic slogans and come to terms with the ultimate jeopardy of the war: death. This peril very much became a part of her own life, owing, in some measure, to the possibility of Leonard's conscription. This possibility became real as reports of deaths continued to pour in, from friends and from relatives—the closest, after Rupert Brooke, being the death of Cecil Woolf and the wounding of his brother Philip in 1917, both "by the same shell" (an irony, as Leonard Woolf would recall, "characteristic of the 1914 war" [*BgA,* 181]).

Faced with the increasing potential for personal death owing to the war, it is little wonder that pretentious phrasemaking seemed more unreal than the sense of natural immunity with which it is juxtaposed in "Heard on the Downs." Leonard had escaped being called up during the first go-round, having come armed with letters, one from Dr. Maurice Craig when he appeared before the tribunal on 30 May 1916 (see Trombley, 314n. 7); but Woolf's anxiety over his potential conscription and the conscientious objector status of Duncan Grant and Lytton Strachey, apparent in her letters, which became increasingly less restrained, caused her to act against the freedom from responsibility civilians were expected to embrace. Writing several times to Lady Robert Cecil, Woolf indulged in what "wire-pulling" was open to her in an attempt to secure a favorable disposition of the case of Duncan Grant, who, with David Garnett, was brought before the local tribunal to support his claim of conscientious objector status, adding in her letter of 16 June 1916 to Lady Robert Cecil, "The war is a nightmare isn't it— two cousins of mine were killed this last week, and I suppose in other families its much worse" (*Letters* 2, 100; see also, *Diary* 1, 87–88 and n. 18).

As a reality and as a threat, then, the war was coming awfully close to home. Woolf saw that the possibility of personal death was real, but, like the village wife, she too felt herself "at the mercy of a force so remote that . . . she [could] hardly figure to herself what the nature of it [was]." In 1917 Leonard Woolf, notwithstanding his being called up a second time, continued his peace efforts, and bombing raids continued, changing the nature of life itself. The raids and rationing and German prisoners walking on the Downs had become part of life, and her references to them are usually clipped and short, like newspaper reports, this a possible effect of her voracious reading of newspapers, which interfered with almost any other activity: "I cant open Dante or think of him . . . the cause being I think partly the enormous numbers of newspapers I've been reading in," she wrote on 2 November 1917 (*Diary* 1, 69).

The truncated diary entry involving the death of Cecil and wounding of her brother-in-law Philip might also be seen as reflecting the journalistic/Northcliffe style of reporting death on the front: "On Sunday we heard of Cecil's death, & Philip's wounds," she wrote on 3 December 1917 (*Diary* 1, 83). This and the omission of any mention of the death of Rupert Brooke during the first year of the war implies a reluctance to endow the deaths with reality by writing about them. Woolf's own safety was continually challenged, and the signals of potential danger were acknowledged; during one "false alarm," for example, she wrote about the "certain knowledge that the extinction of light is in future our warning" (*Diary* 1, 70). False alarms might not continue to be false.

Illusion based on myth and avoiding acknowledgment of the ultimate reality of war death are both central to Woolf's first writings about the war. As these concepts apply to the civilian experience, they indicate Woolf's growing need to recognize and explain a reality that was outside her own experiential frame, this state of mind evidenced not only in her daily reading of newspapers but also in the short fiction published in the last two years of the war. The point is implicitly made in "The Mark on the Wall," in which civilian isolation is formally illustrated as is the depiction of newspapers as unreliable sources of war news. A woman's "train of thought," which is the center of the story, is suddenly interrupted by an intrusive, unidentified presence who, likely parroting an oft-repeated civilian comment, announces: "'I'm going out to buy a newspaper. . . . Though it's no good buying newspapers. . . . Nothing ever happens. Curse this war; God damn this war!'" (83). Suggesting that inner equanimity cannot exist apart from external reality, the story also suggests that newspapers, under the scrutiny of government censors, left the civilian isolated, an effect of what Phillip Knightley calls the "great conspiracy . . . to suppress the truth" (80).

In her short fiction, Woolf demonstrates that from the first the civilian is unable to comprehend the reality of the war. "'What War? . . . What War?'" the women in Woolf's 1921 short story "A Society" cry (127). The lack of the war's reality to civilians is illustrated by omission: a five-year gap in the story from 1914 until the treaty that ended the war is signed in 1919. Tracing the development of the society members' sensibilities before and after the war, the story makes mention of the newly ended war only once, and then ironically, in terms of the Briton's time-honored faith in newspapers as the source of truth: "'I caught [my daughter] only yesterday with a newspaper in her hand and she was beginning to ask me if it was "true." Next she'll ask me whether Mr Lloyd George is a good man, then whether Mr Arnold Bennett is a good novelist, and finally whether I believe in God. How can I bring my daughter up to believe in nothing?'" (128).

Just as the war had killed old values and beliefs, so too had it put into sharp relief the cause of civilian isolation, evidenced in the first set of galley sheets for *The Years,* in the section involving a day in the penultimate year of the war, "1917": "People unfolded their newspapers, spreading the sheets wide, so that 'Three British Cruisers Sunk' was repeated again and again in large black letters on the front page of one newspaper after another. The newspapers were turned over, as if the readers were searching for more information. But they could find nothing more about the disasters, only items" (Radin, "'Two enormous chunks,'" 229). For Woolf, who had used her war diaries in preparing for the writing of the novel, recognizing the consequences of slanted newspaper reports was basic to understanding the illusion of immunity. For Woolf, who embodied her sensitivity to exclusion in her work, invisibility would become a motif in much of her work in the years between the wars, as she recognized that immunity, which was concomitant with incomprehension, also deprived the civilian of a sense of both responsibility and risk.

For the civilian, the only observable evidence of the war is illustrated in "Kew Gardens," written in the last months of the war. Both vibant and placid, in the story Kew Gardens can be seen as a microcosm of London itself. The only evidence of the war in Kew ("'Women! Widows! Women in black—'") is observed as a young visitor wearing "an expression of perhaps unnatural calm," listens to an older companion who alludes to "this war" to reinforce his point about the "spirits of the dead" in heaven and "the ancients in Thessaly" (86). But for this one reference, the ghosts of the past in Kew Gardens, like the ghosts of the past on the Downs, offer the civilians a sense that the secure past is very much a part of the present, as the present would become a part of the future.

Like the visitors to Kew, neither Virginia Woolf nor most of her Bloomsbury friends had seen or experienced the war at the front.[9] Yet, for Leonard,
and surprisingly for Virginia Woolf, there was a sense of loss for having been
left out of it. Virginia later recalled that "we were all C.O.s during the Great
War" (Bell, *VW* 2, 258–59), but Leonard would not have claimed conscientious objector status if he had not received medical exemptions, recalling in
his autobiography that "I have never been a complete pacifist" and that "if
I had not been married or even if Virginia had been well, I should probably
have joined up, because, though I hated the war, I felt . . . an irresistible desire to experience everything" (*BgA*, 177).

Woolf shared something of this longing, albeit for different reasons, as
we see in "A Cambridge V.A.D." (10 May 1917), her review of the E. M.
Spearing memoir *From Cambridge to Camiers under the Red Cross,* which describes Spearing's decision to leave her research chair at Cambridge to join
the Voluntary Aid Detachment (V.A.D.), a nursing service auxiliary to the
armed forces, and serve in a Red Cross hospital in Cambridge and then in
various military hospitals in France. With an admiration that borders on
longing, Woolf describes the case of Spearing, who substituted "the con-
centration of life" for its tedium, who substituted "little time" for too much,
and who experienced "something of the excitement of a student plunged
from books into practical work and finding herself quite capable of it" (113,
112). There is a sense here of empathetic understanding—of "if only I had
been there, I too. . . ." Importantly, what Spearing experienced and Woolf
could but read about and try to appreciate is that "in the nurses and in the
soldiers, such experiences formed deeper thoughts," what Spearing called
"an underlying reality," a "community of suffering." This reality, this community, Woolf would not experience. It is as if this emergence of "[t]he best
qualities, and the most real" (113) were concomitant with responsibility, as
if the civilian illusion of immunity, in contrast, were concomitant with exclusion from responsibility, something that Woolf found increasingly difficult to countenance, particularly in the years between the wars.

If one were to measure the effect of the war, and understand it well
enough to write about it, its reality had to be acknowledged. If a side effect
of the war were to be the shattering of the myth of civilian immunity, a
measure of the reality that war now denoted had to be told. This would explain the comment made by Woolf in her March 1917 review of *Before Midnight* by Elinor Mordaunt. Here Woolf refers to her "prejudice" against "the
war in fiction," which she explains "by the feeling that the vast events now

9. See the appendix.

shaping across the Channel are towering over us too closely and too tremendously to be worked into fiction without a painful jolt in the perspective" ("'Before,'" 87). It seems, however, that here Woolf's quarrel with the war in fiction is not based on a personal, but aesthetic conviction, something we can understand in the context of her major objection to Mordaunt's other stories, which involved the supernatural: "[W]e do not like the war in fiction, and we do not like the supernatural" (87). The writer needed to be in touch with reality, not eschew it, and certainly not to sacrifice her world for one of easy artifice.[10]

This must have struck Woolf the more forcefully after reading the Spearing memoir—which evoked the real thing in a way that Mordaunt, whose work relied on the war as a formulaic device that reminded one of the inconvenience of war without exploring its implications, was unable to do. But, as Paul Fussell and Robert Wohl suggest, even returning veterans were unable to write of the reality of the war, a reality Woolf sought to understand, until ten years after demobilization.[11] In Woolf's case, such a coming to terms, not only with the war but also with her experience of it, was not fully realized fictionally until the 1930s, with *The Years*.

What the civilian was left with when the war ended, as Woolf makes clear in "The War from the Street," her review of D. Bridgman Metchim's *Our Own History of the War from a South London View* (1918), was the sense of "living through four years almost entirely composed of what journalists call 'historic days,'" while knowing that the anonymous "we," the civilian population, will not and never have been a part of history (3). Implicit

10. In her 1916 review of *The Park Wall*, a novel by Elinor Mordaunt, Woolf praises Mordaunt as one of the best of "living novelists," for her originality in creating a "world of . . . her own," where "the story is not the important thing," for her "mastery of her subject" and her "power to strike out characters with solid bodies and clear-cut features" ("'The Park Wall,'": 42–43). Six months later, Woolf's review of Mordaunt's collection of short stories ("'Before Midnight'") suggests that through a handful of stories have something to recommend them, most suffer from "the methods of the conjurer and ask us to be satisfied with a trick" (87).

11. Wohl, for example, reports that "the big year for war books in England was 1929." In that year "some twenty-nine were published"; in 1928 there were twenty-one and there were six in 1926 (106). Fussell calls Graves, Blunden, and Sassoon "three of the great English memoirists of the war" (73). Graves's *Good-bye to All That* was published in 1929, Blunden's *Undertones of War* in 1928, and Sassoon's *Memoirs of a Fox Hunting Man* and *Memoirs of an Infantry Officer* in 1928 and 1930 respectively. Fussell calls the memoir "a kind of fiction . . . [allowing] the ex post facto view of an action that generates coherence or makes irony possible" (*Great War,* 310). Zwerdling references Woolf's reading of "belated 'war books' that appeared around 1930" (298).

in Metchim's perspective, the civilian experience of the war is more ironic than real, and the title of Woolf's review is itself ironic, as Metchim suggests that there was no war from the street. Throughout the war years, life there had remained essentially unchanged, the civilian enjoying both immunity from the reality of war and the illusion of being in on it. As Metchim observes, to end his seventy-one-page *History:*

> By now things were probably beginning to be understood a bit better by everybody than they were in the beginning of the war, and little bits of "secret history" made you say, "Tut tut!" and "Dear me!" as you wondered if they were correct. . . . The Major said that Italy would do the trick, and Austria was as good as out of it, when of course the other enemy countries would go down one after the other, and blood-spattered, cannibalistic Hunland would go smash. He thought, however, that this would not be until about the end of the month, or a day or two later.
>
> You went to bed on 3rd August feeling like some sort of a prophet, and slept the sleep of the just-so.
>
> The sun (not visible at Greenwich) rose on the morning of the 4th of August, nineteen hundred and seventeen.

The fact is, though, that however much truth Woolf saw in Metchim's history, she understood that its effect was belied by what she had observed as the signing of the armistice was imminent. There was "nothing different in the atmosphere," she wrote in her diary; like Katherine Murry (née Mansfield), she believed "most people have grasped neither war nor peace" (*Diary* 1, 215).

Woolf found Metchim's approach to reinforce the division and the literal distance between the experiences of civilians and combatants and more likely to trivialize the civilian experience than to make the horror of the trenches comprehensible and the human cost there and on the streets real. Woolf was not unaware but resentful of the loss of consciousness enforced on the civilian during the war, and like the "shapeless jelly of human stuff" made up of the civilian population, knew that even as reflectors of the workings of the powerful, the mass is inadequate to the task. They in power do—"you in a muddled way reflect what they do in blurred pictures half obliterating each other" ("War in the Street," 4). The result of this is the sense of civilian immunity and, reworking her diary entry, she observes in the review, "Your conviction that nothing is ever going to touch you is profound" (4). What the civilian had been given was "'several versions of The Truth . . . and Real

Facts'" (4). What the civilian had been deprived of was a sense of what the reality was.

Kierkegaard said that recourse to an ironic view makes reality somehow livable, offers a "free[dom] from the sorrows of actuality" (*CI*, 279). It is the *effect* of distancing oneself from reality that Woolf both feared and acknowledged, that she both questioned and countenanced, because she, like Kierkegaard, recognized that irony was a tool used to elicit understanding; as Kierkegaard said, irony is not the truth but the way to the truth (327). What Woolf feared was that rather than being recognized as a means, the irony would be seen as an end, in, for example, Metchim's book, which becomes by turns increasingly ironic and finally satirical and in the poems of Siegfried Sassoon. In her reviews of his war poems in 1917 and 1918, Woolf, calling Sassoon "a realist," overlooks the irony in his poetry, seeing instead "the terrible pictures which lie behind the colourless phrases of the newspapers," the "sordid and horrible experiences" of war ("Mr Sassoon's Poems," 120; "Two Soldier Poets," 269–70).

In fact, the only "peculiar irony" she acknowledged during the war years was that of the "canonisation" of Rupert Brooke ("The New Crusade," 203). The distancing of the civilian from the reality of the war had been an enforced condition of civilian life during its progress, and one with which Woolf had not been comfortable. Sassoon's need to distance himself from the war's reality, from its *actuality,* and make life more livable and death less painful, though understandable as a personal means of coping, added to the civilian's belief in a myth of war, as much as did the myth that grew up around Rupert Brooke. Woolf was not prepared to buy into either popular belief. In the case of Rupert Brooke, she recognized that superficial popular adulation distorted the real complexity of both his being and his vision of the war, and in regard to its mythology, she knew that misrepresenting the lived experience of the war on the front widened the chasm between civilians and combatants. If the experience of the Great War were not to be repeated, either in the trenches or on the street or in the village, Woolf knew that an ironic vision would not serve any more than one skewed by jingoism. The first only sustained belief in the unreality of war and the second trivialized it.

A month after the signing of the armistice, Woolf observed that "the war is already almost forgotten" (*Diary* 1, 227). Yet, for Virginia Woolf, as for Philip Woolf, as for Gerald Brenan, as for Robert Graves, as for Vera Brittain, as for Desmond MacCarthy, and as for Henri Massis, all of whom were survivors, "the war would never cease to mark our work and our days" (284).[12] For Woolf, as for Roger Fry, the experience of the war was a beginning and not an end; for Woolf the war would serve as a touchstone against which life would be judged. What she had learned, and what she would demonstrate in her postwar writings, was that no illusion of immunity served in a world where a distancing ironic vision of war was seen to be its reality. Such illusion, whether in the village or on the streets or from the trenches, could only perpetuate belief in the myth of war. In "The Intellectual Imagination," a review of the Walter de la Mare volume on Rupert Brooke that was published in the *TLS* in December 1919, Woolf begins with a question posed by the author: "'Is life both a dream and an awakening?'" (134). For Virginia Woolf, the experience of the war was sometimes unreal, but it was never a dream. In the end, what the war had taught her was that there is no immunity from its effect.

2

Having witnessed the Armistice Day celebrations in London commemorating the cessation of hostilities (11 November 1918), Woolf suggested to her sister that the shift from war to peace was confusing. "The guns have been going off for half an hour, and the sirens whistling;" Woolf wrote; "so I suppose we are at peace" (*Letters* 2, 290). Only two weeks after the signing of the Treaty of Versailles on 28 June 1919 Woolf began to write about the peace, notwithstanding her disinclination to write an "account" of "the effect of the war" (*Diary* 1, 291).

By 19 July 1919, Woolf was "desolate, dirty, & disillusioned," but determined "to say something about Peace day," which had been declared a hol-

12. In *Promise of Greatness* (Panichas, ed.), a collection of memoirs of and essays involving the war written for the volume (1968), there are thirty-five memoirs among the forty-two represented, and each, in recalling the war, makes clear its indelible impression. Robert Graves ("The Kaiser's War: A British Point of View") is included in a section called "A Total View"; Edmund Blunden ("Infantry Passes By") and Gerald Brenan ("A Survivor's Story") are included in "The Fighting Fronts"; Charles Edmund Carrington ("Some Soldiers") is included in "The Men of 1914," a section that also includes the only memoir involving the civilian experience of the war: Sir Charles Petrie, "Fighting the First World War in London"; Henri Massis ("The War We Fought") and Vera Brittain ("War Service in Perspective") are included in a section called "Awakening." Each of these is noted separately in the bibliography. There is also included an essay written by J. K. Johnstone, "World War I and the Novels of Virginia Woolf," which is one of the earliest essays to note the war imagery in Woolf's novels, and Melvin J. Friedman's "Three Experiences of the War: A Triptych," which involves Bloomsbury, the Woolfs, and the war. See also the appendix.

iday of commemoration (*Diary* 1, 292). Because of the seeming ease with which she habitually validated her experience of public events by writing about it, in her private correspondence and more reliably (and rather less ironically) in her diaries, we discover a trove of observations and reactions, many of which are reconstructed in her professional writings, and particularly in her novels, three in particular (*Mrs. Dalloway, To the Lighthouse,* and *The Years*) having the most direct connection with her experience of the peace (albeit in the shadow of the war). Framing these works, Woolf's first post-peace novel (the first postwar novel to be written during the peace[13]), *Jacob's Room* (1922), and her last (the last to be started before World War II), the posthumously published *Between the Acts* (1941), reveal the author's engagement with ambiguities and realities that blur the lines between peace and war; civilians and combatants; survivors and victims; and, most basically, life and death.

Virginia Woolf was a survivor of the Great War at the home front, while very much being a victim of her own invisibility[14] during its progress—and, significantly, when it was over. What celebrations followed the war to end all war, as might be expected, excluded those who, like her, were civilians. More surprising, perhaps, was the exclusion of survivors who had seen action but were wounded and so joined civilians in being victims—rather than, as one might expect, victors. "It was a melancholy thing to see the incurable soldiers lying bed at the Star & Garter with their backs to us, smoking cigarettes" Woolf recorded in her "account of the peace celebrations" on 20 July 1919 (*Diary* 1, 294). Woolf was alert to the incongruity of the "rejoicings": the theatricality of the proceedings; the role played by the civilian spectators; and the important part, finally, that was played by the weather. "We were children to be amused," she recorded. "Today has left us in no doubt that any remaining festivities are to be completely quenched [by the rain]"

13. *The Voyage Out,* Woolf's first novel, was published during the war, in 1915. *Night and Day* (1919), although published after the war, was probably written 1915–19 (Heine), although J. H. Stape places it somewhat later (1916–19).

14. This term is defined by phenomenological sociologists as a condition of being submerged under twin spheres of social reality and cultural belief systems (Levesque-Lopman, 143); I use this term as it relates to the social reality of the civilian status and the social amnesia encouraged after the Great War. According to Levesque-Lopman, the common focus of a feminist perspective is on making women visible. Yet, the term also signifies death, as well as magic power, and is symbolized by a cloak, mantle, veil and hood (J. C. Cooper, 88). R. D. Laing sees invisibility, in some cases, as controllable, a state dependent on volition, as a defense against danger, for example, and not only the Kafkaesque state of "depersonalization and derealization and inner deadness" (109).

(*Diary* 1, 294). Having all but missed the signing of the Peace Treaty on 28 June (as the Woolfs were negotiating for Monks House in Rodmell), they witnessed the celebrations in London on 19 July 1919 ("Peace Day"). What is clear from her "account," however, is that Woolf was looking less at the actors ("[g]enerals & soldiers & tanks & bands took 2 hours in passing") than at the audience of spectators (*Diary* 1, 292–94).

That Woolf's observation of survivors of the war on the front, such as Philip Woolf or Nicholas Bagenal, or survivors such as her friends Desmond MacCarthy, who drove an ambulance, or even, E. M. Forster, who was a "searcher" for the Red Cross, may have altered her view of the peace remains unacknowledged, in part because of what has been assumed to be her enthusiasm in embracing peace and her optimistic belief that war itself would never occur again.[15] On 11 November 1918, Woolf wrote, albeit without much conviction, to her then pregnant sister: "I cant help being glad that your precious imp will be born into a moderately reasonable world" (*Letters* 2, 290). Pessimistic predictions, such as those articulated as the war began ("It is the end of civilization," for example), and particularly those articulated in and around Bloomsbury and from those actively involved in antiwar activities, were largely forgotten, because, as Clarissa Dalloway would observe (albeit some four years later), "[I]t was over; thank Heaven—over" (*MrsD*, 5).

On 13 November 1918, Woolf observed, more thoughtfully, and with qualification: "Peace seems to make more difference than one could have thought possible, though I think the rejoicing, so far as I have seen it, has been very sordid and depressing" (*Letters* 2, 292). Woolf could only reflect her disappointment that the second round of rejoicings, after the official end of the war, seemed noticeably more calculated and unnatural than the first. Even the newspapers emphasized its staginess. In the "special issue" of the *Times,* published on Monday, 21 July 1919, a photograph captioned in block capitals MEN OF THE BRITISH ARMY PASSING THE CENOTAPH IN WHITEHALL is above one of MEN OF THE ROYAL NAVY PASSING THE CENOTAPH (p. 7), like a mirrored image, except that the second is cropped closer than the first, and "The Glorious Dead," engraved on the stone, is not visible.

Woolf's sense of invisibility owing to the war may, in part, explain her silence in regard to representations of the Peace Day celebrations in the popular press, but it does not suggest either an ignorance of or an indifference to the postwar posture civilians were encouraged to assume. Woolf had stu-

---

15. This belief is widely assumed, and deserves to be looked at again. See Zwerdling's chapter, "Pacifism Without Hope": 271–301.

diously avoided ritualistic and stylized commemoration of the dead, such as she had seen in the case of Rupert Brooke, and to a lesser extent, in the case of Cecil Woolf (in whose commemoration the Woolfs themselves participated—albeit in "the rarest [and least public] of all Hogarth Press publications" [Spater and Parsons 102][16]). Yet, what she found the more puzzling was a studied *resistance* to what she identified as "disillusionment." More curious still was that this willful denial existed not only on the street, where she had expected a "herd" response but also at the 1917 Club.

> There's something calculated & politic & insincere about these peace rejoicings. Moreover they are carried out with no beauty, & not much spontaneity. . . . Yesterday in London the usual sticky stodgy conglomerations of people, sleepy & torpid as a cluster of drenched bees, were crawling over Trafalgar Square, & rocking about the pavements in the neighbourhood. The one pleasant sight I saw was due rather to the breath of wind than to decorative skill; some long tongue shaped streamers attached to the top of the Nelson column licked the air, furled & unfurled, like the gigantic tongues of dragons, with a slow, rather serpentine beauty. . . . I can't deny that I feel a little mean at writing so lugubriously; since we're all supposed to keep up the belief that we're glad & enjoying ourselves. So on a birthday, when for some reason things have gone wrong, it was a point of honour in the nursery to pretend. Years later one could confess what a horrid fraud it seemed; & if, years later, these docile herds will own up that they too saw through it, & will have no more of it—well—should I be more cheerful? I think the dinner at the 1917 Club, & Mrs Besant's speech rubbed the gilt, if there were any grains remaining, effectually off the gingerbread. . . . It seems to me more & more clear that the only honest people are the artists, & that these social reformers & philanthropists [such as Mrs. Besant, president of the Theosophical Society] get so out of hand, & harbour so many discreditable desires under the disguise of loving their kind, that in the end there's more to find fault with in them than in us. But if I were one of them? (*Diary* 1, 292–93)

16. The nineteen-page commemorative volume was hand-printed on the Hogarth Press as a collaborative effort by the Woolfs and surviving brother, Philip. The title page read: "POEMS/by/C. N. Sidney Woolf/Late 20th Hussars (Spec. Res.)/Fellow of Trinity College, Cambridge/Hogarth Press, Richmond/1918." The volume was undoubtedly distributed to the family rather than sold. Philip Woolf "dedicates them [the poems], as they were left, to the memory of the dearest and bravest brother that a man was ever loved by—animae dimidium maeae." The volume is reviewed in "Four Young Poets," in the *TLS*, 23 January 1919, 40. Only two copies of the volume are extant, one in the British Museum. See also Spater and Parsons, 102; and Willis, 23–24.

Even in an account reporting calculation, insincerity, and "sticky stodgy conglomerations," there is a sense that life, among her friends and acquaintances as well as among those outside it, has been affirmed at the expense of death: whatever the pretense, whatever the cost, to survive war is to ignore death—not merely avoid it.[17]

Nevertheless, after 26 July 1919, Woolf observed the curious shadow cast by the war dead over surviving former servicemen, as if the proliferation of war monuments, which glorified death, thereby negated survival and deprived survivors themselves of the right to life. The fact of war death and, moreover, the elevated and dehumanizing acknowledgment of it seems to me to have blurred Woolf's sense of civilian invisibility with a parallel invisibility experienced by ex-servicemen. For many civilians the war had become a reality because of the human costs, but in its wake the glorification of death elicited, particularly among returning soldiers, what might be called a kind of survival guilt, though the term and the concept seems to have originated after World War II.[18] Whatever privation civilians experienced, they had no memory of the life and death experiences that haunted ex-servicemen. Yet, Woolf had displayed some of the same symptoms herself, particularly when she was suffering from the "disease" of "hypersensitivit[y] and introspection" before the war, including absentmindedness and detachment.

Increasingly, the war was being presented as a bad dream—and one from which the populace, civilians and ex-servicemen, could wake, as if the fact of war had been transformed to a fiction and its reality to an illusion. Such wishful thinking must have recalled Woolf's own blurred sense of dream and

17. Ironically, mortality declined among the civilian population during the war (Winter, "Some Paradoxes," 10).

18. Survival guilt, or "guilt over survival priority," is a term that evolved from the Japanese word for survivor, *seizonsha* (Lifton, *Death,* 7). The concept of "survivor syndrome" was formulated and developed by William G. Niederland, who first used the term in reference to the symptoms of survivors of concentrations camps, but is generally applied to the victims of persecution, or man-made or natural disasters. Among the "aftereffects" [*sic*] of survival are depression, expectation of punishment (anxiety), personality change, and identification with the dead (see Niederland, "The Problem of the Survivor" [1961], cited in his "Introductory Notes on the Concept, Definition, and Range of Psychic Trauma" [1971]). Studies on trauma antedate the Great War, but such "loose terms" as "war neurosis," as Niederland points out, were used in the context of medicine and have since been modified and changed (1, 2). Freud wrote "Mourning and Melancholia" in 1915 (published in 1917), but he never specifically related his findings to returning soldiers or used them to study the effects of the Great War. See, for example, "Reflections upon War and Death" (1915) and "Psychoanalysis and War Neurosis" (1919).

reality two days before the armistice: "[T]here is revolution, & a kind of partial reawakenment, one fancies, on the part of people to the unreality of the whole affair. Suppose we wake up too?" (*Diary* 1, 215).

Since 19 July 1919, when the memorial catafalque (renamed the Cenotaph—"the empty tomb"—in time for Peace Day) was made a permanent monument and the Tomb of the Unknown Warrior was situated in Westminster Abbey a year later, followed by approximately forty thousand memorials throughout England (Inglis, 592, 585),[19] civilian invisibility had become blurred with the invisibility of ex-servicemen—and finally overshadowed by trade unionism, a movement that had been forestalled because of the war. When Woolf observed, with some concern, that the railway strike of 27 September–6 October 1919 "broke in to our life more than the war did" (*Diary* 1, 304), she was suggesting that the problem of the invisibility of ex-servicemen was becoming blurred with problems of labor and employment in post-peace England, something she implies by beginning her diary entry of 7 October, the day after the settlement of the strike, with a reference to Peace Day:

> Home [to Hogarth House] yesterday. The 'docile herds' whom I describe [*sic*] on Peace day are not so deluded after all. They have held the country up for eleven days, I think. We did a little to support them too, & kept one man on strike who would have gone back without our pound. Still, what's to be read in the papers is hardly fit for my private page. I wonder if I could expound the railway strike? What they asked, & what they got? . . . There's a private strike to record too. I should like to write philosophically & analyse what is no doubt a sign—dont they call it?—of our times. We must think out our position. The question is, are we to fling off in a new direction? What do we want? (*Diary* 1, 304)

19. The actual number is in doubt. The National Inventory of War Memorials by the Imperial War Museum, begun in 1989, estimates that there are 54,000 war memorials in the British Isles, most of which were erected after the First World War. Some were erected to commemorate earlier conflicts (e.g., the Boer Wars) and some commemorate activity from the Second World War to the present date (*The National Inventory of War Memorials*). See also, Catherine Moriarty, "The Absent Dead and Figurative First World War Memorials." See Homberger for an account of the naming of the Cenotaph (1430) and Cannadine for a variation ("War and Death" 220–21). K. S. Inglis points out that the French inscribe their monuments *MORTS POUR LA FRANCE* and include only the dead. Inglis estimates that 5 percent of the British monuments include names of survivors as well (586).

Woolf seemed to suspect, even in these early months of the peace, that returning soldiers, caught between what Henry Pelling identifies as "industrial unrest and trade-union militancy" (*Short History,* 48), would be numbered among the losers, despite the temporary boom in the postwar economy. It must have seemed clear to her that the conspiracy that had focused on advancing the war effort was now engaged in stifling labor.[20] In fact, conditions simulated those of the war ("The Government make a show of courageous determination. We are on war rations, & told to be brave & good" [*Diary* 1, 301]). "Rumour" again held sway and newspapers, the *Daily Mail* and the *Herald,* in particular, were "untrustworthy in their extreme," while the *Daily News* remained "truthful in the middle" (*Diary* 1, 303). It is not surprising that after the General Strike of 1926 Woolf would come to terms with echoes from the Great War, and in 1930 evoke a military metaphor in describing the Women's Co-operative Guild:

> There was something military in the regularity of the proceeding. They were like marksmen, I thought, standing up in turn with rifles raised to aim at a target. Sometimes they missed, and there was a roar of laughter; sometimes they hit, and there was a roar of applause. But whether the particular shot hit or missed there was no doubt about the carefulness of the aim. ("Introductory Letter," *Life as We Have Known It,* xvi–xvii)

Ironically, Woolf was at a disadvantage, not having served in the war herself nor having had much access to returning soldiers, something that seems also to have occurred to her during the war years proper. Woolf's limited contact with soldiers until she visited Philip Woolf in 1917 at Fishmonger's Hall, where he had been sent to recover after the death of his brother Cecil, may help explain her well-known (and aforementioned) comment to Margaret Llewelyn Davies lamenting "how little one believes what anyone says now [about the war]" (*Letters* 2, 178). Such skepticism, however, does not point to the "involuntary revulsion for the whole business [of war]" that

20. In *A History of British Trade Unionism,* Henry Pelling states: "In the course of 1919 a Restoration of Pre-war Practices Act was passed, which obliged employers to accept the return, for a time at least, of the trade practices which had been put aside by the Treasury Agreement or by the Munitions Acts . . . but the State could no longer compel the enforcement of the decision. . . . [A]t the end of 1919 the only industries still under direct state control were the mines and the railways" (159). After an attempt to reduce wages in the industry, the National Union of Railwaymen (with the aid of the Labour Research Department, "an offshoot of the Fabian Society") called for a national strike in September 1919. After seven days a settlement was reached, although hardly one favorable to the workers, as it called for no increase in wages for another year (162–63).

has long been assumed to explain Woolf's response to World War I.[21] Four months before the letter to Davies, Woolf had publicly dismissed what "people [that is, civilians] say about the war" in "A Cambridge V.A.D."

It is a mistake to assume that either Woolf or Spearing believed that the war would have the salutary effect of "breaking down barriers between the classes" or the equally problematic effect of heightened self-knowledge that the "abnormal conditions" of war presumably elicited (Woolf, "Cambridge," 112, 113). To the contrary, it was Spearing's consciousness of the "sentimental illusions about wounded soldiers and the effects of war on the character which [were] rife in England" (113) that caught Woolf's attention. Certainly, Spearing and Woolf came to have the same concern for returning soldiers.

> "Our demigods in the trenches," as I see one journalist calls them, know perfectly well that in ordinary circumstances they are very ordinary people. . . . They would rather have justice from the Government than charity from outsiders, and their bug-bear is, as many have told me, that when the war is over, and the cheering has died away, they will find themselves maimed and broken selling matches or bootlaces in the street. (Spearing, 81)

Philip Woolf's survival seems central to Woolf's vision of returning soldiers, and what Robert Wohl first identified as "the English *myth* of a lost generation" (emphasis added, *Generation,* 120).[22] At no time was this myth more potent than in commemorating the war dead,[23] and at no other time

21. The difference between what Zwerdling calls her "instinctive pacifism" (272) and her sense of World War I involves the difference between the theoretical and actual (or "real"), which seems to me analogous to what Zwerdling himself calls the "contradictory impulses at work in Woolf's feminism" (244). It seems unreasonable to assume that her experience of the war would be more "instinctive" or less "contradictory." Yet, in some essays in *Virginia Woolf and War* (Mark Hussey, ed.), it is assumed that because of what is universally regarded as her pacifism and her feminism, she can only "identify in a personal way with the families and friends of those who died in the wars" (Bazin and Lauter, 15) or with "female victims of the war" (Usui, 151).

22. Although acknowledging that there is some correspondence to truth in the myth, Wohl argues that the numbers do not bear out the idea of a "lost generation": "of the 700,000 combatants [a number also in dispute] who died during the war, only 37,452 were officers—and yet it is these 37,000 and not the troops they commanded who are enshrined in the myth" (*Generation,* 120–21). See also Wohl, "The Generation of 1914 and Modernism." J. M. Winter, in "Britain's 'Lost Generation' of the First World War," takes the position that there were *proportionately* greater sacrifice of life by the well-to-do and the highly educated (458–59). In any case, as Adrian Gregory puts the case, "Somewhere in the region of three million Britons lost a close relative in the First World War, a substantial number in a population of under 42 million" (19 and n.46).

23. See Hynes, *A War,* 269–82, and Mosse 34–50 and 70–106.

was Woolf's resistance to such ceremony more weak. Having worked with Philip and Leonard on publishing the posthumous volume of poems for their fallen brother, the three were linked in their grief for Cecil's death, although not in the sense of closure that the gesture should suggest.[24] In fact, Virginia Woolf observed with concern that Philip was "wretched" and eager to return to France (*Diary* 1, 123) and it was only with this end in view that Leonard could report him "more cheerful than he had been before" (Spotts, 222).

That Philip Woolf's recovery from his wounds (and not Cecil Woolf's death) made the more profound impression on Woolf has gone unnoticed, not surprisingly perhaps, given both her reticence in regard to Philip and Philip's own reluctance to discuss what he experienced in and because of the war.[25] But Woolf certainly took note of what Jay Winter has called "the unbearable strain of surviving" (*Great War*, 302) evident in Philip—and, perhaps, in Nicholas Baganel. Although it is not clear exactly when Philip was demobilized (a process that was not completed for some months), it is certain that Virginia Woolf was concerned at his being "in the thick of it" as late as October 1918 (*Diary* 1, 200).

It may have been Philip's survival on the front, which Woolf could only know as an outsider, that augmented her sensitivity to what he and other

24. Volumes such as *Poems* by Cecil Woolf were common commemorations for the dead during the war, as war memoirs were attempts by the living to put the dead to rest. Yet, as Paul de Man has argued in another context, "the very need to confess represents a self-justification which can only aggravate the writer's sense of guilt" (see Cobley, 7–9). Certainly, the publication of the commemorative *Poems* by Cecil Woolf had not prevented Philip from grieving for him his entire life. Leonard said that he did not "think that Philip ever completely recovered from Cecil's death" (*BgA*, 182), and Philip's son (who was named for his uncle) recalls in a letter to me that "Cecil's death was something that cast a shadow . . . over the rest of my father's life" (Cecil Woolf, letter to author, 30 May 1991).

25. In *Beginning Again*, Leonard Woolf recalls that Philip "very rarely spoke about his experiences [in the war]" (182). In a letter to me, Philip's son wrote that "Philip seldom spoke of [Cecil's death], but it was something almost palpable that I think we, my mother and my sisters, all lived with. It requires little imagination for anyone who has read about life on the Western Front to understand what five years in the trenches, with so many of your men and brother officers being killed around you—five years of what Unamuno called living in the thought of death, quite literally—what that would do to such an intelligent, civilised, fastidious and highly sensitive young man. In September 1939, when I was a schoolboy, I stood with Philip at the side of Cecil's grave in France, a few days before the outbreak of war, and twenty-two years on it was all as real and horrific to him as it had been in November 1917" (Cecil Woolf, letter to author, 30 May 1991).

returning soldiers were experiencing in postwar London, an empathetic understanding that is apparent in her record of Philip's visit to Asheham in March 1919.

> Asheham was, I suppose, a qualified success only—at any rate for L. because of the discomfort; for me the discomfort such as it was was chiefly due to Philip's presence. . . . I think perhaps Philip felt himself a little of a hindrance, as no doubt, he always feels himself now—an outsider, a spectator; unattached & very lonely. (*Diary* 1, 248)

Like the invisibility Woolf had herself experienced as a civilian, Philip's lack of connection with the civilian world (even of his family) must have left Woolf suspicious of easy characterizations of returning soldiers or of civilians, particularly those that seek to divide them, rather than to understand the common ground upon which they stood.

The peace would teach her that iconization and memorialization were less connected to death in the war than to a popular consciousness born not only of denial and fear but of survival guilt. Woolf observed that illusions of war in the absence of its reality were accepted as reality by those who had lived it as well as by those who had seen it only from the streets or in the village. In her novels in the years between the wars, she explored the distance between experience and memory and between memory and popular consciousness. In the months between the armistice in November 1918 and the Treaty of Versailles in June 1919 and in the years between the first and second world wars, Woolf turned her sharp powers of observation to returning soldiers, seeking insight into the lived experience of the war that none seemed able to forget, and some seemed unable to survive. If we see here early evidence of both the idiom and the idea that Woolf would involve in *Three Guineas* (1939), we also see the direction that her exploration would take her—beginning with the depiction of the prewar world in *Jacob's Room* and ending with the depiction of the prewar world of *Between the Acts*.

"These Are the Plans," an essay written by Virginia Woolf as a book review of two posthumous volumes of poems issued shortly after Peace Day and before the unveiling of the Cenotaph on 11 November 1920, is largely a study in and of incomprehension of war in the trenches, although it is the poetry and lives of two English soldiers to which the essay refers. Because Woolf claims to be able to read "character between the lines" of their books (albeit, she admits, within limits), her vision of Donald Frederic Goold Johnson, the author of *Poems*, and to a greater extent, of Charles Hamilton Sorley, the

author of *Marlborough and Other Poems,* is made with a clarity and authority that neither combatant lived to possess. Johnson was killed in combat in
1916 and Sorley some months before.

The review assumes coincident "feelings" in the reviewer and the writers.
Notwithstanding her incomprehension of the war (still less of the peace that
ended it), Woolf reads into the minds of one, a soldier-turned-poet, and the
other, a poet-turned-soldier. Neither enjoyed a prewar past that prepared
him either for life without a future or a future enshrined as poet or as hero.
Woolf sees and her review suggests that peace, which existed as the back-
drop of civilized discourse and interaction, had been replaced with a context
that challenged life itself in unprecedented ways. Woolf sees that the poets,
accustomed to engagement with books and ideas, language and nature, had
experienced a transformation of their circumstances and found themselves,
in Sorley's words, "behind the lines" watching "the foam and froth of war"
(*Marlborough,* 86, 90). This, Woolf knows, is a most unnatural experience.

It is a deeply felt anger and frustration at this travesty of human behavior
and civilized being that Woolf seeks; yet, it is this "intensity" that Johnson
does not provide. It is a new idiom that she seeks; instead, Johnson offers
"old poetical phrases" that are inappropriate to the new context that the war
has created. Woolf is seeking not something that narrows the gap between
war and peace, but something that informs it. She asks of poetry, as she says
elsewhere, to express the experience of feelings, of emotions in the poetic
present (in this case of the war) naturally and honestly, and without the self-
consciousness that comes of fear ("The Narrow Bridge of Art").

Woolf's sense of the soldiers' inexperience with war is empathetic and
Woolf seeks to understand it in terms of feelings rather than antiquated
poetic conventions, a standard applied as well in "Is This Poetry?" which reviews the wartime poems of civilians J. Middleton Murry and T. S. Eliot.[26]
Unlike this review, however, which in some ways applies what we might call
a standard of poetical correctness in a postwar world, "These Are the Plans"
comes to terms with the shattering of prewar standards with the reality of

26. There is some uncertainty, according to both Andrew McNeillie and B. J. Kirkpatrick, as to the authorship of the review; although the name Virginia Woolf appears on
the manuscript, the review as published in the *Athenaeum,* 20 June 1919, is unsigned, and
there are also two letters in which Woolf implies that the reviews were written altogether
or in part by her husband (*Essays* 3, 57, n.1; Kp C155). Woolf first received and had read the
two volumes by 3 December 1918, shortly after the armistice; they were published by the
Hogarth Press on 12 May 1919, the same day as Woolf's *Kew Gardens* (*Diary* 1, 223; 271
and n. 1).

war in the trenches. Where in "These Are the Plans," Woolf strains to find life struggling with the realities of war, "Is This Poetry?" finds that whatever the "sincerity of [the poets'] passions," it distances them from the realities of postwar life, making them spectators: "stand[ing] upright, survey[ing] the prospect, in which as yet [they] play no part" ("Is This Poetry?" 54).

An irony implicit in "Is This Poetry?" involves not only using poetic impersonality to obscure the human experience of the war and the postwar world but also that both of the up and coming civilian poets have distinct methods of coping with reminders of postwar decay. Murry uses conventional, classical allusions, and Eliot "newness and strangeness" applied "scientifically" (55, 56). Yet, the review is not about the war—or the peace—except by indirection, an approach Woolf herself uses in *Jacob's Room,* where allusions to the war, like the name of the protagonist, Jacob *Flanders* (which immediately calls to mind the region of France and Belgium where much of the fighting and death of British combatants took place), suggest what the author has in mind.

The ironic indirection in "Is This Poetry?" shows the worldly postwar poets under the spell of "ghosts" of prewar poets and terrorized by the "'ordinary man,' the ghostly master . . . of most writers" (54, 55). Common to each poet, however, is the reduction of the war, in the one by reference to a prewar standard, and in the second by an elevation of both the commonplace and the obscure. "[W]hat we require," says the review, is "not the easy beauty that we are used to call inspiration, but a more difficult variety born of friction which, from the effort that it exacts, makes us ask in the midst of our exaltation, 'Is this poetry?'" (55). Whatever her understanding of the enormity of their task, Woolf was less inclined to applaud their efforts than to exhort Murry, in particular, to see the postwar world as it is.

Taken together, these reviews suggest a growth in Woolf's own consciousness of the war and a desire to see beyond Peace Day spectacles to come to terms with constructions of postwar reality. These will finally have less to do with death than with what might be be called the deconstruction of death in the trenches (Winter, *Sites,* 94) and the dissipation of survivor despair. This reality became very much part of her life, owing, perhaps, in some measure, to the survival of her brother-in-law Philip Woolf, particularly as mourning for the war dead more and more took center stage.[27]

27. Adrian Gregory distinguishes bereavement ("the objective situation of someone who has experienced the loss of someone significant to them through death"); grief ("the emotional [affective] response to that loss, [which] includes both psychological and somatic reactions"); and mourning (a culturally determined response to death) (19–20).

Calling the "night of the Cenotaph" (the official unveiling of the monument after the internment of the Unknown Warrior in Westminster Abbey) on 11 November 1920 "a lurid scene, like one in Hell . . . women crying Remember the Glorious Dead, & holding out chrysanthemums" (*Diary* 2, 79–80 and n.8), Woolf saw that the juxtaposition of ceremony and survival had its effect. By 13 November, no fewer than a hundred thousand wreaths had been laid by the empty tomb, and no fewer than a million surrogate mourners visited the site (Eksteins, 255; Cannadine, "War," 224). Philip had escaped physical dismemberment and mutilation, although 25 percent of battle casualties treated in military hospitals were orthopedic cases (Bourke, 33). But Woolf was aware that mutilation is not always visible and although Philip received no treatment after demobilization, according to Leonard, Philip had "a very narrow escape from a booby trap, a mine laid for [his regiment] by the Germans" (*BgA*, 182).

Faced with proliferating war monuments (and other "symbolic gestures of the return of the fallen" [Winter, *Sites*, 27]); the evolution of "the cult of the fallen soldier" (Mosse, 70); and the growth in spiritualism (what David Cannadine sees as the "private denial of death" ["War," 227]), it is little wonder that the incomprehension of civilian poets such as Murry and Eliot would increasingly seem further from the truth than the trench poetry of Wilfred Owen, for example, who was killed a week before the armistice. Philip Woolf had found readjustment a trial, and even went to the Isle of Wright for training in how to be a farmer (*Diary* 1, 277 and n.17), notwithstanding his prewar hope of becoming an artist. Certainly, this was an example of combatant "survival" that Woolf watched with concern and attention. Even Lytton Strachey, to whom she had written of Philip's return, offered to send him a copy of Stephen Graham's *A Private in the Guards* (1919), one of the earliest combatant memoirs and one of the few to admit that "in this war men have craved wounds to get release, and have jumped for death because it was better than life" (7). In sending Philip's address to Strachey, on 30 November 1919, Woolf noted, "Leonard was there [at the farm] yesterday, and found him fearfully dark and dismal, and apparently breaking down in health into the bargain" (*Letters* 2, 404–5).

As a reality and as a threat to life, then, the war was not "over"— it was merely called something else: "reconstruction," for example.[28] Woolf knew

28. Mowat says that toward the end of the war, "reconstruction" was a "magic word" (28). Although "reconstruction" early on referred to the return to prewar conditions, it later referred to the practical problems of demobilization and postwar reorganization.

that death was absolute, but she saw, like Graham, that the reality of survival could be a dismal alternative. In 1921, notwithstanding his ongoing "training" to manage Greenmoor Hill Farm, Philip was "worn & dogged" and, by 1922, Philip had left for India as "an advisor on cattle-breeding" (his official title was "Cattle Breeding Expert to the Government of the Punjab in India").[29] Meanwhile, memorial tributes and "unveilings" continued throughout England (according to Erich Homberger, daily throughout the early 1920s [1430]), almost all without reference to survivors of trench warfare, much less survivors of the war from the streets, notwithstanding the beginnings of ceremonies in the cause of peace and the inclusion of antiwar inscriptions on some monuments—even the one of Edith Cavell, just off Trafalgar Square, to which her last words ("Patriotism is not enough. I must have no hatred or bitterness for anyone") were added in 1924, four years after the monument was erected (McIntyre, 144).[30] (Some years after that, this same statue reminds a character in *The Years* of "an advertisement for sanitary towels" [336].)

Hospitals and recovery facilities and wounded soldiers—spiderlike—had become part of the postwar landscape, and Woolf's references to them are infrequent, not unlike her responses to death during the war. Yet, in a diary entry dated 18 February 1921, three weeks after a visit to Greenmoor Hill Farm, Woolf is finally prepared "to write a historical disquisition on the return of peace," which includes a disquisition on survival.

> It is just perceptible too that there are very few wounded soldiers abroad in blue, though stiff legs, single legs, sticks shod with rubber, & empty sleeves

---

A successor to the Reconstruction Committee of the Cabinet, the Ministry of Reconstruction was established in August 1917 by an act of Parliament and its mandate was broadly defined: "To consider and advise upon the problems which may arise out of the present war and may have to be dealt with on its termination" (5). In 1918–19 the Reconstruction Committee published thirty-eight pamphlets in a series called "Reconstruction Problems, on a wide number of issues, including "The Re-Settlement of Officers" (#12) and "The Classics in British Education" (#21).

29. *Diary* 2, 88; L. Woolf, *BgA*, 182–83; Cecil Woolf, letter to the author, 20 September 1995.

30. Ken Inglis notes that a wreath laid at one such memorial in Cambridge was inscibed with the words IN MEMORY AND HOPE. NO MORE WARS DEMONSTRATION 1922. No More War Day was celebrated for the next few years (602). According to Jill Liddington, the 'No More War' movement, made up of socialists and pacifists, was one of a number of antiwar groups that continued to exist through the twenties and into the thirties (132–33).

are common enough. Also at Waterloo I sometimes see dreadful looking spiders propelling themselves along the platform—men all body—legs trimmed off close to the body. There are few soldiers about. (*Diary* 2, 93)

Invisibility, it would seem, no longer divided combatants and civilians.

Perceptions of death and of war and the popular willingness to afford the war dead a mythical stature—each play a role in Woolf's postwar writings. As these concepts are related to survival, they suggest Woolf's ongoing need to understand constructions of the war and explain their hold on popular consciousness, this state of mind evidenced not only in her reviews but also in her postwar novels, beginning with *Jacob's Room*. Anticipating this concern, two of Woolf's short stories, the unpublished "A Death in the Newspaper" (1921) and "Sympathy" (1919), upon which it is based,[31] involve the meditation of a postwar survivor as it is occasioned by reading a death notice, which is finally recognized to be inaccurate—or inaccurately read.

The train of thought (or feelings), which is the center of each story, is not interrupted until, in the first, "A Death," an invitation arrives to dine at the house of the "dead" man, and in the second, the narrator misspells his name: "Dead! Humphrey Hammond? But Humphrey Hamond spelt his with only one M—Good God are you still alive then? Death how sweet you are! . . . Humphrey's alive! Death what a fraud you are!" (61). Reflecting the effects of four years of reading inaccurate or misleading newspaper reports of death on the front, and similarly inaccurate or belated death notices and obituaries, each narrator apostrophizes death. In "Sympathy," however, the narrator shows impatience with the false alarm: "'Oh don't tell me he lives still! O why did you deceive me?'" (105). In each case, suggesting that death, like survival, has been deprived of a context, the stories also suggest that the lines dividing life and death, reality and illusion, fact and fiction have merged. Yet, neither this blurring nor the war is explicitly mentioned, as if to suggest that its reality and its mythology had already become integrated with the business of living, the pattern of life itself.

In her post-peace novels, and most notably in *Jacob's Room*, Woolf suggests that until the war survivors were perfectly capable of coping with both the reality and the realities of death. Mrs. Betty Flanders, for example, "was a widow in her prime" who had not only managed to survive herself after the death of her husband, Seabrook, but met the challenge of rearing her

---

31. Susan Dick suggests that "A Death in the Newspaper" is a shorter version of "Sympathy" and was probably written in January 1921 (*Collected Stories*, "Sympathy," 292n). "A Death in the Newspaper" is in Jacob's Room Holograph, vol. 3, 61, 63.

three sons alone, in a suburb of Scarborough, with very little money and despite distracting suitors and proposals of remarriage (*JR* 15). The presence of what Lifton and Olson call "an emotional context or system of meaning" (*Living*, 29) is illustrated by the ritual that Seabrook's death had elicited, including the practical dimensions of the burial (which involves a triple seal to protect against graverobbers and internment six feet underground [Roe, 158, n.1]), a context that will undoubtedly be denied the highly self-conscious narrator of *Jacob's Room*: "[W]herever I seat myself, I die in exile" (*JR*, 69).[32]

The novel, which observes the life of the Flanders family (and particularly the growth of Jacob) in the years after the death of Seabrook and leading up to 1914 (when Jacob is, in Kate Flint's words, "swallowed up by the War" ["Revising," 362]), refers to war and war death only in undertones, that is, in allusions, metonyms, and interrupted syntax:[33] "[S]imple young men, these, who would—but there is no need to think of them grown old" (*JR*, 43). Just as the war would interrupt the progress of life, so too would it alter the context that made death acceptable, something that can be seen in Betty Flanders's meditation on Seabrook's tombstone and her transcendent sense of a merging of death and life, in all its manifestations.

> At first, part of herself; now one of a company, he had merged in the grass, the sloping hillside, the thousand white stones, some slanting, others upright, the decayed wreaths, the crosses of green tin, the narrow yellow paths, and the lilacs that drooped in April . . . over the churchyard wall. Seabrook was all that; and when, with her skirt hitched up, feeding the chickens, she heard the bell for service or funeral, that was Seabrook's voice—the voice of the dead. (16)

For Woolf, who had written the novel as the postwar world was presumably returning to normalcy and who, perhaps betraying a reluctant admiration for Mrs. Flanders, was sensitive not only to the effect of ritual but also to what Lady Cecil called the belief in immortality that "the war made . . . difficult" (*Diary* 2, 60). Like Lady Cecil, Woolf may have hoped for the return of the spirit of community she had seen dissipate on Armistice Day

---

32. Barry Morgenstern believes the the novel has two plots: "Jacob's growth and death, and the narrator's learning about him" (97). See also Edward Bishop's "The Subject in *Jacob's Room*" and "The Shaping of *Jacob's Room*"; and Charles G. Hoffman, "'From Lunch to Dinner.'"

33. William A. Evans, whose analysis of the "evolution of language" in Woolf's novels is helpful, but incomplete, says that *Jacob's Room* "shows no especial concern in developing the structures of comparison" and finds little evidence of metonymy and synedoche in Woolf's novels in general and *Jacob's Room* in particular (62–63).

("the whole people . . . concentrated on a single point . . . are once more a nation of individuals" [*Diary* 1, 217]). But it did not happen. "[T]he ceremonial spirit," Woolf observed in August 1920, after attending a funeral in Sussex, "is entirely absent. We never catch fire" (*Diary* 2, 61).

Monuments to the war dead call to mind early ritualized forms that had expressed what Philippe Ariès calls the "anguish of the community," rather than the despair of the individual survivor (582). This was particularly true in the *real* Scarborough, which, considered a "fortified town," as one of the first sites for attack by German warships, erected the Scarborough Monument in 1923.[34] Yet, before the war, for inhabitants of the *fictional* Scarborough,[35] as indeed for much of prewar England, death is part of life: "I never pity the dead," says Mrs. Jarvis. "They are at rest. . . . And we spend our days doing foolish unnecessary things without knowing why" (*JR*, 131).

As has been frequently noticed, evidence of death is everywhere in the novel: a skull on the beach, a tree in the forest, and a butterfly in a net, as well as the Roman fortress beyond Dod's Hill. Yet, for Mrs. Betty Flanders, who often brings her boys to visit Seabrook's gravesite, death and life are fused, and in fact inseparable: "Sounding at the same moment as the bell, her [eldest] son's [Archer's] voice mixed life and death inextricably, exhilaratingly" (16), something suggestive of the kind of spiritualism that vehemently denies the "existence of death" and proscribes mourning (Gorer, 65). The narrator's allusions to death during the war are juxtaposed with reports of life that suggest that distinct categories of being and nonbeing are more apparent than real: "And now Jimmy feeds crows in Flanders and Helen visits hospitals" (*JR*, 97). Finally, Mrs. Flanders's grief for Seabrook is of the same sort as her anxiety over the "loss" of her brother Morty (who had had his troubles) and the loss of her sons, "who were fighting for their country" (175); and her confusion in Jacob's rooms, which she and Bonamy visit without Jacob, is practical: What is she to do with Jacob's shoes? (176).

Originally intending to end the novel with a reference to Mrs. Flanders's seemingly confused response ("They both laughed. The room waved behind her tears" [Jacob's Room Holograph 3, 63]), Woolf omitted this section.

34. Usui, "The German Raid on Scarborough in *Jacob's Room*." The Scarborough memorial, which was unveiled on 26 September 1923, includes the names of twenty civilians (eight men, nine women, and three children) killed during the bombardments of Scarborough in 1914 and 1917 (Boorman, 102).

35. Sue Roe, in the Penguin edition of *Jacob's Room,* suggests that the geography of the actual Scarborough is distinct from that in the novel, although there are similarities. See especially her note 1 (157) and note 8 (159).

It has been suggested that this decision was made because the words were "maudlin", or even "to achieve the effect of action suspended, broken off" (Hoffman, "'From Lunch to Dinner,'" 626; Bishop, "Shaping of *Jacob's Room*," 130). Yet, these readings seem to me to apply only if we accept the idea that Woolf meant to confirm Jacob's death, which I do not believe was her intention. But for the excluded lines, the ending suggests that the implications of the war have not yet been either felt or recognized and the fate of Jacob is made as uncertain as the war; even the highly opinionated narrator is silenced.[36]

Unlike the more than seven hundred inhabitants of Scarborough whose names are engraved on the Scarbrorough Memorial, neither Virginia Woolf nor her husband, nor most of their friends and relatives, had fallen victim to the war. Not surprisingly, perhaps, survival for Leonard, and for Virginia as well, exacted a cost that each paid differently. Although publicly he wrote and spoke volumes on the war and its implications, Leonard would recall in his memoirs some fifty years later only that after the Great War "[o]ne . . . ceased to believe that a public event can be anything other than a horror or a disaster" (*Downhill*, 27). But Virginia Woolf began to recognize its impact on belief much earlier, and beginning, perhaps, with the effect on survivors of public memorialization of the war dead, what Ariès calls "suppression of death," that is, "denying the presence of death in practice, even if one accepts its reality in principle" (579, 580). Mourning is itself a key, Woolf will suggest in *Mrs. Dalloway* and in *To the Lighthouse* especially, not only to acknowledging the reality of death but also to gauging what would be called "the public mood,"[37] something that seemed of constant concern to her, even as she wrote the epistolary, antiwar polemic *Three Guineas* (1938), whose stated purpose is, ironically, "to understand what war means to you" (*3G*, 7).

36. In "The Shaping of *Jacob's Room*," Edward Bishop recognizes that the novel has something to do with "the survivors of World War I," but in emphasizing what he calls the "disturbing lapse in continuity" felt by them, he believes that Woolf emphasizes "the impossibility of making sense of such a death" (130).

37. This function would be filled by Mass-Observation, a group of individual writers (nonjournalists) involved in "self-documentation" of "everyday life and *real* (not just published) public moods" from 1937 on (Harrisson, 11).

2

Life and Death, Memory and Denial
in Postwar London

> I propose to distinguish two among the most potent factors
> in the mental distress felt by non-combatants, against
> which it is such a heavy task to struggle, and to treat of
> them here: the disillusionment which this war has evoked;
> and the altered attitude towards death which this—like
> every other war—imposes upon us.
>
> —Sigmund Freud, "Reflections upon War and Death"

> The social hero-system into which we are born marks our
> paths for our heroism, paths to which we conform, to
> which we shape ourselves so that we can please others,
> become what they expect us to be.
>
> —Ernest Becker, *The Denial of Death*

N OT UNTIL Winifred Holtby's *Virginia Woolf: A Critical Memoir* (1932), the first full-length critical work focusing on her, was *Jacob's Room* called a "war book"; in fact, Holtby stated, "It is as much a war book as *The Death of a Hero* or *Farewell to Arms*" (116). Early reviews of *Jacob's Room* that mention the war, like that of Rebecca West, do so only in passing; others, like the one published in the *TLS,* which compares Jacob to "a little marching soldier," make no mention at all of the war (Majumdar, 95–111).[1] Although Woolf thought the *Times* review "a little tepid," her displeasure was not unmixed with something like relief; she found it "flattering enough" (*Diary* 2, 209).

That the war (and the ironic narrative alluding to it) was missed by so many public voices must have suggested to Woolf that she would be spared the kind of abuse Lytton Strachey had suffered at the publication of *Eminent*

1. Of the sampling offered in Majumdar, only those by Rebecca West (*New Statesman,* 4 November 1922, 142 [100–102], then edited by Leonard) and by Maxwell Bodenheim

Victorians (*Diary* 2, 204, n.16) and given her breathing room. Neverthe-less, her professional sense of relief at the immediate postwar war-silence was not unmixed with a kind of confusion, owing to a similar silence in her friends' responses, even that of Lytton Strachey.[2] She responded tentatively to Lytton's hyperbolic praise of the book, which studiously avoided any mention of the war (this being suspect in the light of the criticism he had re-ceived, particularly in response to "General Gordon"). "I think your praise is extravagant," she wrote him (Majumdar, 94).

She noted privately that it might have suggested some reserve or that it was tinged with an implicit irony: "Lytton praises me too highly for it to give me exquisite pleasure" (*Diary* 2, 207). Woolf did not comment directly on these oversights, but it seems likely that having met with Winifred Holtby in 1931, she would have seen fit to set the record straight, com-menting in her diary, "I'm the hare, a long way ahead of the hounds my crit-ics" (*Letters* 4, 331; *Diary* 4, 45).[3]

Woolf saw *Jacob's Room* as "a necessary step . . . in working free" and vowed that "Mrs. Dalloway" was "to be more close to the fact than Jacob" (*Diary* 2, 208, 207–8). Again, though the war is not mentioned explicitly, she

---

(*Nation* [NY], 28 March 1923: 368–69 [110–11]) mention the war. Curiously, Aileen Pippett, Woolf's first biographer, recognized *Jacob's Room* as a war novel (158) as did James Hafley, *The Glass Roof,* though less decisively (176n. 15). Carolyn Heilbrun, *Toward a Recognition of Androgyny,* considers *Jacob's Room* a war book, and calls it "one of the greatest: the civil-ian *All Quiet on the Western Front*" (164).

    2. Strachey's praise was nothing short of hyperbolic. Although the playful and ironic style is consistent with other letters selected by Leonard Woolf and James Strachey for the volume, Woolf's reaction was clearly divided. Strachey also wrote, "Of course I see some-thing of Thoby in him, as I supposed was intended." Woolf responded, "I breathe more freely now that I have your letter, though I think your praise is extravagant" [*Virginia Woolf & Lytton Strachey Letters,* 144–46]. An edited version of the exchange is published in Majumdar, 93–94.

    3. Woolf wrote a cordial letter to Winifred Holtby on 15 January 1933, after she had read Holtby's book. Although perhaps a matter of civility, the letter also suggests that Mrs. Dalloway of *The Voyage Out* and Mrs. Dalloway of the later novel are the same char-acter: "What an idiotic thing—to give Mrs. Dalloway one father in *The Voyage Out,* and another in *Mrs. Dalloway!* That comes of working from memory" [Joanne Trautmann Banks, "Some New Woolf Letters," 183]. Vera Brittain does not mention a meeting be-tween Woolf and Holtby in *Testament of Friendship,* although she does write of Holtby's admiration for Woolf (315–17). (Woolf, who read the book with some interest, believed "W. H. deserved better" [*Letters* 6, 379]). Brittain also does not include *Jacob's Room* among the war books she mentions in *Testament of Experience* (76–77). Holtby's biogra-pher believes Holtby and Woolf met three times, but I put the count at no fewer than four times (Kennard 109).

is here addressing both the form and substance of the book, which implicitly involves the war. As she "adumbrate[s] . . . a study of insanity & suicide: the world seen by the sane & the insane side by side" (*Diary* 2, 207), she seems to suggest that in the postwar world *sanity* (rather than insanity) is a condition of suicide. Although Woolf's richly ambiguous style may suggest either reading, linking "insanity and suicide" as complements (the usual interpretation) ought not to be seen as her intention.

That insanity and suicide are instead to be read as *contrasts* seems consistent with her more sure vision of the novel eight months later, when, in June 1923, "life & death, sanity & insanity" remain primary concerns. Her vision by this time, however, also includes "the social system," possibly in acquiescence to those critical responses to Jacob that faulted her "'reality' gift" and reinforced her own lack of confidence (*Diary* 2, 248). In any case, it seems to me that her continued "adumbrations," though illustrating the rich ambiguity of her style, also suggest that we may not have fully appreciated either the novel or its provenance. In *Mrs. Dalloway,* Woolf was doing more than affirming her consciousness of the "real world" (Zwerdling, 120). By implicitly stating her intention to show that the definitions of sanity and insanity in the postwar years had been skewed and that their definition ("study") need be informed and altered, Woolf was postulating a relation between sanity and insanity that might only be appreciated by recognizing that the experience of survivors of the war (whether combatants or noncombatants) could lead them to despair (what Kierkegaard called "the sickness unto death") and, possibly, suicide.

Mrs. Dalloway is explicitly dated, in "the middle of June" 1923, a week before the fourth anniversary of the signing of the Treaty of Versailles on 28 June 1919. Unlike *Jacob's Room,* which offers undertones of the war throughout and suggests the *coming* of the war, *Mrs. Dalloway* is overlaid with the war and is more explicitly tied to its experiences and its *effect,* which is, perhaps, part of the "setting free" the earlier novel afforded. Through the offices of a self-conscious, postwar, civilian narrator, who is geographically fixed (leaving Jacob to go to the front unobserved), Woolf had represented incomprehension of the war. *Mrs. Dalloway* exploits the offices of an omniscient and seemingly disinterested narrative voice (which J. Hillis Miller frivolously calls the something "central which permeate[s]" the novel [102]) with the flexibility to report and to enter the consciousness of the characters without reliance on starkly calculated, obvious, and sometimes comic, ironic discourse.

In thus controlling the narrative agency, Woolf seems to have discovered that she did have "that 'reality gift,'" albeit employing a narrative mode unique to her vision. This is not consonant with J. Hillis Miller's vision of the narrator's office: "They thought, therefore I am" (104–5), which would only be true if we accept Daniel Ferrer's assertion that both the characters and the narrator think and speak like middle-class intellectuals living in Bloomsbury.[4] Dorrit Cohn's explanation of the narrated monologue technique (his translation of *erlebte Rede* [97–8]) presumably gives *Mrs. Dalloway* an immediacy not part of Woolf's schema in *Jacob's Room,* where actual experiences of the war are not at issue. But, although exploring the possibilities of indirect discourse in "the twilight realm [of a character's] consciousness" (110), Cohn does not fully take to account Woolf's evocation of what might be called "indirect communication," Roger Poole's term for Kierkegaard's ironic narrative method (537).[5] It seems clear, however, that this term best expresses Woolf's intention in creating a narrative persona whose function in the novel can be seen through the ironic communication of distance from both the war and its experience.

The distance between civilian and combatant experience is explored in *Mrs. Dalloway* where in postwar London the reality of a politician's wife, Clarissa Dalloway (and others who, like Woolf herself, had "seen" the war from the street) is juxtaposed with that of a combat veteran, Septimus Warren Smith—a less privileged Jacob Flanders who had, nonetheless, survived the war. Woolf transformed the physical distance during the war into a physical proximity during the day in the postwar London the novel involves. The

4. Daniel Ferrer finds the narrative ambiguity perplexing owing to a similarity in the voices of characters and the narrative agency: "Throughout *Mrs Dalloway,* idiolects are rare and the level of language remains fairly constant. All the significant characters share with the narrator a certain indefinable accent that might be called Woolfian" (23). He does not find similar similarities in Joyce's *Ulysses* or in Faulkner's *The Sound and the Fury.*

5. Cohn does, however, leave the door open to this possibility by stressing the ambiguities intrinsic to the method: "The degree of association or dissociation between an author and his creature is not always . . . easy to establish. . . . In this respect, the narrated monologue often sustains a more profound ambiguity than other modes of rendering consciousness; and the reader must rely on context, shades of meaning, coloring, and other subtle stylistic indices in order to determine the overall meaning of a text" (112). Roger Poole explains "indirect communication" in phenomenological terms and sees Kierkegaard's use of same signaled through the assumption of personae as having "as its dual axes the total isolation of the individual from his society, and the total obligation to communicate a religious message" (537). See also Poole's "Kierkegaard on Irony."

narrator is omniscient, but only insofar as she knows all about the characters' past and present—as befits one who renders the thoughts and feelings of characters living in postwar England. She does not know the future, and her leitmotif, "The leaden circles dissolved in the air" (a modification of "the leaden coloured clouds dissolved in the air" from an early version of the novel [Notebook labeled "Reviews 1924": 35][6]), is a hope for the future rather than a fact of the present. Through the agency of the narrator, Woolf both presents a picture of a postwar world whose reality is implicitly ironic and portrays the tension that exists between veterans and civilians and, more especially, between life and death, memory and denial.

The distinction between life and death on the sunny day in June the novel involves is sometimes clouded. To what extent can be seen in reference to the characters' experience of the war and experience of the postwar world, that is, to their level of involvement in each. To those who had been civilians in the war, Clarissa Dalloway and Peter Walsh in particular, not only death in the war but also war itself has left them untouched. The first of Clarissa's two "memories" of the war dead does not directly involve the dead at all, but second-hand reports of an inheritance owing to death, and a socially countenanced and applauded repression of death. For Clarissa, "the War was over, except for some one like Mrs. Foxcroft at the Embassy last night eating her heart out because *that nice boy* was killed and now the old Manor House must go to a cousin; or Lady Bexborough who opened a bazaar *they said,* with the telegram in her hand, John, her favourite, killed" (emphasis added; *MrsD,* 5). The war dead are anonymous others and Clarissa spares no thought for anyone killed in the war, finding it "consoling to believe that death ended absolutely" (12).

The belief, if not the sentiment, is also held by Peter Walsh, who has seemingly risen from the dead just in time for the party Clarissa prepares for all day. For Peter Walsh, who had been abroad at one government post or another for the past twenty years and who has not visited England for the past five, the thought of death, particularly Clarissa's, is alarming. When he hears Big Ben striking the hour, "the sudden loudness of the final stroke

6. Most of the manuscripts of *Mrs. Dalloway* at the Berg Collection, New York Public Library, Astor, Lenox and Tilden Foundations (not all of which are in holograph) are dated or in bound notebooks that distinguish them chronologically. The page numbers are ascribed by the Berg Collection. Among the Monks House Papers at the British Library is a holographic manuscript of *Mrs. Dalloway* in three volumes ("Mrs. Dalloway Manuscript"), dated 1923–25; the entire three-volume manuscript is included on reel six of the six-reel microfilm collection *Virginia Woolf Manuscripts from the Monk's House Papers at the University of Sussex* (Harvester).

tolled for death that surprised in the midst of life" he "sees" (in the mind's eye) Clarissa dying, which vision he represses immediately: "No! No! he cried. She is not dead!" (75). In reality, Clarissa is *not dead* and what Peter is doing is, according to Ernest Becker, "a mainspring of human activity," that is, denying "the *idea* of death" (emphasis added; ix). Peter does not deny war deaths; in fact, neither the war nor the war dead enter his consciousness.

The blurring of the distinction between life and death, found in Kierkegaard, is the province of the only born-again civilian in the novel, a veteran of the war in the trenches, Septimus Warren Smith, whose activities that day in June end with his suicide. Continually being reminded by his wife, Rezia, to "look," Septimus sees rather more than is considered normal. When he was in the trenches, living with constant reminders of death, in what Leed calls "a place that dissolved the clear distinction between life and death," he had doubtlessly experienced this "transgression of categories" (21), which explains why he felt nothing when Evans, his officer, died.

That this categorical transgression includes an inability to countenance death as a reality also suggests that activities normally taken to overcome fear of death cease, and the "normal" activity of repression in the presence of death (as seen in the civilian characters) is no longer an operative mode of behavior. What keeps the "normal" civilian population going is what Kierkegaard called "philistinism," which "tranquilizes itself in the trivial" (quoted in Becker, 74). Such is true of Lady Bexborough, "the woman [Clarissa] admired most" (*MrsD*, 13), who assumes a control of possibility, which with necessity makes up "actuality" (*Sickness unto Death*, 66). In the civilian population, living in this "cultural mediocrity," we see evidenced *normal* repression of death. It is the "psychotic" alternative that is evidenced in Septimus, whose behavior can be understood as a "flaunting of reality" (Becker, 75), and who has no sense of possibility because he has no sense of *temporal* reality, death.[7] To Septimus, the numbing finality of death was not a given in the trenches and it is not a given in the postwar world. In fact, Septimus begins the day believing "there is no death" (*MrsD*, 36), only to be momentarily confused in his pronouncement when he "sees" his officer Evans (who had died five years earlier). But it is not Evans who has returned from death to life; it is Septimus who is "taken from life to death" (37).

Septimus does not merely repress death; he *actively* denies its reality. When he imagines "the dead," he thinks of them as *not* dead: "The dead

7. Mark Hussey's explanation of temporal reality is helpful in trying to bridge the gap between what he sees as the circularity of Woolf's vision and her changing "angle of vision." It seems to me that Woolf's understanding of the reality of death owes much to the changing angle of vision caused by the war.

were in Thessaly. . . . There they waited till the War was over" (105). To Septimus, as to Woolf, there is but one time, found in Bergson's idea of durée and as it is applied in Proust, whom Woolf was reading as she began *Mrs. Dalloway.*[8] Bergson says that the present includes both the past and the future (137) and that our personal sense of "reality" is beyond our normal perceptive ability and thus is not dependent on a time-consciousness (145). Taking this one step further, in the character of Septimus, Woolf paints a portrait of one for whom the reality of life and death, of the present, in Bergson's sense, has stopped with the war.

Lacking as well what Husserl calls "internal time-consciousness," that is, lacking a personal sense of time past, time present, and time future, Septimus lacks conscious memory of the war, that is, memory of the war as something past.[9] Husserl is concerned with the *"lived experience* of time" (28–29), measured by an inward sense of time past and time present and, like Septimus, sees the measurement of time as irrelevant. In the trenches, according to Siegfried Sassoon, the combatant lost his sense not of the past, but of the future: "[W]hen I tried to think about the future I found that I couldn't see it. There was no future except 'the rest of the War'" (*Sherston's Progress,* 149).

For Septimus, however, four years after the signing of the treaty, time has no significance at all, and "the rest" of the war has not yet occurred. After Rezia and Septimus had stopped in Regent's Park, en route to their appointment with the nerve specialist, Sir William Bradshaw, the question of time is seen in its effect on Septimus as Rezia's casual comment, "It is time," sets off in him a string of associations: "The word 'time' split its husk; poured its riches over him; and from his lips fell like shells, like shavings from a plane, without his making them, hard, white, imperishable words, and flew to attach themselves to their places in an ode to Time; an immortal ode to Time" (*MrsD,* 105). For Septimus there is but one time, time that is unmeasured, undifferentiated. For Septimus there is only the present; there is no future; there is no past. And if there is no past, there is nothing to remember.

Septimus does not remember the war; unlike the civilian characters, he

8. James Hafley (*The Glass Roof*) was among the first to see evidence of Bergsonian thought in Woolf and to suggest that her reading of Proust may have led her along these lines. Bergson's philosophy rests on the idea of duration (revealed to an individual in immediate experience) and in "pure" rather than measured time. According to Bergson, "our memories form a chain . . . and . . . our character, always present in all our decisions, is indeed the actual synthesis of all our past states . . . [and] take[s] a share in the final decision" (146).

9. For Husserl, memory rests on an internal time-consciousness, distinct from measured time, and thus obviating a correlative sense of chronological sequence. Expectation ("expectational intuition") is an inversion of memory ("memorial intuition") (79).

daily lives with its reality, that is, the war has become his *actuality*. For him, the postwar world has duplicated the war in the trenches—but without the trenches. When Dr. Bradshaw asks him about his service in the war, Septimus responds, the narrator tells us, by "repeat[ing] the word 'war' interrogatively. . . . 'The War?' the patient asked. . . . He really forgot" (145). Although personal death is ordinarily unthinkable, or not thought about, as in the case of Jacob Flanders, the omnipresence of death in war, according to Freud, makes it possible for participants to become "heroes who cannot believe in their own death" ("War and Death," 132), which might have been the case with Leonard's brothers, who were blown up by a shell as they attempted to rescue their officer. Freud's remarks allow for the depersonalization of the *idea* of death, but, removed from the trenches by time and distance, Septimus is no longer a participant and was never seen to be a "hero," the term itself being a societal construct, as Woolf had observed after the death of Rupert Brooke.

The equanimity with which Septimus handled the death of his officer, Evans, is ironically like the equanimity with which civilians, such as Lady Bexborough, managed to cope with war-death at home. To Woolf such equanimity in the face of death, particularly as she experienced it during the war, is an aberration. To Septimus, coping is the same as not feeling, and to him, as to Woolf herself, not feeling is a sin. But, unlike Woolf, and like North Pargeter in *The Years,* who "had been in the trenches" and "seen men killed" (*Years,* 404), Septimus "had gone through the whole show, friendship, European War, death" and at the end, as the narrator tells us, "far from showing any emotion" he had been "taught" by the war that it was better to cope (*MrsD*, 130–31).

That, like Freud, Virginia Woolf had "seen" the war as a civilian (albeit from an opposite "street") and had herself been subject to socially (read societally) motivated diagnoses both before and during the war years may explain certain similarities in their experiences of the war, and their understanding of civilian responses. At the same time, it may explain why Woolf, like Freud, felt compelled to examine more closely the postwar condition of combatants and the postwar "social system" that made their continued survival problematic.[10] Woolf, like her contemporaries who experienced the war

10. Although Freud avoided analysis of suicide in regard to the war, his writings in the postwar years were revised to take into account its experience (e.g., *The Psychopathology of Everyday Life*). According to Ernest Jones, his disciple and biographer, Freud's concern with the treatment administered by Austrian medical doctors during the war led to his "Memorandum on the Electrical Treatment of War Neurotics," for example. See Jones 393–408 and Litman.

from the streets, had coped with news of death on the front through re-pression. Becoming cognizant of the "normalcy" of same in the aftermath of the war, Woolf chose to explore its cultural and psychological *implications* in *Mrs. Dalloway*.

The question of when she began to read Freud in earnest, part of the study by Elizabeth Abel, does not seem relevant here, particularly given the frequency of her meetings with James Strachey and his wife, and Adrian Stephen and Karen Costelloe, all of whom studied with Freud, and the fact that the Hogarth Press became the official publishers of Freud in English after having published the first English translation (by James Strachey) of *Beyond the Pleasure Principle* in 1922.[11] It seems obvious that Woolf applied the principles expounded therein in creating her characters. Freud recog-nized that "[n]o complete explanation has yet been reached either of war neuroses or of the traumatic neuroses of peace" (*BPP*, 10). He nevertheless believed that the denial of death and its repression were part of the same continuum, their distinctions measured by the strength of resistance to what he identifies as the "death instinct" (46–47). Septimus had not only seen men die; he had also seen them deny death in the process.

Virginia Woolf had never seen men die at the front, which may suggest why she spent more time planning and agonizing over the character of Septimus (and to a lesser extent Rezia) than the civilians. In planning the novel, Woolf resolved to "emphasize character" and put weight on the idea of *being seen* as defining the reality of Septimus: "He [Septimus] is only real as she [Rezia] sees him." The emphasis on seeing and being seen becomes a key to appreciating how she intended his character to be understood. "She [Rezia] *feels* him alternatively far & near. [He] might be left vague—as a mad person is—not so much [a] character as an *idea*" (emphasis added; Virginia Woolf, Notebook labeled "Choephori of Aeschylus," 2v, 3). What Woolf ad-umbrates here is not only the indefinition of "madness," as Roger Poole sug-gests, but also the central issue of the ascendancy of ideas over things as a measure of reality. Reality in this context exists in what we see and what we think about what we see, what we do not see, and whether we think about what we do not see.[12]

11. Edward A. Hungerford and Keith Hollingsworth made early contributions to our understanding of Freudian readings of Mrs. Dalloway, but neither pays much attention to the war. Beverly Schlack, in "A Freudian Look at Mrs Dalloway," offers insights that relate to the war, but in seeing Septimus as "Clarissa's double" she overlooks the central importance of the war.

12. See especially Poole's chapter 14, "Was Septimus Smith 'insane?'" in *The Unknown Virginia Woolf* (3d ed., 185–97). See also Lucio Ruotolo's *The Interrupted Moment,* which

Unlike the civilian characters, Septimus "sees" implications, and to see thusly can make him mad. "But he would not go mad. He would shut his eyes; he would see no more" (*MrsD*, 32). When he opens his eyes, he seeks to share his insight: "'I will tell you the time,' said Septimus, very slowly, very drowsily, smiling mysteriously. As he sat smiling at the dead man in the grey suit the quarter struck—the quarter to twelve" (106). To Septimus the man in the grey suit (Peter Walsh) is dead (though death has no reality); to be dead is not to see and the man in the grey suit does not *really* see. Rezia recognizes that the world is "indifferent" to her suffering as she believes Septimus to be (34, 98–99). Septimus judges himself guilty (in the name of "human nature") of the "sin" of not feeling, and believes himself sentenced to death (137). Having recognized, more profoundly than Rezia, that the sin is shared with the civilian population, he also implicitly judges guilty the man in grey, Peter Walsh, who sees, but does not really see.

Peter Walsh, who "always saw through Clarissa" (90), shares war-blindness with other civilians, none of whom have seen the war at all. Although he notices changes in London, he does not so much as consider the possibility that they might have been caused by the war:

> Those five years—1918 to 1923—had been, he suspected, somehow very important. People looked different. Newspapers seemed different. Now for instance there was a man writing quite openly in one of the respectable weeklies about water-closets. That you couldn't have done ten years ago— written quite openly about water-closets in a respectable weekly. And then this taking out a stick of rouge or a powder-puff and making up in public. On board ship coming home there were lots of young men and girls—Betty and Bertie he remembered in particular—carrying on quite openly; the old mother sitting and watching them with her knitting, cool as a cucumber. The girl would stand still and powder her nose in front of every one. And they weren't engaged; just having a good time; no feelings hurt on either side. As hard nails she was—Betty What'shername—; but a thorough good sort. She would make a very good wife at thirty—she would marry when it suited her to marry; marry some rich man and live in a large house near Manchester. (108)

By calling attention to five—rather than to four—years, Woolf makes clear that what changes there were began with the war itself. She particularly calls

---

very much involves how the characters are seen by each other. He compares "the early Septimus" to "some Lawrentian antihero" and believes him "stirred by the idea people represent to him rather than by their presence" (106).

attention to those in the upper (or upper-middle) quadrant of the social system who maintain a prewar sense of the continuity of time, what Fussell sees as the prewar mind-set, which never questioned historical continuity and saw the Great War "taking place within a seamless, purposeful 'history' involving a coherent stream of time running from past through present to future" (*Great War*, 21), as Peter's comment about Betty's future marriage suggests. The "new independence" experienced by women, a holdover from the war, is observed but not considered in the context of the war. However, this, according to Graves and others, is a key to the times.[13]

Given his war-blindness, Peter Walsh's thinking would naturally skirt the issue of the war entirely, this seemingly part of the plan Woolf had for the "tunneling process" that would "build up the *idea* of Clarissa's character" (emphasis added; *Diary* 2, 272; Notebook labeled "Choephori of Aeshylus," 4). Woolf made their relations more ironic by suggesting that though Peter can pronounce Clarissa guilty of "the death of the soul," he does not see a similar guilt in himself. When Peter sees Rezia and Septimus in Regent's Park, his reaction lacks any depth of perception. "And that is being young," he thinks, offhandedly wondering "what awful fix had they got themselves into, both to look so desperate as that on a fine summer morning" (*MrsD*, 106). The narrator's effort to pass this off as typical and unworthy of comment is also ironically intended.

> [W]as there, after all, anything to draw attention to them, anything to make a passerby suspect here is a young man who carries in him the greatest message in the world, and is, moreover, the happiest man in the world, and the most miserable? . . .
>
> To look at, he might have been a clerk. . . . (126)

Hyperbole, litotes, non sequiturs—all suggest ironic distancing, which might seem gratuitous, and too strongly protested, if Woolf were not at this point clearly differentiating the narrative treatment of Septimus from that of the civilian characters. This she does by distinguishing ironic distancing

---

13. Graves makes much of the new independence, rather disapprovingly (*Long Weekend*, 36–49). However, Charles Loch Mowat says that despite the boon in women's employment during the war, by 1919 three-quarters of a million women had lost their jobs (23). Citing Vera Brittain's *Women's Work in Modern England* (1928), Mowat says that most of the women remaining in the workforce returned to service industries, particularly domestic service (23–24). Contemporary interpretations of women's role during and after the war has led to marked disagreement as to the extent of the war's effect on the patriarchal power structure, as seen in Sandra Gilbert's "Soldier's Heart" and Jane Marcus's "The Asylums of Antaeus."

from satirical discourse, which is largely reserved for levels of the social system, from which the Warren Smiths and other living reminders of the war are excluded. The narrator stops just short of saying that it is just human nature to ignore that which is not visibly extraordinary. Further suggesting Septimus's isolation in contrast to the mutual tunneling of memories and observations by Clarissa and Peter (all prewar or not related to the war) is the tunnel Septimus does not share with his wife (whose memories of him begin at the end of the war). Significantly, only the narrator tunnels into Septimus, a signal not only of his isolation as a character in the novel but also of the isolation felt by ex-servicemen returning to the postwar world, an isolation Woolf had observed both during and after the war. Peter Walsh, who observes Rezia and Septimus, is part of the world that Rezia believes "indifferent" to suffering. As Septimus believes that it is "the fault of the world . . . that he could not feel" (133), he sees Peter as its personification, as a "dead man in a grey suit."

When Woolf first envisaged the novel, she planned it to "enclose the human heart" (*Diary* 2, 13–14), a richly ambiguous beginning reminiscent of Ford Madox Ford's *The Good Soldier*. But though Woolf clearly modified and expanded what Charles Hoffman calls her "thematic focus and narrative design through the introduction of Septimus in the novel" ("From Short Story to Novel," 172), she did not abandon her first intention. In February 1922 Woolf had determined that reading the classics, full of "action of the human heart & not of muscle or fate," was "hard going" (*Diary* 2, 169); curiously, about the same time, her trip abroad had to be canceled on the advice of Dr. Harrington Sainsbury, a heart specialist (*Diary* 2, 170).

Woolf may have begun to see that the character of Septimus juxtaposed with those of both Rezia and Peter would require an additional dimension. She modified and expanded the plan privileging "the human heart" to one that would expose "human nature," an expression that can be seen as a denial of culpability, as in "It's just human nature," which is implicit in the narrator's exculpation of the "dead man," Peter Walsh. The narrator suggests, albeit ironically, that Peter cannot be faulted for not paying attention to Septimus, for not seeing the signs that suggest he is still fixated by the war. In the postwar world "business as usual" remained the rule on the street, and veterans, however marginal, were seemingly assimilated in the process (Leed, 209).

In the novel, Peter sees changes in newspapers and in young women, something he (like Robert Graves) rather disapproves of, but (unlike Robert Graves) believes will change back. Peter does not mention survivors of the war, and could not, the narrator suggests, infer Septimus's private history, which had included prewar aspirations inspired by a poetic spirit and an imaginative mind. "London," she tells us, "has swallowed up many millions of young men called Smith" (*MrsD*, 127). In *Now It Can Be Told*, a journalistic commentary written by Sir Philip Gibbs, a war correspondent involved in suppressing war news (for which, subsequently, he was knighted), the changes found by returning veterans are barely touched on. "Something had altered in *them*," he said (emphasis added; 547), implying that they were less manly than their service records would suggest in being ill-equipped to face a world different from the one they had left. But a year later, while restating this observation, albeit with a slightly different emphasis ("They had been utterly changed"), Gibbs also notices that the England to which they returned had been changed "[i]n many subtle ways, not apparent on the surface of things" (*More*, 221, 213).

Peter does not look beyond "the surface of things" and the narrator signals a detachment from that kind of "cheap reality" with which Woolf herself was decidedly uneasy, having come to terms with its limitations both aesthetically (as a narrative method in *Jacob's Room* and as a scheme for characterization in "Mrs. Dalloway on Bond Street" [1923]) and in the real world. Tellingly, on 19 June 1923 Woolf noted her "distrust" of "reality—its cheapness" and resolved in *Mrs. Dalloway* "to go for the central things" (*Diary* 2, 248–49), which very much include the things represented by Septimus Smith, a nondescript veteran whose wounds are not visible to observers and reporters of a "cheap reality."

Like Arnold Bennett and his contemporaries (who Woolf believed reporters at heart, as she made clear in "Mr. Bennett and Mrs. Brown," published a month after *Mrs. Dalloway*), civilians (who rarely see beyond the surface and only occasionally to the heart) and reporters such as Philip Gibbs (who demonstrated how it could be done) look *at* the returning veterans with a lack of sympathy reminiscent of the government's *Report of the War Office Committee of Inquiry into "Shell-Shock."* (Woolf undoubtedly knew of the publication through reports and excerpts in the press and through talk with Leonard, who was then a Labour Party candidate for office [Thomas, 51].) In contrast to the War Office report and Gibbs's reports, Woolf demands that we divide out attention between the narrated monologues of Septimus Warren Smith and the external narrative, which is handled, appropriately, with a Kierkegaardian irony, signaled by an "essentially critical stance" [*CI*, 276]. The condition of the survivors Woolf had seen in hospitals and "homes" (a standard British euphemism, as Woolf herself was aware, for what both Chesler and Showalter refer to as asylums, or the kind of convalescent home Woolf spent time in, mostly before the war, or where combat veterans went to recover both during and after the war) profoundly affected her, as can be seen in their imaginative transfiguation in *Mrs. Dalloway*.

During the war Woolf had seen Leonard's brother, Philip Sidney Woolf, "pass[ing] his days in a dream from which he feels himself detached," while at the same time "wondering why he doesn't feel more," observations that Woolf obviously brought to bear on her creation of Septimus Warren Smith, Philip being a more proximate model than Siegfried Sassoon, whom Elaine Showalter believes to be uppermost on Woolf's mind during the writing of the Septimus scenes (*Female Malady*, 192). What makes Philip a more likely candidate for Woolf's imaginative transfiguration is that, like Septimus, Leonard's brother "enlisted early," witnessed the death of his brother (who, like Septimus, was an *aspiring* poet), and despite his presumed assimilation into the postwar world as a farmer (having given over his aspirations to become an artist) was "worn & dogged, but not much life in him" (*Diary* 2, 88).

Similarly, there is not much life left in Septimus and what there is "he did not want . . . putting from him with a wave of his hand that eternal suffering, that eternal loneliness" (*MrsD*, 37). The life Septimus feels drawn toward in Regent's Park is like a dream: "[A]s, before waking . . . the sleeper feels himself drawing to the shores of life, so he felt himself drawing toward life" (104). The only control Septimus sees is ironically translated through the narrator's tunnel and her report, which employs diction that includes both hyperbole and litotes, what Wayne Booth calls "clues" to ironic intent.

> Up in the sky swallows swooping, swerving, flinging themselves in and out, round and round, yet *always* with *perfect control* as if elastics held them; and the flies *rising and falling;* and the sun spotting now this leaf, now that, in mockery, dazzling it with soft gold in *pure* good temper; and now and again some chime (*it might be a motor horn*) *tinkling divinely* on the green stalks— *all* of this, calm and reasonable as it was, made out of ordinary things as it was, was the truth now; beauty, that was the truth now. Beauty was *everywhere.* (emphasis added; *MrsD*, 104–5)

It is the more ironic that Peter sees life differently, and by comparing it to a human heart: "Like the pulse of a perfect heart, life struck through the streets" (82). To Peter, the reality of the postwar world is reflective of civilization. Septimus can only dream of escaping the postwar world, of leaving its reality, and becoming part of an *un*civilized nature, which, the narrator suggests, is impossible in this life, in this postwar world.

Seemingly having all but disappeared from the street, veterans were over-looked by 1923. Or, perhaps more to the point, given the postwar upheaval civilians and reporters were looking elsewhere. Victims of the war were seen to have no life at all, no existence. Demobilization and discharge had been "mainly completed" by 1920. Yet, while the War Pensions Act of 1921 had begun to be applied to veterans, particularly in Class C ("disabilities not immediately obvious, but emerging after a latent period of varied length, as for example, tuberculosis"), and those approved had begun to receive benefits, these were strictly monitored (Mitchell, 315–16). For the most part sympathy and assistance afforded to veterans had all but ceased by 1921. The Addison Housing Act, designed to help returning veterans, had been "stifled," and "the ideals of the Fisher Education Act destroyed" (Marwick, *Deluge,* 295). And, with the release of the government's report, the term "shell-shock" had been disallowed on the grounds of its being too commonly applied and ill-defined and all but officially proscribed. The War Office Committee (which included Dr. Maurice Craig) had seen it as an excuse for malingering or insubordination. Those who exhibited the least sign of derangement did so at some risk, and like as not would be branded unfit after the fact, that is, seen as unfit for employment.

Little wonder, then, that those who could avoid an immediate return to the reality of the postwar world of London did so, like Gerald Brenan, who went to Spain. Others, whenever possible, left London for quieter, more congenial climes, like Robert Graves, who went back to Cambridge, or Philip Woolf, who sought refuge at Greenmore Hill Farm, or Nick Bagenal, who became a horiculturalist in Kent. Most who could do so were officers and already of some standing in the social system or were financially able to seek private attention to the problems of readjustment, under the care of sympathetic specialists like Dr. W. H. R. Rivers (who treated Wilfred Owen as well as Siegfried Sassoon) or like Dr. Gilbert Anderson in Rebecca West's *The Return of the Soldier.*

The picture we have of veterans returning from the war focuses on officers, not only because, based on statistics, they were seen to suffer proportionately more from the effects of war, particularly from psychological disorders stemming from shell-shock, but also because they published poetry during the war and memoirs afterward.[14] Enlisted men were largely left to

14. In *The Norton Book of Modern War,* for example, Paul Fussell attempts to present a fair cross-section of voices speaking to the horror of modern war. Those chosen to represent the World War I include poets, memoirists, letter writers, and two women (Vera Brittain and Kathleen Tynan). Of the war poets in the collection (Rupert Brooke, Siegfried

fend for themselves, although Graves observed that anyone "who had served in the trenches for as much as five months, or who had been under two or three rolling artillery barrages, was an invalid." Putting "shell-shock" in quotations, no doubt in deference to the report (a standard practice after 1921), Graves states that it was a condition suffered by virtually everyone who had been there (*Long Week-end*, 27). Yet, by 1921 references to shell-shock in medical journals had been abandoned in favor of the term "war neuroses." In the Medical Services study of pensions, the terms "neuraesthenia" and "psychoses," it would seem, are meant to cover the symptoms of the ill-defined condition.[15]

The issue of pensions is not mentioned in *Mrs. Dalloway*, though for most returning veterans, the need for same was gravely felt. There were 1.6 million awards by 1929, but it is impossible to know how many more needed and deserved them. Despite the War Pensions Act, which was administered by the Ministry of Pensions, "allowances" and "awards" were withheld from those not seen to have *visible* wounds or conditions owing directly to the war. The statistics compiled by the ministry suggest not only an absence of thoroughness but also of fellow feeling, both of which came under review at the insistence of the British Legion in the 1930s (Winter, *Great War*, 274–76).

Statistics on mortality, for example, are highly suspect (shocking, in fact), involving only "*pensioners* who died whilst in receipt of some continuing monetary compensation." Though these statistics are widely quoted, "[t]hey do not, *therefore*, include [those who received a] gratuity or a temporary allowance which had expired at the time of death, *the number of these and the cause being generally unknown*" (emphasis added; Mitchell, 317). Certainly, they would not have included someone like Septimus Smith, who is not, apparently, on the governmental dole and who has not been counted in the official statistics involving casualties of the war. There is little to suggest that

Sassoon, Edmund Blunden, Wilfred Owen, Isaac Rosenberg, Herbert Reed, Robert Graves, and Ivor Gurney), all were officers: three were killed, two wrote of the war their entire lives, and one, Ivor Gurney, wrote war poetry in an asylum for the insane until his death in 1937.

15. In the index to the report, psychoses are included under the category of "mental diseases," and neurasthenia is included under "diseases of the nervous system." Thomas W. Salmon, in *The Care and Treatment of Mental Disease and War Neuroses ("Shell Shock") in the British Army*, which he wrote in 1917 for the War Work Committee of the National Committee for Mental Hygiene, includes a bibliography of "references in English to mental diseases and war neuroses ('shell shock') and their treatment and management"; 141 published sources are listed. See also Sue Thomas.

he exhibited any *visible* sign of war-related "disability" during or immediately after the war. As the narrator tells us, "He was right there. The last shells missed him. He watched them explode with indifference" (*MrsD*, 131).

The only real heroes in the Great War were the dead. To have not only his military service but also his survival validated, a veteran needed visible proof of service, like a badge of courage—an amputated limb, for example. Although virtually everything about the Great War was unprecedented (including the number of veterans who sought pensions), the social system and its representative, the Ministry of Pensions, did not accept survival alone as proof of service. The bureaucratic red tape, which must have led many potential beneficiaries of the governmental largesse to forgo the exercise, may explain the steady decline in requests for compensation after 1921 (Mitchell, 312). Before being considered for a pension, one had to have a visible disability that was deemed to have been "consequent upon general demobilisation," and then appear before a medical board appointed by the ministry, which would then "assess the degree of disablement" (309, 311), a task made more touchy when it involved the "'shell-shocks'" (as the ministry self-consciously called them), whose symptoms and disabilities may not have been either immediately visible or obvious. Moreover, if there were a "pre-existing condition," as was the case with musician-turned-poet Ivor Gurney, a petition for a pension could be refused (Kavanagh, 4, 8).

According to the report, a shell-shock was deemed personally culpable, and by the letter of that definition, no hero. By dying, a combatant was grist for the mill of hero makers, the propagandists of the Great War in progress and those who saw to it that survivors and their experience was forgotten afterward. A dead hero provided a cheap reality capable (in the "right" hands) of perpetuating the myth of war. If a combatant did not die, a financial allotment from the ministry in a small way legitimized his service and in a large way kept him off the street.

Personal approbation and "promotion," such as Septimus received, were all but worthless. Even Mr. Brewer, his prewar employer and surrogate father, although proud to have Septimus return, can only say: "You have done your duty" (*MrsD*, 133). "The War" is dismissed by Mr. Bowley with a "tut-tut"; the only heroes to which Mr. Bowley responds (in fact, the only heroes in the novel) are cast in bronze (28). "Death, death—in the service of the Nation. That was the only creditable gift for a man with a wife. It was necessary to kill himself, but so as not to bring discredit on one's wife," are lines Woolf wrote and struck out in the first version of "The Hours," the working title of the novel until its publication (Notebook labeled "Book of scraps of J's R. & first version of The Hours [Mrs. Dalloway]," 159). She also modified a narrated monologue in the 1924 version that said that Septimus "thinks death better than life" (Notebook labeled "Reviews 1924," 21). What these revisions did, finally, in the published version, is to make clear not only that Septimus lacks complicity in the thinking of the world, but is its enemy: "The whole world was clamouring: Kill yourself, kill yourself, for our sakes" (*MrsD*, 140).

Living in the postwar world, a combatant, such as Septimus, who lacked a visible wound was expected "to get on with it" unobtrusively and discreetly. In *Mrs. Dalloway* Woolf suggested the burden placed on such "unsung heroes" by obliquely punning on the expression, by having Septimus see the "quick[ening of] trees into life" as reminiscent of "plumes on horses' heads, feathers on ladies" and to "[t]he sparrows fluttering, rising, and falling in jagged fountains" (32). To Septimus these are "part of the pattern" (33) of a harmonious and, in Buber's terms, an integrated and relational life. They are not seen as such, if they are noticed at all, by the rest of the postwar world. Septimus and others like him were kept from disrupting the apparent harmony of life that had been changed by the war, but in ways so "subtle" that most civilians had not noticed or, as in the case of Peter Walsh, brushed aside in anticipation of an eventual return to prewar normalcy.

Woolf alerts us to a different view of things through the narrated monologues, particularly those of the civilian characters from whom the narrator effects distance. Narrative irony is a double-edged sword, demonstrating the incongruity implicit in their visions of the war itself and in their observations of Septimus—who had been there. Since his return to London from Italy and until some weeks before his suicide on a sunny day in June 1923, Septimus Warren Smith had lived admirably, becoming assimilated into the postwar world by displaying the same sangfroid as that exhibited by civilians like Mr. Brewer during the war. Mr. Brewer's vision of the war in progress was myopic, if quasi-mythic, as the narrator tells us with an ironic disdain: "[S]omething happened which threw out many of Mr Brewer's calculations, took away his ablest young fellows, and eventually, so prying and insidious were the fingers of the European War, smashed a plaster cast of Ceres, ploughed a hole in the geranium beds, and utterly ruined the cook's nerves" (129–30). Referring to the cast of Ceres (the goddess of corn), the narrator, though suggesting, as Beverly Schlack believes, "the life-death antithesis that pervades the novel" (*Continuing Presences*, 52) more subtly personifies the power of the war itself, as if its effects stopped when it ceased to be. The power of the war to effect changes more damaging than the loss of a plaster statue and a flower bed is seen only by the narrator, who tells us that "in the trenches the change which Mr Brewer desired when he advised football was produced *instantly;* he [Septimus] developed manliness" (emphasis added; *MrsD,* 130).

"Manliness" is what happens in war when what Freud calls a "parasitic double" overcomes the fear of death, a fear that returns "as soon as the peace-ego realizes what danger it runs of losing its life" ("Psychoanalysis and War Neurosis," 217). The universal fear of death is thus denied during the war, but the peace-ego does not return to Septimus, who is expected to retain his manliness in the postwar world. Unlike the condition of heroism, which demands death, manliness demands the *apparent* death of feelings, that is, their denial in combat and their repression in the postwar world.

When Septimus *identifies* his inability to feel after Evans's death, he does not "lie," as Lee Edwards believes (105), and the death of Evans did not cause the death of his feelings, but awoke his consciousness of it. Septimus had not been feeling for a long time before Evans was killed, probably in an explosion. This explains why, when Septimus hears the backfire of a car in postwar London, the same "violent explosion which made Mrs. Dalloway jump" (19), his reaction is not unlike that of the inmates at the Star & Garter, "waiting for the noise to be over" (*Diary* 1, 294).

As Freud explains, in war the "reality principle" exists in curious relation to the death instinct, both of which are kept in check in ordinary circumstances. The trauma of war can lead to behavior typical of "subjective ailments," like melancholia (*BPP,* 10–11). Under the strain of combat, primitive instincts, particularly the "double feeling" of love and hate against someone who died, becomes manifest and leads to the feeling of guilt (*Totem and Taboo,* 83). Septimus exhibits signs of each, crying, for example, several times during the day. But this alone cannot explain Septimus, arguably the most complex and important combatant character in all of Woolf, and certainly the most difficult to penetrate, in part because of what A. Alvarez calls "psychic numbing," an extreme form of denial of death (*Savage,* 263). After the "explosion" caused by the backfire, Septimus sees the "gradual coming together of everything to one centre before his eyes, as if some horror had come to the surface and was about to burst into flames" and this "terrified him" (*MrsD,* 21). The war from the beginning of his day is clearly part of Septimus's actuality.

Septimus, who anticipates Buber, was taught by the war that there is no life if there is no love and there is no love if there is no relation. Septimus learned from the solitude of his experience in the trenches: "The War had taught him. It was sublime" (130). What Buber says, in fact, both informs and is informed by Septimus Warren Smith. Smith, more than any character in war literature, demonstrates that, as Buber says, "Feelings dwell in man, but man dwells in his love" (*I and Thou*, 66). Unlike Rezia (and Clarissa) Septimus does not believe "[t]o love makes one solitary" (*MrsD*, 33). To Septimus, love makes one whole, complete, in much the same way as it does to Buber: "The world is merely a setting for experience; it does not play an active part in experience. The world objectifies; experience is subjective" (*I and Thou*, 56). Buber's philosophy is based on the ascendancy of love, of relation.

Septimus, who experiences "thunder claps of fear [that] he could not feel" (*MrsD*, 131), does not lie (as one cannot fear without feeling, any more than one can weep). Rather, he bemoans the lack of relation in his life, the unfulfilled need to love, the need to communicate. He writes down revelations on the backs of envelopes, but he comes to understand, unlike Rezia and like Buber, that language merely objectifies relation. What is needed is a language that will catch more than "one corner of actual life" (*I and Thou*, 69). "So, thought Septimus, looking up, they are signalling to me. Not indeed in actual words; that is, he could not read the language *yet*" (emphasis added; *MrsD*, 31). The war had made a mockery of both the need for relation and its possibility, in reaction to which Septimus developed what the world saw as manliness. The manliness he developed denied the possibility of death and led the way for heroism, which could be achieved only in death.

Unlike the civilian characters, Septimus does not fear death any more than it is feared by Kierkegaard or by Montaigne, whom Woolf was reading in preparation for a review that was eventually part of the first *Common Reader*. Yet, the fear of death occupies much of the civilian characters' thoughts (particularly those characters having the least contact with or consciousness of the war). Septimus does not even fear the dead, or their communications, something suggesting that societal taboos involving death and the dead, as discussed by Freud, do not play a role in Septimus's postwar life, any more than they did in the trenches, any more than they do in Montaigne. In fact, both Montaigne and Septimus spend much time planning for death.

Montaigne believes (and throughout his essays shows how) we should detach ourselves from the numbing finality of death and recognize that what "we principally fear in death is pain, its customary forerunner" (*CW*, 37). This is something that also occurs to Septimus: "[H]ow does one set about it, with a table knife, uglily, with floods of blood,—by sucking a gaspipe?" (*MrsD*, 140). Montaigne believes that a mocking attitude toward both death and fear of same is the way to go (*CW*, 35). He has no patience with those who live only to worry about death: "He who has not the courage to suffer either death or life, who will neither resist nor flee, what can we do with him?" (*CW,* 47). Clarissa loves life (*MrsD,* 5) and finds death "unbelievable" (185). Both Montaigne and Septimus address death openly and find it a consoling prospect. What anxiety Septimus feels does not concern death, but life in the postwar world, life in a world where language is ineffectual, where appearance means more than essence.

In the postwar world, Septimus has learned that there is no relation and no direct communication. Only "Evans was speaking. The dead were with him" (140). Had Septimus made any attempt to share his war experiences, his efforts would have been met with ignorance, particularly from his wife, who, unlike the recruiting poster, never asked Septimus what *he* did in the Great War. The war had no special significance to Rezia, who remembers the war years fondly, as a time of making hats with her sisters in Italy and meeting English soldiers in cafés.

An illusion of civilian immunity, Woolf implies, was not an exclusively British trait and one that had little relation to proximity to the fighting. Rezia, though married to a veteran, had seen little of Septimus's suffering in Italy (222) and knows nothing of his experience other than the public record that "'he served with the greatest distinction'" and "'he was promoted'" (145). Having met Septimus shortly before and married him shortly after Evans (like Wilfred Owen and Isaac Rosenberg) was killed, just before the armistice, Rezia saw nothing unusual in his reserve and thought it a particularly admirable English trait (133). When five years after their marriage Septimus shows signs of emotion and a seemingly fanatical need to communicate, "Rezia could not understand him" (139).

Faced with this postwar fact of life, Septimus, unlike Clarissa and like Woolf herself, gives reality to his "revelations" by writing them down. As the only combatant character in Woolf to do so, he suggests a relation to the war poets, who also wrote things down so as to communicate what Woolf herself had "seen" only in the "colourless phrases of the newspapers" ("Two Soldier-Poets," 269–70). Since he returned to England with his wife, Septimus's attempts at direct communication have met with ignorance, not only from Rezia but also from the "indifferent" world. So, he talks to the dead man, Evans, his officer at the front.

We see here a resemblance to Montaigne, whose *Essais* were written to communicate with his dead friend Boitie, who had died during the civil war that Montaigne lived through. According to Donald Frame, "the reader takes the place of the dead friend" (*CW,* v). Lacking a reader for his writings and a listener to his revelations, Septimus continues to talk to Evans, perhaps the only one to whom he could ever relate, ironically, in the war. The irony is the more pronounced when we consider that the comradery that is an inextricable part of his being makes the war a living reality as well, when to the civilian characters it has all but been consigned to history. In the postwar world both the visibly wounded and the "incurably diasabled" were isolated from the public, and largely kept out of view. The "dreadful looking spiders propelling themselves along the platform—men all body—legs trimmed off close to the body" that Woolf had observed at Victoria Station in 1921 (*Diary* 2, 93) had seemingly disappeared. In this world Septimus might be seen as a reminder of the war, more particularly that part of the war that civilians had not seen. Even Rezia, who has been spared the horror of war, is unable to cope with observing Septimus and leaves him alone on a bench in Regent's Park because she fears that "people must notice" (*MrsD*, 33). People must see.

However, other than Peter Walsh and Maisie Johnson (who thinks not only that both of them seem "queer," but that "[e]verything seemed very queer" [38]), no one so much as glances in Septimus's direction. No one, that is, other than the all-seeing nerve specialist Sir William Bradshaw (who has rather exclusive vision), sees anything wrong with Septimus and this he sees only after having read (and reread) the "most generous terms" of Mr. Brewer's letter to him ("Mrs Dalloway Manuscript," 127) and asks Septimus about his service in the war in such an offhand matter that Septimus is confused. The narrative irony is palpable: "[Bradshaw] could see the first moment they came into the room (the Warren Smiths they were called); he was certain directly he saw the man; it was a case of extreme gravity" (*MrsD*, 144). The rest of the world overlooks him entirely.

Even Dr. Holmes, the general practitioner, who had come to see him "quite regularly every day" for six weeks, found "nothing whatever seriously the matter with him" (139, 31). Lacking the requisite symptoms exhibited at the requisite time, Septimus lacks a pension and is largely overlooked by the civilian population, even by doctors, who, as Kierkegaard observed, cannot see inner health.

> Commonly a person is assumed to be healthy if he himself doesn't say that he is ill; even more so if he says he is well. A physician, on the other hand, looks on the illness differently. And why? Because the physician has a definite and articulate conception of what it is to be healthy, and tests a person's condition against this. (*Sickness unto Death*, 53)

In like manner, a "psychic expert" will accept an individual's assertion as to whether he is depressed (or, in "despair") (54).

What is clear in *Mrs. Dalloway* is that Septimus thinks himself neither and would undoubtedly agree with Montaigne's medical metaphors. War, like medicine and those who administer it, "carries infection" (*CW,* 796). The only one who sees Septimus as "mad" is Rezia, her diagnosis based not on what Septimus does, but on what he says. In earlier manuscripts, Septimus *says* he fears madness.[16] In the published version, he actively struggles against it, which we learn through the narrative tunnel, as he witnesses the passing of "a maimed file of lunatics being exercised or displayed for the diversion of the populace (who laughed aloud), ambled and nodded and grinned past him, in the Tottenham Court Road, each half apologetically, yet triumphantly, inflicting his hopeless woe. And would *he* go mad?" (*MrsD,* 136). As long as Septimus was silent he got along fine in the postwar world. Civilians did not want to hear any more than they wanted to see reminders of the war; least of all did they want to be reminded of the ultimate reality of the war in the trenches: death. Only as Septimus reminds civilians of death is he seen as threatening. His talking to the dead is a clue to what civilians find most disturbing, for, as Freud pointed out, fear of death was preceded by fear of the dead, to whom were attributed malevolent designs on the living (*Totem & Taboo,* 79).

Rezia does not have a lot of patience with her husband when "he talks to a dead man," which she sees as analogous to marriage: "Every one has friends who were killed in the War. Every one gives up something when they marry" (*MrsD,* 99). Unable to face the reality of death, she sees her situation and her suffering as comparable to that of Septimus: "She had . . . seen him . . . suffering sometimes through this terrible war, but even so, when she came in, he would put it all away" (222). She only begins to think him "mad" when he speaks not only of killing himself but also of a double suicide in which she is invited to participate, in which she could share and establish relation, as she had not done during the war, and which she had not done in the postwar world.

Although in a curious way this anticipates the situation Woolf herself would face in 1941 when without Leonard she commits suicide, it also points to her awareness of and sympathy for those who lived with veterans of the war, as she demonstrated in her response to witnessing Barbara Bagenal, a possible model for Rezia, trying to cope with her husband, Nick, a veteran,

16. See the notebook labeled "J's Room & First Version of the Hours," 159; "Mrs. Dalloway Manuscript," 103, 134; and the notebook labeled "Reviews 1924," 25.

after the war. "Poor Barbara," she recorded in her diary after a visit in 1920. "Such a grind & a drudge her life is as fills me with pity—seeing human life a thing to be put through the machine by necessity" (*Diary* 2, 50–51). Woolf, like Kierkegaard, understood that "actuality is the unity of possibility and necessity" (*Sickness unto Death,* 66). For Rezia, as for Barbara Bagenal, in the postwar world, there was little possibility. After the years she had spent in London, Rezia knows no one other than Septimus. When Septimus recognizes the necessity for death in the absence of possibility in life that he kills himself. As Camus wrote, "There is only one liberty, to come to terms with death. After which, everything is possible" (quoted in Alvarez, 283).

During the war, killing and death were the defining activities of life, and of the 8 million mobilized in Great Britain, 950,000 lost their lives (Ferro, 227), some in circumstances that Claire Tylee calls "nauseating" (62). During wartime, however, suicide is rare, not only in the trenches but on the home front, where individuals feel themselves part of the greater good. After the war, as Woolf noted, the communal effort and the communal spirit died. But the idiom and standard of manliness remained, which explains Rezia's sense that "it was cowardly for a man to say he would kill himself, but Septimus had fought; he was brave" (*MrsD,* 33). Bravery, that is, killing the enemy, led to promotion and honor during the war.

In the postwar world, this is no longer the measure of the man, and suicide, a word not used in the novel, was (like shell-shock) considered evidence of cowardice and a crime against the state. C. E. M. Joad said that "in England you must not commit suicide, on pain of being regarded as a criminal if you fail and a lunatic if you succeed" (quoted in Alvarez, 66). This attitude explains Bradshaw's concern with what Septimus had said about killing himself, which gave Bradshaw the legal right (nay, obligation) to put him in a "home." Septimus "'must'" go to a home, Rezia explains to him, "'because you talked of killing yourself'" (*MrsD,* 223). It also explains Holmes's exhortation "'The coward!'" (226) after Septimus does the deed in a manner so brutal as to evoke the horror of the war itself. What Woolf was clearly showing was that in postwar London, death could be as brutal as life, something the civilian characters did not recognize.

For the civilian characters, signs of health are overlooked in favor of symptoms of insanity which, Bradshaw acknowledges (to himself), "we know nothing about" (149). Irony involving these characters is not self-generated, but effected by narrative tunneling or commentary. The civilian characters lack a sense of the ironic. They lack the ability to distance themselves from their sense of self-importance and to see themselves in absurdist terms, as espoused by Kierkegaard, who sees irony as signaling control of self in relation to the world. In Septimus's case, ironic discourse signals the beginnings of health, not in society's terms or in terms of human nature, but in Kierkegaard's.

To Bradshaw, "health is proportion" (149). When Septimus asks an ironically intended (or, as the narrator tells us, a "sneering") question ("'One of Holmes' homes?'") (147), it is a "symptom" to be noted on a card (a pink card in an earlier version ["Mrs Dalloway Manuscript," 129]). This leaves Bradshaw with "a distasteful impression," suggesting that Holmes was more right than he knew (or than Woolf intended) when he says in the published version that "health is largely a matter in our own control" (*MrsD*, 138). His comment in the 1924 version that "health is largely in our own actions" (Notebook labeled "Reviews 1924," 25) might be more consistent with the picture Woolf is painting of his character. That Woolf meant Septimus's question to signal a healthy response and one that demonstrates a control not apparent in Septimus theretofore can be seen in the ironic narrative treatment of the interview as well as in Bradshaw's obtuse reaction. The only civilian comment identified as ironic is made by Holmes, who looks "ironically round the room," inferring the Warren Smiths' standard of living and implying that a Harley Street doctor is financially and socially out of reach for them (*MrsD*, 142).

That economic and social factors play into what was seen as "health" of ex-servicemen is clearly a point being made here. What is less clear is that Woolf is suggesting that the same social system was operative during the war in the trenches, something more clearly seen in early versions of the novel. Septimus does not refer to Evans as a "friend" in the published version, though in the 1923 version he tells Bradshaw, "my friend Evans was killed at Virney Ridge" and also believes Evans "commanded" him from beyond the grave ("Mrs Dalloway Manuscript," 135, 137). This consciousness is not included in the published version of *Mrs. Dalloway*, as notwithstanding Septimus's belief in the need for relation, what he shared with Evans was only friendship in the context of the war. There is nothing to indicate that the association would have lasted beyond the war, which may suggest another reason why the war has not ended for Septimus.

The social system, which was even in effect in prisoner of war camps, as Jean Renoir makes clear in his film *Grand Illusion*, was alive and well in the trenches also.[17] The idea of an officer as a "friend" to an enlisted man is palpably absurd and an infantryman of Septimus's rank and background would never presume. That Septimus uses Evans's surname rather than his given name in addressing or referring to him may also suggest that their comradery was little more than the avuncular relationship (such as Graves experienced with his "men" or Sassoon with his), notwithstanding the intensity of the love Septimus feels for Evans, and the "incommunicable" love he had felt for Miss Isabel Pole before the war.

To Septimus, Evans represents a father figure (replacing Brewer), as Miss Pole may have represented a mother figure. In an earlier version, both Evans and Septimus's dead father speak to him from the grave ("Mrs Dalloway Manuscript," 120, 137) and Evans is very much in command, maintaining his authority, like the father to whom he is implicitly identified. We see this also as Septimus responds to Evans's speaking to him with a mixture of love and hate. This response is, in fact, the kind Freud found in children who commit suicide after the death of a parent, and that Woolf herself had experienced.

Although the prewar psychological bases for Septimus's suicide are clearly indicated, revisions to early versions suggest that Woolf did not want these to be seen as central. Death did not stop with the war and in her life she was seeing more and more evidence to suggest that though suicide was not an answer to the indifference of the postwar world, it could be a viable alternative to living in it. The death of Katherine Mansfield in 1923 had left Woolf with the numbness she had experienced during the war. But perhaps more striking still was the incidence of suicide, considered by, among others, Ralph Partridge's father two years earlier, something she mentions to Vanessa in a letter. Interestingly, after giving Vanessa this rather shocking news, Woolf waxes poetic about her meeting with Beatrice Webb, with whom she "got onto terms of humanity" (*Letters* 2, 453).

The question of insanity is not part of her writings involving suicide, but is categorically separate from them, as in her record of Clive Bell's prewar affair with a woman who was "now imbecile" (*Diary* 2, 89). To Woolf, the question of being a lunatic was distinct from the question of suicide the novel raises; the group of lunatics Septimus sees (based on her own observation of lunatics during the war [*Diary* 1, 13]) bears on Septimus's character only as it references the social system and his resolve *not* to go mad. That

17. See Leed, 80–105. Leed explains that soldiers in the trenches came to see "that their conception of the war as a community of fate in which all class differences would be submerged was an 'illusion,' a function of their initial innocence and idealism" (81).

Woolf wanted to show that Septimus's psychological condition is not only related to but also finds its beginnings in the Great War is more obvious still in a deleted reference to Septimus's mother: "She was insane" (Notebook labeled "Reviews 1924," 23). Charles Hoffman overlooks this revision and others that bear directly not only on what Woolf was saying about the war but also on what she was showing about the postwar world.[18]

Whatever psychological underpinnings were apparent in Septimus during the years leading up to the Great War (and his immediate enlistment), the experience of the war in combination with the experience of the postwar world leads Septimus to suicide. In making this point, Woolf anticipates Emile Durkheim, whose *Suicide: A Study in Sociology* remains definitive and involves three categories of suicide: egoistic, altruistic, and anomic. Had Septimus killed himself before the war, he might have fit into the category of egoistic suicide, which is a category for outsiders, those who have not been integrated into society. Before the war, Septimus's poetic spirit moved him to leave home to find himself and fulfill his aspirations in London

18. Hoffman's interpretation of the manuscript revisions focuses on those bearing on the theme of "authority and irresponsibility" ("From Short Story," 173). Hoffman neglects mention of both the war and the postwar world, although the manuscript provides evidence that these became increasingly important in the evolution of the published version of the novel. Some of these revisions bear indirectly on the characterization of Septimus. For example, Woolf deleted references to Holmes's admiration of young women, and particularly Rezia ("Mrs. Dalloway Manuscript," 116ff), which suggest jealousy as a motive for Septimus's hate and for his calling Holmes a "brute"; by effectively erasing this consideration, Woolf suggests that Septimus's aberrational behavior is not caused by personal considerations and feelings, of which he lacks consciousness, but by the wider cultural changes in humane values, and, importantly, Septimus's sense of powerlessness in the postwar world. This is further supported by Septimus's lack of concern for Rezia, particularly in regard to his suicide, and by the manuscript revisions that make this clear. Several are narrated monologues involving the "dishonor" his wife would suffer if he killed himself.

Hoffman notes the creation of Septimus and then of Rezia, but does not involve Septimus's experience of the war or of the world suffering from what Bernard Blackstone calls "war-shock" (98). Hoffman believes that Woolf sought to find a "sympathetic and poetic approach to Septimus 'insane truth'" (175), but by not considering Septimus's status as a veteran, overlooks the possibility that Woolf's struggle with Septimus's character reached a turning point when she decided to make him a veteran of the war, something that she had opposed on principle. Feeling conflicted over the war as a historical fact, Woolf's efforts to come to terms with it and the eventual centrality of the war to her vision of the novel may explain why Septimus begins to win her sympathy once she gives his war service a more prominent position in his characterization. Hoffman does not mention the increasing importance of the war in the 1923 and 1924 manuscripts, and in the explicit references to the war in the published novel. Additional study of the early manuscripts yields even fuller appreciation of the war in her vision.

where, lonely and isolated as newcomers (such as Maisie Johnson) are, he falls in love with his teacher (this love is described as "incommunicable" in the 1923 version) and wins a "father" in Mr. Brewer (who is concerned with his future owing to the state of his health—"he looked weakly" [*MrsD*, 129]). But other than these quasi-normal problems of growing up and relation (and this is how they are presented, as the deletions to earlier versions make clear), there is little to suggest a hopelessness sufficient to move him to suicide before the war. Septimus's eventual suicide is not intended to owe very much to the prewar period of his youth, and were it not for narrative background, we would assume that Septimus's life began with Evans's death.

Had he killed himself during the war, Durkheim might have called the suicide "altruistic," except that in the 1923 version it is directly stated: "He [Septimus] was no patriot" ("Mrs Dalloway Manuscript," 106). Durkheim would classify his postwar suicide as anomic, based on the "regulative action" of society, its power to control (*Suicide*, 241).[19] After the war, during the day in June on which Septimus commits suicide, his behavior is clearly seen to be grossly lacking in manliness and rather than finding the sustenance he needs through what Durkheim calls society's "reflective conscience" that matches and supports his own (297), he is left without a correlative to his moral sensibility. This "collective conscience," as George Simpson calls it in his introduction to the book, sounds very much like what Zwerdling calls the real world and what Woolf calls life itself: "the totality of beliefs and practices, of folkways and *mores*. It is the repository of common sentiments, a well-spring from which each individual conscience draws its moral sustenance" (16).

When Peter Walsh observes the ambulance taking away the mangled body of Septimus, he calls it a "triumph of civilisation" (*MrsD*, 229); issues of conscience have nothing to do with him or with what he calls civilization. Even had he known that the body being transported in the ambulance was the young man he had seen several hours earlier, there is nothing to suggest that Peter would consider or acknowledge that civilization is something to which Septimus can aspire only in death. Woolf would agree that suicide "shows up a deep crisis in modern society" (Durkheim, 17). But Woolf saw the modern crisis growing out of the Great War.

19. In his chapter on anomic suicide, Durkheim discounts "economic distress" as leading to suicide, asserting that increased comfort may even contribute to a heightening awareness of "disturbances in the collective order" (245–46). He suggests that "moral consciousness" of society is what moves men to obey its precepts and that a sense of individual progress is necessary for individual well-being (249). "However," says Durkheim, "one does not advance when one walks toward no goal, or—which is the same thing—when his goal is infinity" (248).

The proximate cause of Septimus's suicide is the arrival of Dr. Holmes. The remote cause is the Great War. And the underlying cause is the prospect of continuing life in a postwar society informed by indifference to the war and self-serving power over its survivor-victims. On 29 June 1920 Woolf saw the residual effects of the war in generational terms: "Our generation is daily scourged by the bloody war" (*Diary* 2, 51). This comment curiously prefigures Septimus's awareness of the lack of sensitivity in the postwar world: "The world has raised its whip; where will it descend?" (*MrsD*, 20). To Woolf, a civilian who did not experience the war in the trenches, the war beats the world. To Septimus, the character created to represent its continual present, it is the world that beats the war.

What becomes apparent in *Mrs. Dalloway* is that for Woolf, as for Montaigne (and, indeed, for Septimus), suicide does not signal denial of life, but the affirmation of a life that was impossible in the postwar world, something that is not part of her first novel, which involves accidental death. Nor is it part of her first postwar novel, which suggests not only her own denial of death owing to the war but also, in a sense, denial of the war itself. Dr. Holmes is certainly one of the civilian characters who has most efficiently expunged evidence of the war from his professional (that is, diagnostic) consciousness. His arrival at the Smiths' Bloomsbury home for no apparent reason ("'My dear lady, I have come as a friend,' Holmes was saying" [225]) and his forced entrance into their living quarters signals to Septimus not only the incursion of societal insensitivity but a loss of individual autonomy in the name of what Septimus calls "the brute"—Dr Holmes—or human nature.

The postwar world to which Septimus returned might be called, in Buber's terms, an It-world "in a sick age," that is, a world in which there is no relation and no awareness of its own sickness (*I and Thou*, 102). Virginia Woolf, conscious of this on personal as well as societal levels, wrote to Vanessa in 1921, "[Y]ou don't believe in other people's humanity," adding, ironically, "I wish I didn't" (*Letters* 2, 453). Septimus did not return from the front believing the age was sick, but that there was a sickness inherent in him, which he saw manifest in his sins against human nature. The "worst" of these sins was the first: "He had not cared when Evans was killed" (*MrsD*, 137), for here he had demonstrated what Helene Deutsch calls "absence of grief" or "omission of affect" (*Neuroses and Character Types*, 226, 228). Freud has explained that this sense of sin is guilt. That Freud also was aware that memory was central to coming to terms with guilt may explain why, as he observed of neurotics, memory rarely plays into their fixations (*BPP*, 12).

In the years after the end of the war, during the evolution of a postwar value system, Septimus had gradually become aware that human nature was but another name for human cruelty (*MrsD*, 213). This awareness leads him finally to reject the manliness he had developed in the trenches and which had served him with success in the postwar world. He had spoken of his crime against human nature, an abstraction, until he allows Rezia to call for Dr. Holmes. This leads Septimus to see human nature personified and empowered through him and subsequently through Dr Bradshaw. After his interview with Bradshaw, he sees that human nature seeks to perpetuate its own sickness—the lack of relation: "'The people we are most fond of are not good for us when we are ill,'" he *remembers* Bradshaw saying (223).

"[I]n sick ages," says Buber, "it happens that the It-world, no longer irrigated and fertilized by the living currents of the You-world [of relation], severed and stagnant, becomes a gigantic swamp phantom that overpowers man" (*I and Thou*, 102). When Septimus becomes conscious of this, when for the first time he *remembers,* he truly shows signs of realizing a control of self over society that had been intimated during his interview with Bradshaw. This control, not only of his view of the postwar world but also of himself, gives him the freedom to recognize his powerlessness against its will and to assume the freedom to kill himself. His suicide is not a cure for the sickness of the postwar world, which had been indifferent to his life and ignores his death; it is his final capitulation to its power.

Woolf signals the development of Septimus's character not through Rezia, who was originally to be seen as the measure of his reality, but through a shift in the narrative tone and agency, as if the tunnel to Septimus, to which only the narrator had access and which was infused with the narrator's own personality and interpretive powers, is no longer needed. The power to judge and condemn, which Septimus had seen to be the province of human nature, is no longer considered. The power comes from within, from the human heart: "Fear no more, says the heart in the body; fear no more" (*MrsD*, 211). The narrator becomes a reporter rather than an interpreter, as Septimus opens his eyes.

> Why then rage and prophecy? Why fly scourged and outcast? Why be made to tremble and sob by the clouds? Why seek truths and deliver messages when Rezia sat sticking pins into the front of her dress . . . ? Miracles, revelations, agonies, loneliness, falling through the sea, down, down into the flames, all were burnt out, for he had a sense, as he watched Rezia trimming the straw hat for Mrs Peters, of a coverlet of flowers. (216)

Septimus, who had gone into the war an innocent, had had experiences too horrific to remember. Only after seeing Dr. Bradshaw does he begin to come to terms with the reality of the postwar world and see its possibilities. Septimus left the front with experiences that made sense only in the context of war, yet in the postwar world he keeps the standards of acceptable behavior that had been taught him in the war. He returns unable to read Shakespeare, in whom he sees evidence of the same either-or, life-denying vision that is concommitant with war. But, as he comes to recognize that Shakespeare is not but one thing, that the world is not an abstraction, he begins to discover an equilibrium in dealing with it and recognize a higher power.

> At every moment Nature signified by some laughing hint like that gold spot which went round the wall—there, there, there—her determination to show, by brandishing her plumes, shaking her tresses, flinging her mantle this way and that, beautifully, always beautifully, and standing close up to breathe through her hollowed hands Shakespeare's words, her meaning. (211–12)

The world that since the war had seemed so filled with death and oppression that Septimus again and again shut his eyes and looked within; as he opens his eyes he discovers life.

As Septimus comes to terms with life in the postwar world, he loses his sense of his own "sin" and sees that life itself may be a workable alternative to living in the continual past of the war: "He began, very cautiously, to open his eyes. . . . He would not go mad" (215). Life is no longer seen in a dreamlike dimension, but in everyday, domestic reality, in the reality of the hat Rezia makes for Mrs. Peters: "So she sewed. When she sewed, *he thought,* she made a sound like a kettle on the hob; bubbling, murmuring, always busy, her strong little pointed fingers pinching and poking; her needle flashing straight" (emphasis added; 218). As he comes to terms with domestic reality ("It was so real, it was so substantial, Mrs Peters' hat"), life itself is no longer described by the narrative tunnel in abstractions, but in concrete terms, and Septimus's thoughts become concrete. It is the only memory he has that leads him for the first time to waver between life and death, as for the first time he sees them as separate dimensions.

As he wavers between death and life, both the death instinct and the survival instinct become manifest. The dead seem to have left him: "As for the visions, the faces, the voices of the dead, where were they? . . . 'Evans!' he cried. There was no answer" (220). As he remembers the postwar past (albeit the immediate past), he seeks to destroy what remains of the war itself. He orders Rezia to destroy all his writings, those on the war, those communications to and from Evans after his death. It is as if by destroying the past, he is seeking the will to embrace the future, which includes death: "The table drawer was full of those writings; about war; about Shakespeare; about great discoveries; how there is no death" (212). He becomes as obsessed with destroying them as he had been in writing them.

> Burn them! he cried. Now for his writings; how the dead sing behind rho-dodendron bushes; odes to Time; conversations with Shakespeare; Evans, Evans, Evans—his messages from the dead; do not cut down trees; tell the Prime Minister. Universal love: the meaning of the world. Burn them! he cried. (224)

It is as if, deserted by the dead, he has resolved to obliterate their thereto-fore continual presence. It is as if, faced with the reality of life in postwar London, the limitations of which Bradshaw represents, he "sees" himself joining them.

According to A. Alvarez, "a man who decides to commit suicide puts a full stop to his being, he turns his back on the past, he declares himself to be a bankrupt and his memories to be unreal" (269). For Septimus, who begins to recover his ability to remember and demonstrate a consciousness of the future as well as the past, life is no longer experienced in a dreamlike dimension; he sees it in the reality of the hat Rezia makes for Mrs. Peters. Life itself is perceived in real terms, rather than in abstractions: "The sun might go in and out, on the tassels, on the wall-paper, but he would wait, *he thought*" (emphasis added; *MrsD*, 218). Although it is not clear here what it is for which Septimus waits, Woolf makes it clear eight pages later, that in the earlier reference he is willing to wait for death, that he is here thinking of life: "[H]e would wait till the very last moment. He did not want to die. Life was good. The sun hot. Only human beings—what did *they* want?" (226).

Woolf, in the essay on Montaigne that she completed as she was in the final stages of writing *Mrs. Dalloway*, agrees with him that "[t]his soul, or life within us, by no means agrees with the life outside us" ("Montaigne," 19), and suggests that suicide is a valid alternative, if not a cure, to living in untenable circumstances. Like Kierkegaard, Septimus understands a higher power, which he calls Nature, which Kierkegaard calls the infinite. In Kierkegaard, suicide might be seen as evidence of despair brought about by anxiety: a "self-deceptive despair." In Kierkegaard's dialectic, the self reaches synthesis only when the inner self can combine freedom with prohibitions imposed on it by the outside world: "[A] genuine human being, as a synthesis of the finite and the infinite, finds his reality in holding these two factors together" (cited in Mullen, *Kierkegaard's Philosophy*, 47).

John Douglas Mullen sees Kierkegaard differentiating between "pathological anxiety," which is curable through therapy, and "existential anxiety," which is not (53). This suggests that a sympathetic therapist might not have kept Septimus from suicide, unless he took to account the dilemma caused Septimus in the anomic terms of Durkheim, unless he took to account the changes Septimus saw realized in postwar society. In Kierkegaard's terms, the state of innocence is lost and anxiety begun with the introduction of prohibitions that make us conscious of freedom (*CA*, 40, 123). To resolve this existential dilemma, Kierkegaard posits a *leap* over the chasm between societal demands and the interior world of memory and dream. For Septimus this duality leads to a breakdown of the tenuous synthesis, occasioned not only by his experience of the war but, more especially, by his experience of the postwar world.

Septimus's suicide is the climax of his development and is not the result of insanity, but of a profound sanity such as that extolled by Montaigne, quoting Pliny: "A quick death is the supreme good fortune of human life" (*CW*, 460). In demonstrating this, Woolf effected a Kierkegaardization of Montaigne whereby asserting a final gesture of control, Septimus leaps to his death. It is Septimus's memory, not of the war, but of Bradshaw's pronouncements involving freedom that moves Septimus unstoppably to suicide: "So he was in their power! Holmes and Bradshaw were on him! The brute with the red nostrils was snuffing into every secret place!" (*MrsD*, 223). His own power, he sees, is no match for the collective *in*conscience and unconsciousness of the social order. As Rezia's efforts to keep Holmes away from Septimus prove unsuccessful, Septimus, in a final act of free will, "flung himself vigorously, violently down on to Mrs Filmer's area railings" (226).

His last words, seemingly addressed to no one, are ironic, a final demonstration of what we can see is Kierkegaardian control: "I'll give it you!" The antecedent of "you" is ambiguous. Whether its referent is Holmes, who has "come upstairs," or the old man opposite, who stops to stare as he is "[c]oming down the staircase" (226), what "they" as representatives of the social system want is the death of Septimus. His death is his offering, his gift to Holmes, who had looked at Septimus but did not see and at the old man, who had looked too late.

Septimus's death bears out Montaigne, who, like Lucretius (whom Montaigne cites) believed that in dying "true words surge up from deep within our breast,/The mask is snatched away, reality is left" (*CW*, 55). To Woolf, Septimus's suicide is pregnant with meaning, not only in its reality but also in the civilian responses to it, which may be seen in their lack of response to the war. Except for Rezia, no civilian sees the dying Septimus or wants to: "Rezia ran to the window, she saw; she understood" as Mrs. Filmer "made her hide her eyes in the bedroom" (*MrsD*, 226–27). Dr. Holmes absolves himself (and everyone else) of responsibility for the mangled body of Septimus ("A sudden impulse, no one was in the least to blame (he told Mrs Filmer). And why the devil he did it, Dr Holmes could not conceive") and, predicting death ("her husband . . . would not recover consciousness"), tells Rezia that "she must not see him" (227).

Septimus in death (which is determined by Holmes from his upper-story view), as in life, is hidden as far as possible, both his death and mangled body potentially giving rise to memories of the war. But only Rezia seems to recognize that the war had continued for Septimus (if not for her) after the fighting in the trenches stopped. It continued in postwar London: "She had once seen a flag slowly rippling out from a mast when she stayed with her aunt at Venice. Men killed in battle were thus saluted, and Septimus had been through the War. Of her memories, most were happy" (227–28). Septimus was killed in the battle between his self and the postwar world, where the war had continued. Of Rezia's memories, most do not involve the war.

As the importance of the war in the creation of the postwar social system became more central to her vision of the novel, Woolf diminished Rezia's importance in relation to Septimus and to his decision to kill himself. Even in the 1924 version, Septimus considers the effect his suicide might have on his wife, something that does not enter his mind in the published novel. What is of importance to Woolf is not the effect of the suicide on Rezia, but the absence of effect in the postwar world. Septimus's suicide thus is a more significant though unnoticed gift to postwar life than is Clarissa's party, *her* "offering."

What is important to seeing the development of Woolf's vision in the published novel is understanding that the very life of Clarissa's party reaffirms the chasm between civilians and combatants. As she heard of death on the front, Clarissa hears of postwar death second (or third) hand, as she is told of a telephone call involving the suicide, much as Woolf had heard of Rupert Brooke's death from Leonard. That the nameless young man had been a soldier does not affect her in the least: "Oh! thought Clarissa, in the middle of my party, here's death, she thought" (*MrsD*, 279). Septimus's name is never mentioned, though he is identified as one who served in the war. Civilians in peacetime as in war prefer the dead either to be heroes or anonymous—sometimes both. Septimus (like the mass of veterans) has no identity. For Richard Dalloway, the member of Parliament, with whom Bradshaw discusses a bill for victims of "deferred shell-shock," veterans of the war lack reality and he thinks of the war only in terms of the "thousands of poor chaps, with all their lives before them, shovelled together, already half forgotten" (174). To Richard, as to other civilian characters, the only victims of the war are the dead.

The reason for Septimus's suicide is not as Bradshaw assumes owing to *shell*-shock, but to the shock occasioned by recognition of the power of the postwar world to ignore or to suppress. To assume (as Bradshaw does) that Septimus was suffering from deferred shell-shock is to neglect to acknowledge culpability and responsibility. Deferred shell-shock does not cause his death, as Woolf makes clear by putting this opinion in the mouth of Dr. Bradshaw. What causes his death is Smith's recognition of individual powerlessness in an indifferent postwar world.

Although the war and its effects are "something central that permeate" the novel, they are unnoticed by Clarissa Dalloway. That Woolf chose to provide Clarissa with a suggestion of war-consciousness (though not Great War–consciousness) may be seen in her bedside reading (the memoirs of Lord Marbot). That Clarissa overlooks Lady Asquith's *Memoirs* in a bookshop window[20] implies a lack of interest in any experiences of the war. By the time Woolf wrote the final typescript and corrected the final proofs, she had modified her earlier plans and decided that the characters could best be understood and could best inform her purpose in the novel in their awareness of the war.

That her earliest intentions changed while writing the novel suggests that Woolf was taking to account the changes brought about in the wake of the war, and considering on whom the effect could be seen. Clarissa's suicide, which Woolf acknowledged was her earliest plan,[21] was abandoned, I think,

20. Lady Asquith's "memoirs" (*Diaries 1915–1918*) were not published until 1968 but, according to Beverly Schlack, members of Woolf's circle of friends knew that Lady Asquith was keeping a war diary (*Continuing Presences,* 144). Besides Siegfried Sassoon, T. S. Eliot, and Rupert Brooke, Lady Asquith was on friendly terms with Desmond MacCarthy and Vita Sackville-West.

21. The passage in question says that in the first version Septimus did not exist and "that Mrs Dalloway was originally to kill herself, or perhaps merely to die at the end of the party" (*Mrs. Dalloway,* Modern Library [1928], vi). I agree with Daniel Ferrer, who believes that the importance of this comment is not to be found in what it literally says ("There never was a first version as described in the preface" [9]), but in Woolf's reasons for making it. I disagree with Ferrer's reasoning, which is based on Kitty Maxse as the model for Mrs. Dalloway and a confusion of Maxse's presumed suicide with that of Clarissa Dalloway. The preface has similarities to "How Should One Read a Book?" which Woolf first published in 1926 and continued revising until it was included in the *Second Common Reader* (1932).

as the central importance of the war and the postwar world became obvious to her. As Josephine O'Brien Schaefer says, "without the presence of Septimus, Clarissa's emotions might seem minor and trivial" (86). That Clarissa, who leaves the party after the shock of this "news" overcomes her, had little awareness of the war is consistent with her myopic view of life itself. As John G. Hessler demonstrates in "Moral Accountability in *Mrs. Dalloway*," "for Clarissa, the best life is the unexamined life" (131).

The only kind of "warfare" she knows is the metaphorical kind she has with the only obvious victim of the war on the home front, Doris Kilman, the woman whom Clarissa admired *least*. She sees Doris Kilman as "some prehistoric monster armoured for primeval warfare" (*MrsD*, 190), as "her enemy" (265), using the war imagery that has been part of life itself since the Great War. In answer to Phyllis Rose's question, "what is her [Doris Kilman's] particular function in this novel?" (*Woman of Letters*, 147), we must look at her experience of the war, which was comparable to that experienced by D. H. Lawrence's wife, Frieda, and her experience of the postwar world, both of which are disallowed by Clarissa Dalloway. Here we see not only Doris Kilman's function but also Clarissa Dalloway's.

Clarissa's view of Miss Kilman points to her status as an outsider by birth and, like Septimus, as a survivor. Mrs. Dalloway not only "lacks the . . . generosity" of a Mrs. Ramsay, as Suzette Henke notes ("*Mrs. Dalloway*," 133). As Clarissa demonstrates a Kierkegaardian philistinism, her narrated monologues, like Browning's dramatic monologues, point to the narrative distance from both Clarissa and the social system she represents, through an irony that is widely regarded as social satire.

> Miss Kilman would do anything for the Russians, starved herself for the Austrians, but in private inflicted positive torture, so insensitive was she, dressed in a green mackintosh coat. Year in year out she wore that coat; she perspired; she was never in a room five minutes without making you feel her superiority, your inferiority; how poor she was; how rich you were; how she lived in a slum without a cushion or a bed or a rug or whatever it might be, all her soul rusted with that grievance sticking in it, her dismissal from school during the War—poor embittered unfortunate creature! (*MrsD*, 16)

Exploiting Clarissa's patronizing attitude and disregard of Kilman's professional qualifications as tutor to Elizabeth (which Richard Dalloway sees) and her personal suffering (which he, like his wife, does not notice), Woolf suggests how far Mrs. Dalloway represents her sense of what has been called "the road not taken." Mrs. Dalloway casts a cold eye at the economic suffering that faced the indigenous German population of England during the war and in its aftermath, when the distrust that the government and its propaganda organs had taken such pains to instill was alive and well in postwar London: "For it was not her one hated but the idea of her, which undoubtedly had gathered in to itself a great deal that was not Miss Kilman; had become one of those spectres with which one battles in the night" (16).

Woolf's sensitivity to the emotional and economic cost exacted from civilians of German origin must have led her to use Louise Matthaei, who was dismissed "'under a cloud'" from Newnham College, Cambridge, because her father was German, as a model for Doris Kilman.

> It is easy to see from her limp, apologetic attitude that the cloud has sapped her powers of resistance. We skirted round the war, but she edged away from it, & it seemed altogether odious that anyone should be afraid to declare her opinions—as if a dog used to excessive beating, dreaded even the raising of a hand. She and L[eonard] discussed their business, which has to do with W[ar]. & P[eace]. & may result in an offer to her of a place on the staff. She has to earn her living. 'I must tell you one thing, she said, when the talk was over, my father was a German. I find it makes a good deal of difference—it is a distinct hindrance commercially.' L. agreed that it was. She is a lanky gawky unattractive woman, about 36, with a complexion that blotches red & shiny suddenly; dressed in her best, which was inconceivably stiff & ugly. But she has a quick mind, & is an enthusiast; said she loved writing. (*Diary* 1, 135–36)

Just as Woolf had given Mrs. Dalloway the eccentricities of Ottoline Morrell without her political commitment, she used the situation and appearance of Louise Matthei without endowing Miss Kilman with her passivity. To isolate Septimus Smith as the doppelgänger of Clarissa Dalloway is to miss the importance of Doris Kilman, for "Miss Kilman did not hate Mrs. Dalloway" (*MrsD*, 189); she understood Mrs. Dalloway and her limitations all too well.[22]

By juxtaposing Kilman's need for relation, as manifest in her fanatical religious zeal (that begins at about the same time as Septimus's aberrational behavior became manifest) and her seemingly unhealthy attachment to Clarissa's daughter Elizabeth, Woolf suggests that the war-blindness (which

22. Compare Kenneth Moon's "Where Is Clarissa? Doris Kilman in *Mrs Dalloway*," which sees Miss Kilman as informing the character of Mrs. Dalloway, and the novel itself "as an exercise in characterization, as primarily a search for the whole Clarissa" (147).

on the home front was manifest through a propaganda campaign designed to isolate and demean those of German origin) was alive and well in postwar London. This may also suggest why, as she was completing the final text, she changed the working title of "The Hours" to *Mrs. Dalloway*. Mrs. Dalloway is a survivor of the war, but unlike Lady Bexborough, who had suffered from death, and even Miss Parry, who during the war had a bomb dropped "at her very door" (271), Mrs. Dalloway ends the day as she began it, believing the war is over. Henke is certainly right in seeing the title of the novel as ironic, "since, in actuality, there *is* no Mrs Dalloway" (*"Mrs. Dalloway,"* 130). But, I would suggest, the irony is found in more than her "romantic" vision of the war; it is found in her blindness to its effects, an isolation Woolf suggests graphically, at the end of the novel:

> It is Clarissa, he said.
> For there she was. (*MrsD*, 296)

The isolation of Clarissa Dalloway owes nothing to the war. That of Rezia and, more especially, of Septimus Smith and Doris Kilman does. For Clarissa Dalloway the war did nothing to alter either the workings of the social system or life itself. For Rezia, Septimus, and Doris, the alterations were a matter of life and death. That much is made of Clarissa's spiritual communion with Septimus signals a lack of responsiveness to the reality of the social system she represents. Miss Kilman is not invited to the party that gathers the governing class around the prime minister, its "symbol," and Septimus would not have been noticed (much less invited) even if Clarissa, like Peter Walsh, had seen him. If, as Claire Tylee says, Clarissa feels a spiritual bond with Septimus, it is because Woolf makes clear that it is the only kind she is capable of feeling. Clarissa did not only enjoy an illusion of immunity from the war; she also, like the other civilians represented in the novel, believes herself immune from its effects and evidence of them in the postwar world.

In *Mrs. Dalloway* Virginia Woolf sought not to endorse suicide as an answer to living in the postwar world, but to dramatize a situation that had long been ignored and allowed to become more widespread and harmful. That this was not a conscious part of her original plan for the novel is not surprising. But whether her sense of the postwar atmosphere was given reality to her by writing it down is not really at issue. The centrality Septimus assumes in the final novel cannot be disputed: he not only begins his day while Clarissa's is going on but ends his day as her party gets under way. The juxtaposition of life and death there, part of her notes for the novel in 1923

("All must bear finally upon the party at the end; which expresses life in every variety . . . while Septimus dies" (Notebook labeled "Choephori of Aeshylus," 2), became important in showing further that death itself has become part of the myopia typical of postwar London.

Virginia Woolf in what must clearly be recognized as a war novel was here indeed a hare far removed from the critics her hounds, as well as from her friends and readers. The novel aroused much discussion and disagreement, most of which focused on character. Friends and reviewers alike were divided between negative readings of Mrs. Dalloway (Lytton Strachey was especially biting in his response) and of Septimus Warren Smith. What neither her friends or reviewers or even the critic Winifred Holtby saw was the irony that operated throughout the novel, an irony intended to invoke the war and her vision of it through a Kierkegaardian indirection.

In "Cinema," an essay written two years after the publication of *Mrs. Dalloway*, Woolf said, "The war sprung its chasm at the feet of all this innocence and ignorance but it was thus that we danced and pirouetted, toiled and desired, thus that the sun shone and the clouds scudded, up to the very end" (269). In *Mrs. Dalloway* Woolf had shown that the music had stopped with the war, but no one seemed to listen—or see. The leaden-colored clouds, the leaden circles might dissolve—but they remained a barrier in the postwar world.

3

The Language of Memory as Time Passes

War creates a broken human syntax.
—Margaret R. Higonnet,
"Not So Quiet in No-Woman's-Land"

The corruption of language is war's first casualty.
—Jane Marcus, "Corpus/Corps/Corpse"

HAVING PUBLISHED "The War from the Street" in the *Times Literary Supplement* seven years earlier, Woolf was recalled to her own civilian experience by Rose Macaulay, who had been commissioned by the *New York Times* to write an article that might have been called "*After* the War from the Street." Recounting her reaction to the news and suggesting the chain of response that followed from it in her diary entry of 24 February 1926, Woolf (uncharacteristically) made use of a war/sports metaphor: "It is [this] sort of thing that one distrusts in her. Why should she take the [battle/playing] field so unnecessarily?" But it seems that Woolf immediately regretted having written with territorial animus. She subsequently reasoned that even "leading lady novelists" (a class to which Woolf herself aspired) were subject to "do[ing] as they are asked" (*Diary* 3, 61), sometimes by editors other than Bruce Richmond, and even if it involved writing about a topic that Woolf had (unconsciously) claimed as her own.

Not only would Macaulay identify the civilian experience as central to her point of view in the article ("The New London since 1914") but she frankly admitted her unease in identifying the war as the cause of "considerable changes" in the postwar world: "[I]t would be difficult to assert with confidence which of the changes were caused by the European war . . . but changes there certainly were" (171). To Woolf, who had used *Mrs. Dalloway* to portray seemingly inconsiderable (and/or unconsidered) changes, this was a familiar sentiment in and around Bloomsbury, and one that may suggest why writing *Mrs. Dalloway* was "all agony but the end" (*Diary* 3, 59). It may well have been because of that agony that Woolf looked forward to her next book with such eagerness and anticipation.

Woolf could not have forgotten that for all the postwar recognition afforded Macaulay (including being awarded the *Femina-Vie Heureuse* Prize in 1922), she would not have garnered such distinction had her reputation depended on the reception afforded to her civilian war novel *Non-Combatants and Others* (1916), an antiwar book so blasted by the wartime press that when the smoke cleared, Macaulay had lost not only her publisher but her readers.[1] As with Elinor Mordaunt's *Before Midnight*, which Woolf had reviewed during the war, Macaulay's book may have caused "a painful jolt in the perspective" that readers were not prepared to accommodate ("'Before Midnight,'" 87). To avoid a similar fate with *To the Lighthouse*, the civilian postwar novel that she was then writing, Woolf would circumvent such a potential loss in readership, not because she was "uncommitted" to historico-political reality (even if, as Jane Marcus points out, she sounded that way ["'No More,'" 269]), but because she (like Macaulay) recognized the power of language and (unlike Macaulay) could suggest it indirectly.

That Macaulay had only just agreed to do her historical article when Woolf was two months short of finishing the first part of her novel ("The Window") may ultimately have helped her in coming to terms with the difficult central section of the novel ("Time Passes"), the one that involved dislocating what she remembered of her grief at the death of her mother and offered a unique challenge to both her artistic control and her use of language. Ten years after the war, Macaulay was moving beyond the pain of loss during the war to analysis of it, as if she were illustrating what happens when the memory of death is "objectified" (to use Husserl's terms [27]) and the disposition to melancholy (in Freudian terms) is controlled or transformed "in a normal fashion" ("Mourning," 585). As if to suggest (unconsciously) that she had had a similar success in dislocating her memories in ways she had not attempted before, after writing the first draft of "The Window," Woolf forgot to note the thirtieth anniversary of the day her mother died, 5 May.

1. Jane Emery says that "*Non-Combatants and Others* was not a conspicuous success with home-front readers" and cites one particularly hostile review from the *Englishwoman*, which accuses the novelist of "belittling those who fight." Although Emery cannot confirm the reasons why *Non-Combatants* was the "last book Rose was to publish with Hodder & Stoughton" (*Rose Macaulay*, 155), it may be inferred that the house was not eager to publish another. Alice Bensen says that the novel is as much a product of "serious journalism" as a novel, and cites a "handbook" of the time that lists it under "Essays" (50); a review in *Punch* ("Our Booking Office," September 20, 1916) calls it "a gloomily didactic tale" (212). The popularity Macaulay was beginning to enjoy before the war was not restored until the publication of *Potterism* (by W. Collins, London) in 1920.

In the early going, before Woolf had given her ideas for *To the Lighthouse* time "to simmer," the autobiographical bias (which is widely believed to be the animating force behind the entire novel[2]) is most apparent and can be seen in references to the "characters" of her mother and father and to the setting as "St. Ives" (where the Stephens had spent their summers) rather than the "Isles of Skye" (its not so subtle echo) (*Diary* 3, 18).[3] It may have been this same confusion of her personal history with the fictional one that led to her brief flirtation with the idea of making up the category of "elegy" to classify her postwar novels (*Diary* 3, 34).[4] But when Woolf conceived of the tripartite structure on 20 July 1925, she had modified her first idea and was viewing the novel in impersonal and even journalistic terms because she hesitated to involve a "theme [that] may be sentimental" (*Diary* 3, 36), or overly concerned with emotion.[5] Woolf was not so naive as to believe that clues to her own life would be missed, and although ten days later the writing was again postponed ("I am inclined to wait for a clearer head" and, it seems, a clearer sense of the "character of father"), there were no subsequent alterations in conception. Woolf was coming to terms with the demands of the "task" she had in mind: "I think I might do something in To the Lighthouse, to split up emotions more completely. I think I'm working in that direction" (*Diary* 3, 37, 38).

2. The tone is set in Jane Lilienfeld's "'The Deceptiveness of Beauty'" (1977), which points "not only [to] the autobiographical origins" of the novel but also claims that they "impelled" the writing of the novel itself: "Virginia Woolf uses the characters of Mr. and Mrs. Ramsay in *To the Lighthouse* as surrogates for her parents, Leslie and Julia Stephen" (345).

3. Susan Dick believes this to be a mistake, reflecting Woolf's "unfamiliarity with th[e] Scottish setting" ("Introduction," *To the Lighthouse*, ed. Susan Dick, xxxv, n.7); to the contrary, I think the evidence suggests the choice to be intentional. Future references to Dick's edition of the novel will be to "*TL*, Dick" and indicated parenthetically in the text.

4. Gillian Beer offers a cultural definition of *elegy*, as it informs the novel, calling death "the special knowledge of her [Woolf's] entire generation, through the obliterative experience of the first world war," but sees strong evidence of Woolf's "special knowledge" of death ("Hume," 77). However, I think that Woolf's "special knowledge" can be more suggestively seen in her subsequent abandonment of the classification "elegy" and by the fact that it became increasingly difficult to identify what the war had "obliterated." Zwerdling (180–81), Knox-Shaw, and Corsa also explore Woolf's use of "elegy" in the diary, though with only passing reference to the war.

5. Leslie Hankins ("A Splice of Reel Life in Virginia Woolf's 'Time Passes'") suggests that Woolf embraced the term "sentimental" in her aesthetics and deeply resented "emotional strait-jacketing or patriarchal silencing of sentiment" (93).

In a more detailed plan for the novel on 6 August, it is clear that despite her anxiety to begin writing the novel, she was being held up by part 2, which she vaguely saw as "an interesting experiment" that would include "the sense of 10 years passing" in ways that were still unclear to her, the more so as she had also considered eliminating any "specification of date."[6] What she finally decided was to set aside her plans and plunge right in, describing the writing on 5 September 1925 ("22 pages straight off in less than a fortnight") with an allusion to military engagement, one of the inconsiderable (though not entirely unconsidered) effects of the war:[7] "I have made a very quick and flourishing attack on To the Lighthouse" (*Diary* 3, 39).

Yet, some six months later, when Woolf recorded that she was reading Beatrice Webb's *My Apprenticeship* (1926) with some interest and with some discomfort, it may well have been because in dealing with Webb's early years (1858–93), the edited diary had (indirectly) reminded Woolf of her mother (1846–95), who was already on her mind as Mrs. Ramsay. Webb, who also considered using her life as the basis of a novel, had lost her mother in 1882 (the year Woolf was born) and admitted that the writing of her "personal history" (vii) had offered only "tentative answers" (viii) to the internal and external controversies that she subsequently faced. Although reading Mrs. Webb's book left Woolf "headachy" on 27 February, Woolf turned to her own *postwar* diary of 1923, which may have reminded her that while she lived at some remove from the "causes" that moved Beatrice Webb, her own historical position offered its own challenges (*Diary* 3, 62). Not comfortable with showing life's relation to history, as Webb does in her memoir,[8] and still less with the self-conscious posturing she saw in the published *Letters of Walter Raleigh* (which she reviewed for *Vogue* at this time[9]), Woolf tried an

6. Susan Dick, ed., *Virginia Woolf's "To the Lighthouse": The Original Holograph Draft*, 2. Future references to this version will be indicated parenthetically in the text: (*Holograph*, Dick,).

7. See, for example, Rose Macaulay's *Potterism* (1920) and *Catchwords and Claptrap* (1926), the latter published as a Hogarth Essay by the Woolfs' Hogarth Press. See also Fromm, "Re-inscribing *The Years*," 295–97.

8. This was not an unusual practice, though not one shared by Bloomsbury in general or the postwar Memoir Club (one of its manifestations) in particular (see Hussey, *A to Z*, 158). As Barbara Caine points out, "The approach which Beatrice Webb took to her autobiography necessitated not only careful control of her material but also a sense of order being shown in her search. The *Diary*, by contrast, points to the sense of purposelessness she often felt and to the chaos involved in her quest" (83).

9. Woolf's review of the *Letters*, which was published in *Vogue* (May 1926) under the title "A Professor of Life" (reprinted as "Walter Raleigh"), fairly drips with irony. Woolf ends it by noting the actual irony of Raleigh's life, that though "his chance of life [that

approach to "The Window" effectively demonstrating that memory (like history, and like language itself) is in what Husserl calls continuous states of modification (129).[10]

The first draft of "The Window," which Woolf completed on 28 April 1926 (less than a week before the General Strike began on 2 May[11]) suggests Woolf's rather naive confidence that her fiction could compete with Webb's nonfiction. Even in her diary entry of 11 April 1926, Woolf refers to what she has written of the novel as her "life," in much the same way as she had earlier referred to "mother" and "father" as characters in her book. In writing that "Mrs Webb's Life makes me compare it with mine," Woolf was looking at "The Window" as something of an answer to Webb (*Diary* 3, 74). In contrast to her restlessness when she began reading the memoir six weeks earlier, Woolf's confidence here owes something to the control she had asserted in the novel over autobiographical (cum historical) material, having refused during the writing of the novel to consult the Stephen "archive," what Alex Zwerdling calls the "'documentary evidence'" (181): her parents' letters, for example, and Leslie Stephen's *Mauseleum Book* (*Letters* 3, 379). She did not even look at her own Cornwall diary, or, as far as we know, her memoir of the time, "Reminiscences" (1908). Yet, when she reread "The Window," Woolf found it to approximate life as she remembered it fairly and non-

---

is, fighting in a war] had come too late . . . [t]o his infinite satisfaction he consorted with soldiers," and although he died a week after visiting Baghdad, "The professor of English Literature had lived at last" (318). Lytton Strachey, who knew him as a family friend and as a lecturer at Cambridge, was rather less critical, and when he saw Raleigh on a visit to Roger Fry's house in 1916, found him "far less outré and bloodthirsty about the war than I'd expected" (Holroyd 662).

10. Husserl explains that each modification after the primal impression brings us further from it. In other words, primal memory is continuously "d[ying] away," to be replaced by an infinite series of modifications (130).

11. Dating of the General Strike is not generally clear. The strike is variously said to have been called on 2 May and ended on 12 May or to have begun on 4 May and ended on 14 May. It is referred to as a nine-day strike, a ten-day strike, and an eleven-day strike, although the miners, on whose behalf the General Strike was declared, went out on 26 April and remained on strike until six months after the General Strike was settled (to the disadvantage of the workers). For example, Kate Flint calls it a ten-day strike in her "Virginia Woolf and the General Strike." Flint sees Woolf's reaction as part of her "desire for peace and reconciliation" (323). Anne Olivier Bell is correct is saying that the "General Strike was proclaimed by the Trades Union Congress on the evening of 2 May 1926 in support of the mineworkers who had struck on 1 May" (*Diary* 3, 77, n.1), yet Woolf herself calls "Monday night" (which would have been 3 May) "the night of the strike" (*Diary* 3, 79). Most labor historians (e.g., Margaret Morris, R. A. Florey, and Henry Pelling), agree with Woolf, and say that the strike (Pelling calls it "the so-called General Strike" [*A History of Trade Unionism*, 173]) lasted nine days.

judgmentally; "This is not made up: it is the literal fact," she recorded on 30 April 1926 (*Diary* 3, 76).

Woolf recognized that depending on memory for her raw material was tricky. In fact, in an ongoing process of what Husserl calls reproductive modification or "presentifying modifications of consciousness" (115–16), memories of the past affect perceptions in the present and perceptions in the present affect memories of the past. That Woolf herself would come more and more to appreciate memory this way[12] may owe something to how her memory of the Great War was recalled by the General Strike. Having found writing "The Window" to be all but effortless (and accomplishing it at "3 times the speed" [*Holograph,* Dick, 3]), Woolf anticipated a similar ease with "Time Passes." So sure was she of facility with the writing that she no sooner finished the first part than she began the second, albeit with less satisfactory results: "I cannot make it out," she recorded in frustration, after having "rush[ed] at it & at once scatter[ed] out two pages" of "Time Passes" (*Diary* 3, 76). It may be because of this false start that she seemed genuinely relieved to put it aside for the duration of the General Strike, and she did not begin writing the novel again in earnest until 14 May, two days after she recorded "Strike settled" (*Diary* 3, 84).[13]

Although she had "finished—sketchily [she] admit[ted]—the second part of To the Lighthouse" on 25 May, and planned to work at having a complete draft in hand "by the end of July" (*Diary* 3, 88), "Time Passes" continued to be a stumbling block, going through no fewer than three versions (and possibly more) before the novel was published, and leaving her unsatisfied for months afterward.[14] Although Woolf often had second thoughts after completing a manuscript, it becomes increasingly apparent that her misgivings

12. See "A Sketch of the Past," 66–67.

13. The only attempt to continue during the strike was on Sunday, 9 May, the day after a "quarrel" with Leonard (*Diary* 3, 80). In all, she wrote two paragraphs and then gave up writing what Dick identifies as "Chapter 5. Mrs McNab" (*Holograph,* Dick, 215–17; Appendix D, 61).

14. On 28 September 1926 Woolf recorded parenthetically that the first draft of *To the Lighthouse* had been "finished, provisionally, Sept. 16th" (*Diary* 3, 111). By 25 October, she was revising and retyping "(some parts 3 times over)" (*Diary* 3, 123) and some time before January 1927 she had sent what James Haule calls the "intermediate version" of "Time Passes" (which she subsequently called her "story") to Charles Mauron for translation into French for publication in the Winter 1926 issue of *Commerce* (Haule, "'Le Temps Passe'"). Although she claimed to have finished the novel on 14 January 1927, she continued her revisions well into February 1927, including "correcting two sets of proofs" (the American and the English—see Lavin) and, particularly, punctuation, as she wrote to Vita Sackville-West (*Letters* 3, 333). Although she had presumably entered "finished [on] 16

here had something to do with her memories of the war. During the ten years covered in "Time Passes" as the war begins and ends, Woolf suggests that liminality on the Isle of Skye determines both the range of perception and, significantly, the sweep of language. Woolf thus presents the distaff side of the war, and foregrounds what we might call (modifying Elaine Scarry's term [135]) the indeterminate meaning of language *on the home front*. This is apparent not only through what Mitchell Leaska calls shifting "angles of perspective" (*Lighthouse* 98) but through the use, finally, of typographical and syntactical signals that call attention both to geographic distance from the fighting and to lexical resistance to representing it accurately. Woolf was coming to see how liminality of experience could be recalled and with what difficulty memory was transformed into art, something that had undoubtedly been too great an obstacle for Beatrice Webb, and, perhaps, for returning combatants-become-civilians, many of whom did not begin publishing their stories until 1928.[15]

The third part of *To the Lighthouse* ("The Lighthouse") suggests that the potential for life and growth in the postwar world involves validation of civilian memory as well. By choosing the visual artist Lily Briscoe as the "governing consciousness" of "The Lighthouse" (*Lighthouse*, 114), while allowing Augustus Carmichael, the poet, to sleep (thereby depriving him of consciousness), Woolf avoids the dilemma she faced in writing "The Window." Here she creates a fair representation of the prewar world while testing a postwar idiom (in ways not considered even by John Burt, whose analysis somehow overlooks language itself). At the same time, she successfully negotiates the challenge caused by remembering war and death in a world intent on forgetting them both.

In *To the Lighthouse* Woolf suggests the need to assuage frustration by using memory of the past to create something new, in a sense making good

---

March" on the title page (*Holograph*, Dick, Appendix D, 62), she records uneasiness with the ending on 21 March, and even after it was published, significantly on 5 May 1927, she remained concerned over "Time Passes" (*Letters* 3, 374, 377–78).

15. Edmund Blunden's "Introduction" to *A Booklist on the War 1914–1918* (1929), compiled by Blunden et al., suggests that the reason for the delay in "a real account of the War" was that "[l]oyalty, as we nationally conceived it, co-operated with the censor in enforcing a silence and in trying to indicate by smiles that war was not a hopeless disaster" (1–2). Blunden's book list, the first since the war, provides "a candid statement of the broad and particular nature of war experience, such as we can awaken the imagination of those who missed it, or revive the memory of those who passed through it" (2). The introduction to the eleven-page publication, which reprints the book list published in *The Reader* in 1928, antedates Sassoon's *Memoirs of a Fox-hunting Man* (1928) and H. M. Tomlinson's *All Our Yesterdays* (1930).

a pronouncement she entered into her diary after finishing *Mrs. Dalloway*. "It's life that matters!" she wrote on 8 April 1925. "Enough of death," also from Montaigne, was, she said, implicit: "I do not any longer feel inclined to doff the cap to death" (*Diary* 3, 8 and n.5; *Diary* 2, 301; *Diary* 3, 7). From "The Window," which begins in medias res, as the Ramsays are observed at their summer house in the Hebrides for the last time before the war, to "Time Passes," which begins with the departure of the Ramsays and their circle before the war and ends with the return of the surviving characters after the war; through "The Lighthouse," which ends with the surviving Ramsays' completion of the trip planned before the war and Lily Briscoe's completion of a painting outside the house in the Hebrides, the novel itself moves toward closure. In so doing, it seems to me that rather than "creat[ing] a form of immediate memory for the reader," as Gillian Beer suggests, the novel works *through* what Beer generally calls "the obliterative experience of the first world war" ("Hume," 75, 77), to create possibility out of its memory. The novel, and particularly "The Lighthouse," thus anticipates *A Room of One's Own* (1929) in ways not appreciated before.

The war had made Woolf aware of what Elaine Scarry calls the "language of 'by-product'" (73), whereby consequences of the war (like death) are depersonalized and obscured, or deemed sentimental. That such sentimentality, as Leslie Hankins suggests, would have been effectively, if "subtly," censored by her friends in Bloomsbury (92), may have led Woolf to feel the need for indirection in *Mrs. Dalloway*. There Septimus Smith is himself a "by-product," not only of the war, but of his belief in the need to expose its reality, albeit in a language that is inadequate to the task.

In postwar London, words themselves have variable "objective correlatives," a reality we witness as Smith reviews the seemingly commonplace steps he must follow to commit suicide, while simulataneously understanding that he has run out of time: "There remained only the window, the large Bloomsbury-lodging house window, the tiresome, the troublesome, and rather melodramatic business of opening the window and throwing himself out. It was their idea of tragedy, not his or Rezia's" (*Mrs.D*, 226). The division here between civilians (like Holmes) and combatants (like Smith) is suggested in the metonymy, as modifiers (like those discussed by Scarry) effectively trivialize by delimiting: window=suicide/tragedy=melodrama. The portrait of Smith, even as he "fling[s] himself vigorously, violently down on to Mrs. Filmer's area railings" suggests that not death, but the problem of survival is the more troubling by-product of the war. Rezia is told (by Holmes) that she should *think* of him as dead because although he is not dead, he is "horribly mangled, [and] would not recover consciousness" (227).[16] In postwar newspeak: death = unconsciousness. In "The Lighthouse," even the poet Augustus Carmichael will only respond to the "mercifully . . . instantaneous" (*TL,* 201) death of Andrew Ramsay during the war with a kind of living death, or unconsciousness.

  To the Lighthouse houses a sense that displacement of earlier (and sentimental) habits of mind may have been an additional (and not entirely unwelcome) by-product of the war. Woolf's early notes for the novel imply how impoverished such sentiment had become by using "The Charge of the Light Brigade" in "Mr. R[amsay's] . . . discourse on sentimentality" (*Holograph,* Dick, Appendix A, 12). Even as Mr. Ramsay, in the first version of "The Window," assumes the identity of one "Rhoderick Ramsay," he is drawing on the same sentimental myth of war that moves Jacob Flanders and Septimus Smith and the eldest Ramsay son, Andrew, to enlist and, like Rhoderick, die: "But it was intolerable. He had died upon the heights of Balaclava—Stormed at by shot & shell boldly we rode and well—flashed through the valley of death—volleyed & thundered" (*Holograph,* Dick, 60).[17]

  In the published novel there is no Rhoderick Ramsay, and only the artist, Lily Briscoe, acknowledges the possibility of death in what has been called the Crimean War's most bungled battle: "Indeed, he almost knocked her

  16. Lifton's *Death in Life* offers valuable insights as to survival guilt in World War II that might be applied to the experience of World War I. See my "Virginia Woolf and Returning Soldiers."

  17. Christopher Ricks explains that "The Charge of the Light Brigade" (1854) was written by Tennyson after he read a *Times* report of a charge taking place during the Crimean War in which "some one had blundered" appeared (*Poems of Tennyson,* vol 2, 510). The phrase is repeated seven times in the novel. The holograph is more explicit "about Mr. Ramsay" and "how . . . he could cherish illusions. . . . Here he was . . . charging at the head of an army, receiving . . . wounds of which he died gloriously on the heights of Balaclava" (*Holograph,* Dick, 27–28). Tennyson's sequel, "The Charge of the Heavy Brigade" (1882), was on the poet's mind for nearly thirty years (vol. 3, 92–95). Jerome Hamilton Buckley explains that Tennyson was privately pleased that the combatants in Crimea found "curious consolation in chanting—rather subversively perhaps—that 'Some one had blundered'" (134). Tennyson did support the combat in the Crimea and elsewhere in the Empire, which may explain why he was not a close friend to Leslie Stephen. Yet, Stephen and Tennyson were undoubtedly agreed on the misrepresentations by newspapers, particularly as it involved the use of litotes (or understatement) in reporting on the Battle of Balaclava. Woolf was aware of Leslie Stephen's acquaintance with and opinions of Tennyson, who was among the luminaries photographed by Woolf's aunt, Julia Margaret Cameron. There are two extant versions of Woolf's *Freshwater: A Comedy* (1923, 1935) in which Tennyson is a character; in the 1935 staging of the play, Julian Bell played the role.

easel over, coming down upon her with his hands waving shouting out, 'Boldly we rode and well,' but, mercifully, he turned sharp, and rode off, to die gloriously she supposed upon the heights of Balaclava" (*TL*, 29). It is as if in the first construction the mythical ideal of war had been personified, and then, finally, idealized in the published version to form a sentimental construct where Mr. Ramsay himself remains as unconscious of the possibility of death as his wife. Even as Mrs. Ramsay "gave meaning to words which she had held meaningless in her mind," she concludes that "it sounded ridiculous—'Some one had blundered'—said like that . . . without any conviction, melodiously" (48, 52).

Woolf would make the connection with meaning, sound, and value more directly in *A Room of One's Own* (1929), where it is in "the value of . . . words themselves" that Woolf presents evidence of change that might otherwise be missed.

> Nothing was changed; nothing was different save only—here I listened with all my ears not entirely to what was being said, but to the murmur or current behind it. Yes, that was it—the change was there. Before the war at a luncheon party like this people would have said precisely the same things but they would have sounded different, because in those days they were accompanied by a sort of humming noise, not articulate, but musical, exciting, which changed the value of the words themselves. (*Room*, 12)

The war, Woolf suggests, had shifted the balance between sound and value, between the inarticulate and the articulate: Nothing was changed/nothing was different; people would have said precisely the same things/they would have sounded different. The war had happened, Woolf suggests, but no one seems to have noticed.

Woolf's sense of sentimentality in the *prewar* world of "The Window" has largely been overlooked, or misread, and its relevance to the rest of the book ignored. E. M. Forster, condemning Woolf with faint praise in 1927, finds it reasonable to absolve her of the label of "sentimentalist" in all but "her latest work, *To the Lighthouse*" (*Aspects of a Novel*, 37). And Leslie Hankins in 1993 asks, "What are the cultural politics of emotion?" and goes on to suggest that "strategies for circumventing the sentimental were uppermost in Woolf's artistic project of the twenties," a response brought on by reviewers hostile to *Mrs. Dalloway* ("A Splice," 91, 96). It is easy enough to see that the novel follows a strategy in part designed to confute her detractors. But in some critical attempts to show this as a reaction to her contemporaries, "The

Window" has, I think, mistakenly been seen as reflecting a sentimental longing to recover (or construct) the kind of prewar life that she described in her
1909 memoir as "ordered with simplicity and regularity" ("Reminiscences,"
28). However modified with reference to the therapeutic value of the sentimental journey, this reading seems to me too narrow to be wholly defensi-
ble.[18] The first section of the novel should, I think, be recognized as an attempt by Woolf to embody the pervasive sense of sentimentality and myth
that invited participation in and support for the Great War, but disallowed
its reality.

The setting of the novel can be seen as providing us not so much with
Woolf's memory of her family, as with the ways in which the language of
the time reflected a prewar mythology: when "little warfares" denoted sib-
ling rivalry and Talland House in St. Ives was a place that connoted "the
golden enchantments of Tennysonian sentiment" ("Reminiscences," 28, 32).
It follows that any apparent stability was not without its distortions and its
illusions, as Woolf pictures it in "The Window," which involves a day in mid-
September 1909.[19] The unity of place that begins here signals not the idea of
"simplicity and regularity" or "golden enchantments," but a deconstruction
of linguistic conventions that had ceased to enliven even prewar characters
for the postwar reader.

In our first look at the Ramsays and their guests, the evening before the
trip to the lighthouse, the youngest son is cutting pictures from an army
and navy store catalogue, an activity whose implications are realized only
in "Time Passes" as the eldest son, Andrew, is reported to be among the
"[t]wenty or thirty young men . . . blown up in France" (*TL*, 201) and then
all but forgotten by the much reduced chorus of survivors in "The Lighthouse." Unlike the chorus in a Greek tragedy, to which they might be compared, what separates the members of the Ramsay circle is finally more important than what brings them together, something that even Mrs. Ramsay

18. Louise DeSalvo (*Virginia Woolf: The Impact of Childhood Sexual Abuse on Her Life
and Work*) and Roger Poole (*The Unknown Virginia Woolf*) have also reacted to the limitations of such valuations.

19. See Jane Lilienfeld, "Where the Spear Plants Grew," 149–50. Lilienfeld makes
"explicit Woolf's hints about the novel's time scheme. Part III takes place in 1919 as the
Great War has ended; in it Mr Ramsay tells Macalister that he is seventy-one. Since Mr
Ramsay was over sixty in Part I, we know that Part II covers ten years, making Part I occur
in 1909." It is worth noting that after considering "seven years passed" in the second part
(*Diary* 3, 36), Woolf's notes and outline for the novel involve "ten years passing" in "Time
Passes" (*Holograph,* Dick, 2 and Appendix B; and *TL,* Dick, xix).

knows, though her hyperbolic vocabulary and convoluted syntax may suggest how sentimental and myopic her instincts and vision are.

> The real differences, she thought, standing by the drawing-room window, are enough, quite enough. She had in mind at the moment, rich and poor, high and low; the great in birth receiving from her, some half grudgingly, half respect, for had she not in her veins the blood of that very noble, if slightly mythical, Italian house, whose daughters, scattered about English drawing-rooms in the nineteenth century, had lisped so charmingly, had stormed so wildly, and all her wit and her bearing and her temper came from them, and not from the sluggish English, or the cold Scotch; but more profoundly, she ruminated the other problem, of rich and poor, and the things she saw with her own eyes, weekly, daily, here or in London, when she visited this widow, or that struggling wife in person with a bag on her arm, and a note-book and pencil with which she wrote down in columns carefully ruled for the purpose wages and spendings, employment and unemployment, in the hope that thus she would cease to be a private woman whose charity was half a sop to her own indignation, half a relief to her own curiosity, and become what with her untrained mind she greatly admired, an investigator, elucidating the social problem. (*TL*, 17–18)

Woolf suggests her own difficulties in putting word to vision and vision to construction in "Mr. Bennett and Mrs. Brown" (1924). To present character (be she a Mrs. Brown or a Mrs. Ramsay), the writer must discover a new grammar, a new syntax, and even a new vocabulary, because, Woolf argues, "the convention [has] cease[d] to be a means of communication between writer and reader, and become instead an obstacle and an impediment . . . [to] telling the truth" (334–35).

It is in the situation of language that we see the connection between what Susan Dick vaguely calls "hints of the destruction to come" (*TL*, Dick, xix) and reference points from which to gauge the *effect* of the war on prewar language—and on postwar thought.[20] No one reading the book in 1927, for example, would miss the anachronistic use of "no-man's land" in a narrative description of Mrs. Ramsay in "The Window," or fail to recognize that this earlier meaning had been displaced by the experience of the war.

---

20. Barthes suggests that by situating words in a given context, the writer creates a tension between the intended contextual meaning and its historical meaning. See his *Writing Degree Zero* and Wiiliam Ray, *Literary Meaning*, 171–185.

Lily Briscoe watched her drifting into that strange *no-man's land* where to follow people is impossible and yet their going inflicts such a chill on those who watch them that they always try at least to follow them with their eyes as one follows a fading ship until the sails have sunk beneath the horizon. (emphasis added; *TL*, 127)

However obscured in an imagistic and syntactic maze of eyes and ships and sails and "fading . . . beneath the horizon," after the Great War, "no-man's land" could only refer to one thing, whatever the modification.[21]

At no time since the war was Woolf more challenged by and cognizant of what was happening and what was being said inside and outside Bloomsbury than during the General Strike of May 1926, something clearly evident in her resolve to keep an "exact" diary of its progress (*Diary* 3, 77). Begun on 5 May, in medias res, as it were, the diary records the impact on her and on her friends of the charged atmosphere and unsettled conditions that left Roger Fry fearful of walking the streets, presses without printers, the country without newspapers, and Leonard Woolf very nearly without friends. Woolf did not intend to use her strike diary, which tested her skill as a reporter/journalist, in *To the Lighthouse* or in the essay she was then writing on Thomas De Quincy. But as the pages in the strike diary show, she was constantly responding to what was happening on the streets of London and inside her home at 52 Tavistock Square (*Diary* 3, 77).

21. The *Oxford English Dictionary* identifies "no man's land" as "a piece of waste, or unowned land; in early use as the name of a plot of ground lying outside the north wall of London and used as a place of execution"; a second nautical meaning from the eighteenth century is also included (*Compact Edition*, vol. 1, 183). Malcolm Brown explains: "The space between the trench lines on the Western Front—and in all theatres where the same situation applied—was given a memorable and chilling name: No Man's Land. In the Middle Ages, as 'nonesmanneslond,' the term defined disputed territory— an area over which there were legal disagreements. Later it was the specific name of a plot of ground lying outside the north wall of the city of London assigned as a place of execution. In the days of sail it was an area of deck containing blocks, ropes, tackle and other equipment that might be required on the forecastle. Towards the end of the nineteenth century it began to appear in a military context—sometimes in the variant of No Man's Territory. By the beginning of the 1914–18 war it had acquired the meaning which now dominates all others: the terrain between the front lines of opposing armies. From the beginnings of entrenchment onwards it was in constant currency—usually, though not always, spelt with initial capital letters as though it were a precise location on a map, which in a sense it was, for most of four years" (*Imperial War Museum*, 57).

This effort to report eventually proved so suggestive that it comes as no surprise that the exercise affected her deeply, if indirectly. What she wrote in "The Cinema" (1926) about the relation between film and the real world seems equally to describe the strike diary and the General Strike: "The eye wants help. The eye says to the brain, 'Something is happening which I do not in the least understand. You are needed'" (268).[22] The continuous challenge to what powers of observation she possessed was so all-consuming and ultimately so informed her own memories of the war that it is not surprising that her sense of what was happening *on* the street and *in* her drawing room would finally affect her approach to the novel in general, and to "Time Passes," the section of the novel she had only just begun to write, in particular.

Both before and after the strike, newspapers, periodicals, and "historians' histories" recalled the Great War in images, idioms, and expressions. On 26 April the *Times* had published an article highlighting "efforts for peace" in the coal crisis; the *Daily Telegraph* mounted a placard announcing WAR on 3 May when negotiations broke down and the Trades Union Congress (T.U.C.) called the General Strike; and the "official government organ," the *British Gazette*, with Winston Churchill in charge, called the workingmen "the enemy" and demanded an "unconditional surrender."[23] This response was neither idiosyncratic nor reserved for papers supporting the governmental position, and even the usually evenhanded (though labor-friendly) reporters of the *Daily Herald* acquiesced.[24] As Kingsley Martin recalls, "On the morning of the strike [it] countered with, 'If it be war, so be it'" (65).

When the dust cleared and the printers had joined the strike, there were only five large daily newspapers (and a handful of regional ones) remaining, out of the more than two thousand that were published in the United Kingdom in 1926:[25] the *British Gazette* (the government's strike paper, which took

22. See also Hankins, "A Splice of Life."

23. A. J. P. Taylor finds it somehow fitting that Churchill would repeat this demand "more appropriately, against the Germans in the second World war" [sic] (*English History,* 246).

24. Several reporters from the *Daily Herald* wrote for the labor-run *British Worker* during the strike, but were rarely identified. On 5 May 1926, the first day of publication, there was one article, "Would You Believe It?" written by C. L. Everard, who was identified as the "'Gadfly' of the 'Daily Herald,'" and a poem, "We Have Not Chosen Lightly," "By 'Tomfool,' of the 'Daily Herald'" (4).

25. In 1910 there were 2,331 newspapers in the United Kingdom, including 414 in London; in 1928 there were 2,150 newspapers. In this number is included morning and evening dailies, and specialized journals, e.g., the *Jewish Times* and *Lloyd's Daily Index* (Tracey, *British Press,* 26).

over the press of the *Morning Post*); the *British Worker* (the T.U.C.'s answer
to the *British Gazette*); the *Daily Mail* (but only the Continental edition,
which had to be flown in from Paris); the *Scotsman;* and the *Times,* which
Woolf called, macabrely, perhaps, but accurately, one of the "various skeleton papers being sold" (*Diary* 3, 78).[26] On 15 May, the *Nation* published "An
Analogy of War" and, in *The British Public and the General Strike,* published
by the Hogarth Press that October, Kingsley Martin uses "war" and "strike"
interchangeably. Forty years later Leonard Woolf would recall the strike in
terms of the ubiquitous recruiting poster from the Great War: "What did
you do in the General Strike?" (*Downhill,* 217).

Woolf's strike diary is itself informed by this analogy. Beginning two days
into what she calls "this horror" in a letter written from "this doomed city"
(*Letters* 3, 259),[27] it assumes a posture not terribly different from the one she
had tried in the early days of the war. Framing eight entries in her diary
(*Diary* 3, 77–86), the lived experience of the strike is demonstrated through
observation, sometimes from a window of the house, as if sustaining Woolf's
sense that such a record would at least be "interesting" (*Diary* 3, 77). It is difficult to understand why critics such as Thomas Mallon overlook the strike
diary altogether, given her sense of purpose in starting it, while others, such
as Kate Flint, use it to provide evidence that Woolf's "position" vis-à-vis the
General Strike, was like that of John Galsworthy ("Virginia Woolf," 322).

Much of the strike diary can be read as a parody of the kind of writing
(particularly the kind of history and journalism) Woolf rejected, possibly one
of the activities she had planned to assure that she "become more independent and stoical as the days go on" (*Diary* 3, 78). On 6 May, as Woolf describes
a scene replete with rumors and what we would call sound bites, even the
syntax suggests a comical balance that may, perhaps, anticipate the mock-

26. In *The General Strike,* Martin discusses the press and the strike on pages 59–89. On
4 May 1926, in its last complete issue, the *Times* published "London Evening Papers, Stoppages Yesterday," reporting few stoppages, and directly beneath it "'Daily Mail' Printed
in Manchester" and "Movement of Troops, Use Strictly Limited" (10). Even the *Times,*
after an abbreviated four-column issue on 5 May, published in only four pages and irreg-
ularly until Tuesday, 18 May, when regular daily publication was resumed. Meanwhile,
although the *British Gazette* included a daily count of newspapers being published, of the
dozen or so that managed to publish, most were, like the others, only four pages, and
included little if anything other than strike news.

27. On 5 May, the first day of Woolf's strike diary, both the *British Gazette* and the
British Worker published their first numbers. The *British Gazette* ceased publication after
eight issues on 13 May, announcing in a box that *The Morning Post* would resume publication the next day. The *British Worker* continued publication for ten issues, ending on
15 May.

heroic style Woolf would use in her portrait of Percival in *The Waves* (1931):[28] "'everyone is pro-men'"/"'everyone is pro-government'"; "'Churchill is for peace'"/"'Churchill is for tear gas bombs, fight to the death'"; "it will be cold & windy tomorrow (it is shivering cold today)/there was a warm debate in the Commons"; "I notice how frequently we break of[f] with 'Well I don't know'"/"According to L. this open state of mind is due to the lack of papers" (*Diary* 3, 78, 79).

Yet, the tension underlying these snippets, orts, and fragments of public discourse carries into the private conversations of the Woolfs that are reported in the diary and seem clearly to have recalled the Great War. During the strike, Virginia Woolf avoids as far as possible confrontations with the constant stream of visitors to their Bloomsbury home/headquarters and makes a point of remaining alone when listening to the morning broadcast of the Voice of Britain, "to *wh.* we can make no reply" (*Diary* 3, 77; emphasis added). The diary suggests, however, that like the Voice itself (is it a person? a thing? does "wh." = which? whom?), words had become unstable and inexact, inadequate to the task: "It is all tedious & depressing, *rather like* waiting in a train outside a station"; "It feels *like* a deadlock"; "it is *like* a house where someone is dangerously ill" (*Diary* 3, 77, 78, 79; emphasis added).

Her accounts of the "spectacle" of arguments inside the house at 52 Tavistock Square—some between Leonard and various assistants, neighbors, and friends—are not directly related to outside events so much as to the sense of distance from them, of being trapped in an "odd pale unnatural atmosphere—great activity but no normal life" (*Diary* 3, 77, 78). It is almost as if, in Barthes's terms, the continuity of language were disrupted at this time of national/historical crisis.[29] The entries in the diary suggest that the use of language for propaganda during the war was analogous to its function during the strike, and with the same effect.

Inside the house, meaning is dislocated, sometimes in direct response to the historical moment. "Taking a cup of tea" meant "an hour and a half's talk about the Strike"; yet, "minding *this* more than the war" could refer to the absence of reliable information or to the loss of wages or to the strike itself; and Leonard's ironic claim that "if the state wins & smashes T[rades].

---

28. See Little, 74–78, and Graham's "Manuscript Revision and the Heroic Theme of *The Waves*." In an early version of *The Waves,* it maybe implied that Percival dies in the war, as Rhoda "proclaims" civilian immunity: "Look at the street now that Percival is dead. . . . I am immune" (*The Waves: The Two Holograph Drafts,* 556, 560, 562). See also Usui, "A Portrait of Alexander," 122.

29. See Barthes, *Writing Degree Zero.*

U[nion]s he will devote his life to labour: if the archbishop succeeds, he will be baptised" (*Diary* 3, 80) may be less an example of the "Bloomsbury sneer" as some historians assume (e.g., Mellor et al., 345), than an effort to cope with what Woolf calls in "De Quincey's Autobiography" the "two levels of existence": "the rapid passage of events and actions [and] the slow opening up of the single and solemn moments of concentrated emotion" (6). Referring to a "quarrel with Leonard" on 8 May (the only day during the strike not represented in the diary), Woolf suggests that even they had descended to meaningless name-calling: "I dislike the tub thumper in him; he the irrational Xtian in me" (*Diary 3, 80–81*).

Reportage in the diary reflects the frenetic energy of the first days of the strike and a loss of energy at the end. But between the events and the emotion is a sense that history has been displaced by current events, the four years of the Great War by the ten days of the General Strike, an ironic observation given Dangerfield's comment that "the great General Strike of 1914 [was] forestalled by some bullets at Sarajevo" (400). Conscious memory of the Great War emerges at the crucial moment when she has begun to doubt the value of her diary: "I believe it is false psychology to think that in after years these details will be interesting. The war is now barren sand after all." Yet, Woolf must have felt that this was in some sense an inappropiate response, as she immediately modifies the analogy: "But one never knows" (*Diary* 3, 83). Significantly, by the time she writes to her sister, she seems prepared to relieve herself of the tension created in her effort to avoid vitrification, as if in repeating the offending language privately, she had freed herself from the associations the words elicited publicly. "It beggars description," Woolf wrote to her sister the day the strike was settled. "Recall the worst days of the war. Nobody can settle to anything—endless conversations go on—rumours fly—petitions to the Prime Minister are got up" (*Letters* 3, 260).

Neither the General Strike nor the Great War was ever really "business as usual," though in each case civilians were made to believe that it was, particularly if they read the *British Gazette*.[30] That Woolf had reached this dismaying conclusion even as skeleton newspapers were boldly declaring

---

30. The *British Gazette* encouraged readers to beware the "danger of rumours" (1), thereafter encouraging "normalcy" by daily reports on vital services (including railway schedules) and sporting events (including ice hockey in Canada) and by disputing reports in the *British Worker* under the heading "False News." By 10 May, a headline in the *British Gazette* announced "NORMAL!" (3) and three days after that, it announced the "unconditional withdrawal" and "surrender" of the T.U.C. (1).

"victory" was more disturbing than she let on. Certainly, her letter to Vanessa implies a seemingly happy end to it all. "Strike settled 1 p.m. This has just been broadcast. . . . Everyone is in the greatest spirits . . . jubilant and almost hysterical," she wrote on 12 May. "We're going to have a strike dinner and drink champagne with Clive, the Frys, and other spirits" (*Letters* 3, 262). But privately Woolf recorded little real change in the atmosphere and the Woolfs remained "gloomy . . . because the Strike continue[d]" despite celebrations like those greeting the end of the war (complete with "armoured cars" and "soldiers in tin helmets . . . one stood with his hand at the gun which was pointed straight ahead ready to fire") on 12 May (*Diary* 3, 85). The fact is that the miners remained on strike and, as R. A. Foley makes clear, the class war continued for those (like the printers) who did return to work, as well as for those (like the miners and railwaymen) who did not.[31] That the scene Woolf describes recalls those that followed the end of the Great War could not have escaped her notice. "Such sights I dare say I shall never see again; & dont in the least wish to," she reports, betraying a feeling of fatigue and perhaps of resignation, or, perhaps, repressing a sense of déjà vu (*Diary* 3, 85).

By the time Woolf returned to "Time Passes," the same techniques that had been aimed at "cutting the war down to size" (what George Mosse calls "the process of trivialization"[32]) had come to seem a fact of life. What made this the more noticeable was that unlike what happened during the Great War, there had been no noticeable "jolt in the perspective" during the strike, either as the population relied on skeleton newspapers, or faceless voices on the wireless—or afterward:

> The Strike was settled about 1.15—or it was then broadcast. I was in Tottenham Court Rd. at 1 & heard Bartholemew & Fletcher's megaphone declaim that the T.U.C. leaders were at Downing Street. . . . 5 minutes later,

31. For many, the strike continued. Anne Olivier Bell points out that for the miners and the railways workers, to name only two groups of workers, there was no resumption of work (*Diary* 3, 85, n.27). In the last chapter of his book *The General Strike of 1926*, "The Class War Intensified: Battle, Betrayal, Rout and Reprisal," R. A. Foley makes clear the class war continued for those who did return to work, as well as for those who did not: 119–168. On 14 May, the *British Worker* reported "EMPLOYERS BLOCK THE WAY TO PEACE/ Attempts to Victimise Strikers and Impose New Conditions" (4); it continued publication until Saturday, 15 May, with one final issue.

32. Mosse explains that trivialization disguised the reality of the war "even if it was not transcended." His analysis of trivialization involves the tangible *kitsch* of the war: souvenir postcards, for example, as well as "trashy literature" and tin soldiers, whose popularity declined in England "while in Germany it remained high" (126–56).

the wireless. They told us to stand by & await important news. Then a piano played a tune. Then the solemn broadcaster assuming incredible pomp & gloom & speaking one word to the minute read out: Message from 10 Downing Street. The T.U.C. leaders have agreed that Strike shall be withdrawn. (*Diary* 3, 84–85)

The next day's entry, juxtaposing idiosyncratic and impersonal reports, suggests that like returning soldiers, labor will suffer: "[N]o railwaymen back: vindictiveness has now seized our masters. Government shillyshallies. . . . Labour, it seems clear, will be effectively diddled again, & perhaps rid of its power to make strikes in future" (*Diary* 3, 85). It may well have been that Woolf had seen *The British Worker* that same day:[33] WHY WORK DID NOT BEGIN/Employers Make Fresh Attack upon Trade Unionism & Workers Standard of Life/MILLIONS STILL OUT, says the headline on the front page. Meanwhile, the headline to *The British Gazette* announces a peace that runs parallel to the terms set forth in the Treaty of Versailles: General Strike Off/Unconditional Withdrawal of Notices by T.U.C./Men to Return Forthwith/Surrender Received in Downing Street/Negotiations to be Resumed in the Coal Dispute. Such headlines must have suggested to Woolf that since the war the idiom of irony had become the idiom of truth, and the idiom of war, the idiom of the real world. When Woolf self-consciously noted that "nothing need be said of the Strike" on 18 May, she may have been speaking out of frustration (*Diary* 3, 86). Or, perhaps, because she was thinking of what Montaigne calls the "vanity of words" (that is, the eloquence that flourishes "when affairs were in the worst state and agitated by the storm of civil wars" [*CW,* 221, 222]); or, perhaps, because of what Rose Macaulay calls in *Catchwords and Claptrap* (published by the Hogarth Press five months later) "nimbuses of associations" (7).

The sense of wartime language functioning in a postwar context so affected Woolf that it undermined her ability to continue writing the novel, at least temporarily. In the last entry in her "Strike diary" on 13 May, she predicts

33. Other Britons may not have been so lucky. Graves and Hodge point out that the limited means at the disposal of the T.U.C. were no match for the resources available to the government-supported *British Gazette* (164), which nonetheless printed a daily tally of "circulation," which on 12 May was reported at 1,801,400 for the previous day, up from 232,000 on 5 May (3). Nevertheless, Samuel Hynes points out that however many copies of the *Gazette* were printed, the numbers are deceiving and do not represent readership: "distribution was apparently a matter of dumping bundles of papers on to street corners and from RAF planes on to mining villages" (*A War,* 410).

that "all pages devoted to the Strike will be skipped, when I read over this book. Oh that dull old chapter, I shall say. Excitements about what are called real things are always unutterably transitory" (*Diary* 3, 85). Such fears for the readability of even her private writing must have reminded her that the changes in language during the war had left postwar England with a leaner and sparer sense, not only of "real things" but of discourse. In a letter to Edward Sackville-West on 15 May, she admits to being "all over the place trying to do a difficult thing in my novel ["Time Passes"]" (*Letters* 3, 262) and is finally so frustrated by the effort (and so clearly unsatisfied with the "sketchy" results) that she declares it "finished" ten days later (*Diary* 3, 88). It may have been, indirectly, the unusually public nature of the writing and revision of this section in particular (including the publication of a translated version of "Time Passes" as a "story") and particularly Roger Fry's criticism of it as "poeticize[d]" that ultimately leads her to establish the link with the war as giving the "empty house . . . [some]thing to cling to" (*Diary* 3, 76). Finally, only in the published novel is Woolf able to modulate narrative authority in "Time Passes" by shifting the center of consciousness as the war begins and as it ends. And in the published novel Woolf suggests her understanding that the problems facing the postwar world were not so much a limitation, as a challenge requiring reorientation.

To the Lighthouse is finally an expression of a quasi-Dadaistic anxiety over the postwar future not only of language but of art itself.[34] In "Time Passes," Woolf informs this deep concern by including, ironically, something of the purposeful "detachment" of Roger Fry, a sense of detachment that is realized in the same kind of "scattered and incongruous fragments" she would include in "The War Years" chapter of *Roger Fry: A Biography* in 1940 (214, 213, 200–15). But in "Time Passes," which might be called "the war years" section of the novel, the narrative represents a noncombatant experience that cannot transgress its geographic and lexical limitations. Unlike Roger Fry, who had found "translating" governmental propaganda "into something real" an amusing diversion (*RF*, 210), Woolf would include six bracketed reports of news (which Roger Poole calls "public reality" ["'We all,'" 83]), all but the first from the world outside the house on the Isles of Skye, which signal the translation of something real (such as death) into the kind of idiom found in the Northcliffe-controlled *Daily News,* or, more recently, in *The British Gazette.* "Time Passes" thus illustrates this lexical dilemma by jux-

---

34. Quentin Bell, in his review-essay "The Biographer, the Critic, and the Lighthouse," says *"To the Lighthouse* is cubist writing" (98).

taposing a prewar mode of discourse with the "new journalism" that controlled popular newspaper reports during the war, and very nearly reduces
the entire section to a *great war of words* (to use the title of Buitenhuis's study
and subtitle to one of Gilbert and Gubar's), with the civilian experience at
the center. Mrs. Ramsay dies, we are told in brackets, "rather suddenly the
night before"; and Prue Ramsay's death in childbirth "was indeed a tragedy."
But Andrew Ramsay's death in combat "mercifully, was instantaneous" (*TL,*
194, 199, 201).

It is, I should think, a distortion to see "Time Passes" as involving the war
only metaphorically—or figuratively, though such figures of speech are included here, as they are in *Mrs. Dalloway* and *Jacob's Room,* partly to suggest,
as Woolf does in *Roger Fry,* that "a break must be made in every life when
August 1914 is reached." Woolf offers a modification to the metaphor that
would seem to inform "Time Passes" as well: "But the fracture differs, according to what is broken" (*RF,* 200). Critics, even those who see the section
to be "about the war," have stressed the metaphorical or figurative dimension of "Time Passes," and certainly this position is not without support.[35]
But the figurative or "literary" language is found not only in the unbracketed narrative but in the bracketed reports, which represent the wartime
press. Woolf makes the timing apparent in the first bracketed report, which
suggests that newspaper reporting before the war was more reliable—or, at
least, verifiable: "[Here Mr. Carmichael, who was reading Virgil, blew out
his candle. It was midnight]" (192). This point is made the more clearly by
the deletion of the modifier in the earlier (English) version, which is the
same, but for the last line: "It was past midnight" (*TL, Dick,* 201). The last
bracketed report is the first one to refer directly to the war, albeit in similarly
ambiguous language: "[Mr. Carmichael brought out a volume of poems
that spring, which had an unexpected success. The war, people said, had revived their interest in poetry]" (*TL,* 202). But Woolf's point is clearly that
newspaper reporting is selective and incomplete, something suggested by
the omission of the fact that Carmichael's poems had been written some
thirty-five years before the war (288). As an avid wartime reader of newspapers herself, Woolf found sloppy and unreliable coverage of the war on the

35. See, for example, Makiko Minow-Pinkney: "What is literally destroying the house
is rain, rats, and wind, but what is figuratively destroying it is the First World War" (99).
Essays in *Virginia Woolf and War* (Hussey, ed.), particularly those by Haule and Bazin/
Lauter, also stress the figurative over the historical. Michael Tratner, on the other hand,
says that "'Time Passes' is of course about World War I'" ("Figures in the Dark," 3), and
rather leaves it at that.

front even more disturbing: "[A shell exploded. Twenty *or* thirty young men were blown up in France, among them Andrew Ramsay. . . .]" (emphasis added, 201).

The narrator of "Time Passes" seems to frame her own (unbracketed) observations of the empty house (and the area she surveys from a window) in terms of war, even from time to time using an anachronistic Great War idiom. "Were they allies? Were they enemies? How long would they endure?" she asks, rhetorically, to refer to "certain airs, detached from the body of the wind . . . [to] venture indoors"; subsequently, "those stray airs" are reconstructed more definitely as "advance guards of great armies" (190–91; 194). To see these passages as suggesting consciousness of the war, even (as James Haule suggests, "to write for the first time about the war 'from our point of view'" ["*To the Lighthouse*," 166]), is, I think to miss the crucial point Woolf is making about the lack of consciousness: "Nothing it seemed could break that image, corrupt that innocence, or disturb the . . . silence" that is contained by the house (195). The house withstands assaults of nature (the "clammy sea airs . . . reiterating their questions—'Will you fade? Will you perish'"), maintaining "the peace, the indifference, the air of pure integrity" (as if the questions are not only figurative but also rhetorical): "we remain" (195). Yet, notwithstanding the increased frequency of the military imaging (culminating in chapter 6 of "Time Passes"), the narrator seems to have no clue as to its context, or the meaning of what J. K. Johnstone calls "the [geographically] distant sounds of war" ("World War I," 535), which are described in mythic terms, "as if a giant voice had shrieked so loud in its agony that tumblers stood inside a cupboard vibrated too" (*TL*, 200).

Such metaphors do not merely invite the reader to question the authority of the civilian point of view represented by the narrator; they also undermine the authority of what Foucault calls "literary language" that the narrator employs (*The Order of Things*, quoted in *Language* 19). It is as if narrative authority is intentionally undercut, not only by bracketed news from the outside or by what Michael Tratner calls "a complete change of cast" ("Figures," 3) but also by losing the sense of civilian immunity that prewar language embodied. The narrator is limited, quite literally, by time and place. And she can no more transcend these boundaries than can Mrs. McNab, the caretaker of the house, or Mrs. Bast and her son George, who help her. Woolf's narrator observes Mrs, McNab "tearing the veil of silence with [her] hands" and "grinding it with boots," although what she is doing is humming and dancing to a tune she remembers from before the war. Removed from their context, however, the words, not only of the song but also of the text, are "robbed of meaning" (*TL*, 196), and suggest a linguistic unease like that found in combatant narratives that struggle to move away from mythic configurations and, as Cobley says, "tell it as it had been" (6).[36]

Howsoever the narrator's struggles with liminality inform the civilian experience of the war, they remind us as well of Woolf's struggle to establish her authority as a postwar novelist in a market that was just beginning to see a second wave in the publication of Great War books, some of them written by noncombatants, and some printed on or published by the Woolfs' own Hogarth Press during what J. H. Willis refers to as the "peak years" of 1923, 1927, and 1928 (34, 363, 369).[37] There were starts and stops in writing and revising the novel, and "Time Passes" in particular (including time off to see to the Hogarth Press's *Victorian Photographs of Famous Men and Fair Women* by her aunt, Julia Margaret Cameron [1926], for which she also wrote an introduction). Yet Woolf, repeatedly and uncharacteristically, found the courage to expose her work-in-progress to scrutiny not only privately but publicly and most obviously in the intermediate version of "Time Passes" translated by Charles Mauron and published in the French magazine *Commerce*. Just how much this affected her is the subject of some debate, but it seems to me that the changes made in the final version indicate that her memories of the strike had begun to blur with those of the war, as if the one had ultimately clarified the other.

By the time the novel finally went to press she had added both the bracketed reports and development of the narrative voice, a variation on E. M. Forster's definition of a "round" (or developed) character in *Aspects of the Novel* (1927). In Woolf's review of *Aspects* for the *Atlantic Monthly* she omits this definition, but notes that "[a]lmost nothing is said about words [themselves]" ("Art of Fiction," 54), as if calling attention to what she calls in "How Should One Read a Book?" (1926) "the dangers and difficulties of words": "[W]hen you attempt to reconstruct [a whole vision] in words, you will find that it breaks into a thousand conflicting impressions" (2).

36. James Haule is certainly on to something in noting the changes in Mrs. McNab's characterization from the earlier drafts (particularly from what he calls the "intermediate" version to the published novel), but where I think he errs is in neglecting to consider how the "tightening form and narrowing focus of her words" are not only stylistic or aesthetic considerations (which he finds in all her novels) ("*To the Lighthouse*," 175); they also bear on what Woolf was saying about the effect of the war not only on language but also on life itself.

37. Willis finds a number of "peak years" in his study, and those of 1927 and 1928 followed the "peak year" of 1923, which saw the publication of T. S. Eliot's postwar "The Waste Land"; and former servicemen Herbert Read and Robert Graves, both war poets.

As if illustrating this problem of reconstructing in words, Woolf follows the bracketed report of Andrew Ramsay's combat death (along with "[t]wenty or thirty others") with an unbracketed admission: there is "something out of harmony with [the] jocundity and [the] serenity" of nature, an "intrusion" that "[i]t was difficult blandly to overlook"; it was still more difficult to subscribe to the Romantic belief that "beauty outside mirrored beauty within" (*TL,* 201). In juxtaposing this "literary" observation with a personification of Nature, typical of prewar, nineteenth-century thought ("Did Nature supplement what man advanced?" [201]), Woolf alters the narrative voice, something not appreciated, even by "deconstructionists" (see Laurence, 95–96). In so doing, both the lyrical language and the reliability of narrative observation is questioned ("That dream, of sharing, completing, of finding in solitude on the beach an answer, was then but a reflection in a mirror, and the mirror itself was but the suface glassiness which forms in quiescence when the nobler powers sleep beneath?"). It is finally nullified by death, the ultimate reality of the war—the one that newspapers relegate to lists of names and deprive of the tragedy that the numbers should imply: "contemplation was unendurable; the mirror was broken" (*TL,* 202).

The bracketed report of the wartime publication of Carmichael's poetry is the last attempt to juxtapose newspaper reports with the "literary language" it all but replaces. In the second line, which attempts to explain the "unexpected success" of the publication, we are told: "[. . . The war, people said, had revived their interest in poetry]" (202). But the unpoetic statement that reduces reading to "interest," and "success" to sales, illustrates the limits of newspaper reports. And, after one last effort to discover a literary language for the war at home, the unbracketed narrative voice seems to fade into oblivion as it is reduced to parentheses.

> Listening (had there been any one to listen) from the upper rooms of the empty house only gigantic chaos streaked with lightning could have been heard tumbling and tossing, as the winds and waves disported themselves like the amorphous bulks of leviathans whose brows are pierced by no light of reason, and mounted one on top of another and lunged and plunged in the darkness or the daylight (for night and day, month and year ran shapelessly together) in idiot games, until it seemed as if the universe were battling and tumbling, in brute confusion and wanton lust aimlessly by itself. (202–3)

The withdrawal of the narrative voice is an implicit admission of the inadequacy of words, which is explicitly seen in the absence of the *word* "word" in "Time Passes" and "words" in relation to the war.[38] The withdrawal would seem to be based on the assumption that the war would make "impossible" the ability to "read in the littered pieces the clear words of truth" (*TL*, 193).

In her postwar novels to date Woolf had treated the war as a combatant experience, the reality of which was beyond the power of her pen to describe and the power of civilians (particularly in the village) to understand. A well-known passage from *Jacob's Room* suggests how detached Mrs. Flanders is, with her worries about the poultry (like Mr. Brewer and his geraniums in *Mrs. Dalloway*), even as we are told that "her sons [were] fighting for their country."

> "The guns?" said Betty Flanders, half asleep, getting out of bed and going to the window, which was decorated with a fringe of dark leaves.
>
> "Not at this distance," she thought. "It is the sea."
>
> Again, far away, she heard the dull sound, as if nocturnal women were beating great carpets. There was Morty lost, and Seabrook dead; her sons fighting for their country. But were the chickens safe? Was that someone moving downstairs? Rebecca with the toothache? No. The nocturnal women were beating great carpets. Her hens shifted slightly on their perches. (*JR*, 175)

Yet in "Time Passes" this sense of civilian detachment is modified. Without further bracketed reports of the outside world, the published novel suggests that Woolf had discovered a strategy for representing the effect of the war not only on language but on life itself. This strategy had been lacking in the earlier drafts, which had too emphatically rested the future of the postwar world on the shoulders of Mrs. McNab, whose consciousness finally accounts for only 16 percent of the section (Leaska, *Lighthouse*, appendix B, 208).[39] By putting the narrative under the control of a working woman's vision and vocabulary, Woolf no longer "poeticizes" or "exaggerates," weaknesses that Fry saw in the intermediate version translated by Mauron (Fry, *Letters* 2, 598). Instead, she describes changes owing to the war in the con-

---

38. In his *Concordance to "To the Lighthouse,"* James Haule notes that "word" is used thirteen times in "The Window" and seven times in "The Lighthouse"; "words" is used twenty-eight times and fourteen times. In "Time Passes," the one use of "words" ("read in the littered pieces the clear words of truth" [*TL*, 193]) comes after the first bracketed report: "[Here Mr. Carmichael, who was reading Virgil blew out his candle. It was midnight.]" (192).

39. Compare Haule, *"To the Lighthouse"* (172–74), and Dick, "The Restless Searcher" (322–23).

crete, nonliterary terms of lived experience: in the availability and cost of goods and services ("there was plaster fallen in the hall" and "the carpet was ruined quite"); in the impediments to travel ("travel being so difficult these days"); and in the frequency of death: "every one had lost some one these years" (*TL,* 203–5). Finally, only because Mrs. McNab cannot do her work ("The books and things were mouldy, for, what with the war and help being hard to get, the house had not been cleaned as she could have wished" [203–4]) does she realize the task is too much for her and leaves "the house alone, shut up, locked" (206).[40]

"Time Passes" gives us the sense, nevertheless, that the war had affected not only memory of the prewar past but also understanding of the postwar future, in what Husserl might call "an immanent now" (38–39). This becomes most clear in the last two chapters of "Time Passes," not only because all mention of the war is deleted but because they suggest that like the war, the peace somehow happens and is outside both *human* control and *human* comprehension: "Poppies sowed themselves among the dahlias" and "peace had come" (*TL,* 207, 213). What we are shown is that if it had not been for "a force working," both the prewar house and its contents would have lain "upon the sands of oblivion" (209). But confidence in the power of the caretakers to "fetch up from oblivion all the Waverly novels" (209), for example, is juxtaposed with Mrs. McNab "wantoning on with her memories" (211), as preparations are made for the return of the Ramsays and their circle to the house in the Hebrides. For Mrs. McNab, who was unable to find the help she needed to care for the house during the war, it is only because of the return of Mrs. Bast and her son George from Glasgow (possibly after riots over demobilization and the forty-hour general strike there in January 1919 [Marwick, *Britain,* 66]) that the house is restored. If Mrs. McNab on the Isle of Skye relied on rumors, observation, and gossip for news during the war years, Mrs. Bast, in the city, had access to newspapers, which left her feeling better informed: "The young gentleman [Andrew Ramsay] was dead. That she was sure. She had read his name in the papers" (*TL,* 210).

This greater knowledge leads Mrs. Bast to predict that despite efforts to restore the house to its prewar state, as dictated by Mrs. McNab's "unwound . . . ball of memories" (particularly of Mrs. Ramsay), the family would "find it changed" (*Holograph,* Dick, 231; *TL,* 211). Yet, awareness of the changes caused by the war are obscured in the narrative and the war itself seems relegated to oblivion as we are told (parenthetically) of the return of Lily

40. Lucio Ruotolo believes that Mrs. McNab notices further "details of war" not present in *The Original Holograph Draft* (134, 247n).

Briscoe "in September" 1919. The signing of the Treaty of Versailles that ended the war in June 1919 is transfigured to "[m]essages of peace breathed from sea to the shore" to begin chapter 10, and the meaning of it all is obscured: "[B]ut what mattered if the meaning were plain?" (213).

It is finally not the seemingly ageless and all-knowing poet Augustus Carmichael (whose return is also set in parenthesis) who will actively seek the balance needed to survive in the postwar world, but the forty-four-year-old artist, Lily Briscoe. It is Lily Briscoe who remembers having heard that after learning of "Andrew Ramsay's death . . . Mr. Carmichael had 'lost all interest in life'" (289). Not surprisingly, Mr. Carmichael notices nothing different in the house and falls asleep that first night thinking that "it all looked . . . much as it used to look" (214). Yet, for Woolf, who worried about the effectiveness of "Time Passes" long after publication, it is finally not life that the war obscured, but death, something suggested as "Time Passes" ends with the word "Awake" (214).

Though the war is never explicitly denied in the postwar world of "The Lighthouse," as the occasional references to it confirm, the effects of peace are undercut by the unrelenting presence of death and the dead. Lily Briscoe repeats: "Mrs. Ramsay dead; Andrew killed; Prue dead too" (219). And as she hears orts and fragments of Mr. Ramsay's mantra ("Perished" and "Alone"), she realizes that "like everything else this strange morning the words became symbols" (219). On the first night back to the house in the Hebrides, a curiously unchanged Mr. Ramsay says "You [will] find us much changed" to a Lily Briscoe who had already "felt that . . . it was a house full of unrelated passions" (221). "The Lighthouse" begins by confirming that postwar life picks up where prewar life (almost literally) stopped, something Woolf had herself observed right before the armistice (*Diary* 1, 215).

Yet, in the novel, something *is* different. And what is especially disturbing is that Lily can find no way to describe her feelings, "nothing that she could express at all"; even "What does it mean?" was "a catchword" she had "caught up from some book" (*TL*, 217). Even the easiest of tasks seem out of reach, a simple list of things to bring on the trip to the lighthouse beyond her abilities.

Nancy [Ramsay] burst in, and asked . . . in a queer half dazed, half desperate way, "What does one send to the Lighthouse?" . . .

What does one send to the Lighthouse indeed! At any other time Lily could have suggested reasonably tea, tobacco, newspapers. But this morning everything seemed so extraordinarily queer that a question like Nancy's

—What does one send to the Lighthouse?—opened doors in one's mind
that went banging and swinging to and fro and made one keep asking, in a
stupefied gaze, What does one send? What does one do? Why is one sitting
here, after all? (218)

The questions are symptomatic of a kind of dementia, which, like war neurosis (or shell-shock), seeks clarification in repetition. What clarification
Woolf achieves in *To the Lighthouse* is due less to relieving the burden of the
war felt in her earlier novels, than to recognizing it as a form of what we now
call survival guilt.[41]

It is not surprising, then, that "The Lighthouse" stresses the unrelenting
consciousness of death and the dead on only one character, Lily Briscoe, the
artist. And though Lily "could remember the look on Mrs. Ramsay's face"
(*TL,* 224) and, in an earlier draft, remembers visiting her gravesite during
the war with Prue and Andrew (*Holograph,* Dick, 304), neither the few other
guests nor Mr. Ramsay and his surviving children (including James and
Cam, who accompany him on the trip to the lighthouse), show any consciousness or explicit memory of either the war (which was responsible for
the loss of Andrew) or death (which claimed both Mrs. Ramsay and Prue).
It is as if the house in the Hebrides symbolically absolves the Ramsays and
their guests of the burden of the postwar "world of woe," as "[t]hey stood
there, isolated from the rest of the world" (*TL,* 227, 228). Yet, it offers no
such comfort to Lily Briscoe, whose "remembering the symbol [of the
kitchen table] which . . . Andrew had given her," evokes the parenthetical
thought that "[h]e had been killed by the splinter of a shell instantly" (232).

If, on the way to completing her prewar painting ("She had never finished
the painting. She would paint that picture now" [220]), Lily Briscoe becomes the novel's "most reliable witness," as Alex Zwerdling suggests (200),
it may be because she is the only survivor who remembers not only what she
witnessed during the war but also, significantly, what she missed. Her success in arriving at a vision that provides the "razor edge of balance" between
the prewar and postwar worlds can thus be attributed not only to her memories but to what Bertrand Russell calls "memory-beliefs." In other words,
her memories are not only composed of home front events she had herself
seen but of "hypotheses" that allow her to remember what was outside personal experience (*Analysis,* 159).[42]

41. See note 18 to chapter 1. See also Levenback, "Virginia Woolf and Returning
Soldiers."
42. In "Memory and the Past," Norman Malcolm suggests that however "skeptically"
conceived, "memory-beliefs" are "logically tenable" and may rely on G. E. Moore's *Philo-
sophical Papers* for authority (188–89).

If this device blurs or obscures the actual wartime experiences of Lily Briscoe, whose life had continued apart from the house in the Hebrides, it may be part of Woolf's plan to make "some use of symbolism" to overcome her "dread of 'sentimentality'" (*Diary* 3, 110). "[T]he war," we are told parenthetically, "had drawn the sting of her femininity" (*TL*, 238), but Lily remembers an antiwar rally, for example, not unlike the one held at Kingsway Hall on 4 August 1914, two days after Keir Hardie addressed a larger one in Trafalgar Square, and only hours before Britain declared war on Germany (Liddington, 78):[43] "She had gone one day into a Hall and heard him speaking during the war . . . preaching love from a platform . . . in the half-empty hall" (*TL*, 292–93). Resisting the urge to repeat the past, Lily Briscoe had set up her easel "not too close to Mr. Carmichael, but close enough for his protection. Yes, it must have been precisely here that she had stood ten years ago" (220–21). But there is a difference: "She set her clean canvas firmly upon the easel, as a barrier . . . to ward off Mr. Ramsay" (223), where before the war she had believed it a target. Woolf chose, however, to exclude Lily Briscoe's question about what the late Mrs. Ramsay "would have thought about the War," perhaps because the artist herself had to "step back to get her canvas at a due distance" (*Holograph*, Dick, 296).

Woolf did not, however, intend "The Lighthouse" to show us the artist at odds with the postwar present and the prewar past. When Woolf admitted on 21 March 1927 that however much she "like[d] the end" of the novel she was not entirely comfortable with changes she had made to Lily Briscoe (*Diary* 3, 132), she may have been reconsidering how she had used the artist to inform survival guilt. Having chosen in "Time Passes" to juxtapose the "sudden" death of Mrs. Ramsay with the "instant" death of Andrew Ramsay, Woolf must have thought it prudent to delete a reference to the death "in battle" of both Andrew and his younger brother, Jasper, and to reduce the description of Andrew Ramsay's friendship with Augustus Carmichael, both having been included in Lily Briscoe's "memories" of the war in "The Lighthouse" (*Holograph*, Dick, 241, 330–31). Yet, in retaining Lily's memory-belief involving Carmichael "march[ing] through Trafalgar Square carrying a big stick" after he learns of the death of Andrew, Woolf may have herself been remembering the Peace Day celebrations that had taken place there on 19 July 1919, two months before "The Lighthouse" is set. Woolf might also have been suggesting that Lily and Mr. Carmichael shared the kind of union

43. As Woolf was writing the novel, the Peacemakers Pilgrim Council and the Women's Cooperative Guild began to plan with the Labour Party for the Disarmament Conference of 1932 (Liddington, 143–45), something about which Woolf would likely have known.

that she had herself experienced with the artist Jacques Raverat, even as he literally (like Carmichael spiritually) had lived with death in life:[44] "She did not know what he had done, when he heard that Andrew was killed, but she felt it in him all the same" (*TL*, 289).

In "The Lighthouse" the war theme (not unlike the war itself) is easy enough to miss. Yet even as the surviving characters (excepting Lily Briscoe) repress memories of death and the war, they remain members of the same postwar community, linked through what they remember of the prewar past. Some treat the prewar past with indifference: neither Augustus Carmichael (who was a guest before the war) nor Mrs. Beckwith (who was not) has any memories of it at all, and Cam Ramsay denies the past altogether and embraces the immediate present, with a repetition that betokens clarification— or survival guilt ("She was thinking how all those paths and the lawn, thick and knotted with the lives they had lived there, were gone: were rubbed out; were past; were unreal, and now this was real; the boat and the sail with its patch; Macalister with his earrings; the noise of the waves—all this was real" [248–49]). For James Ramsay, prewar memory makes postwar closure problematic: "Something, he remembered, stayed and darkened over him; would not move; . . . something arid and sharp descended even there, like a blade, a scimitar, smiting through the leaves and flowers even of that happy world, making it shrivel and fall" (276). For Lily Briscoe, "tunneling her way into her picture, into the past" (258), she comes to terms with the problematic present: "For how could one express in words . . . that emptiness there?" (265). The last part of the novel is not only interested in exploring survival guilt among civilians—as *Mrs. Dalloway* had explored survival guilt in Septimus Warren Smith—but in assembling a world broken apart for ten years and without so much as the lexical tools to put it back together. Yet each of the four central characters in his or her way works toward a goal, each in one way or another reaching the lighthouse, an archetypal symbol of personal epiphany, in a postwar world where "nothing was simply one thing" (277).

Postwar instability and change in "The Lighthouse" does not, however, limit the artist so much as offer new challenges. There is an ironic balance offered at the end of the novel that underscores changes "between the [prewar] past and the [postwar] present," which are seen as "disconcerting" in

44. Virginia Woolf shared a close, spiritual relationship with the poet and "Neo-Pagan" Jacques Raverat, something that can be seen in their correspondence and in a gesture that was never repeated: in February 1925 Woolf had sent him the proofs of *Mrs. Dalloway*, which he was finally too ill to read himself. He died a month later.

Woolf's 1926 essay "How It Strikes a Contemporary" (158). In the novel, even as the more cynical or hopeless responses are neutralized (Mr. Ramsay smiles his approval to James) or overcome (Lily Briscoe has "a vision"), these moments of triumph are undercut by mock-heroic narrative: "[Mr. Ramsay] rose and stood in the bow of the boat, very straight and tall, for all the world, James thought, as if he were saying, 'There is no God'" (*TL*, 308). And Lily's naive assertion that "nothing stays; all changes; but not words, not paint" (267) is shown to be an exercise in self-delusion, barely balanced by her moment of completion.

> "There it was—her picture. Yes, with all its greens and blues, its lines running up and across, its attempt at something. It would be hung in the attics, she thought; it would be destroyed. But what did that matter. . . . It was done; it was finished. Yes, she thought, laying down her brush in extreme fatigue, I have had my vision" (309–10).

Yet if the creative impulse seems to end anonymously and in "extreme fatigue," it is not because there is no future, but because like the past, the future has to be acknowledged—in its own terms.

As Woolf says in the review-essay "The Narrow Bridge of Art," published three months after *To the Lighthouse,* "for our generation and the generation that is coming the lyric cry of ecstasy or despair, which is so intense, so personal, and so limited, is not enough . . . [and] it is in this atmosphere of doubt and conflict that writers have now to create" (218–19). Woolf, whose sensitivity to death during the war was challenged by the difficulties of postwar life and postwar language, seems to have used "The Lighthouse" to suggest contextualization of its memory. By using memory to juxtapose the prewar past and the postwar present (as she would do with greater authority and less indirection in *A Room of One's Own*), Woolf suggests that a balance may be found not in individual experience of the war, or even in one's memory of it, but in recognizing how best to accommodate changes that it brought about. As *Non-combatants and Others* helped Macaulay come to terms with the reality of death during the war, *To the Lighthouse* allowed Woolf to come to terms with the reality that it left behind. Although combatant writings of the time might suggest that former soldiers were coming to terms with their memories of the front, Woolf learned that whether expressed or repressed, memories of the war on the front or at home do not die.

4

Remembering the War in the Years Between the Wars

> How far was one justified in making use of one's immunity?
> . . . Had one any right to be immune?
>
> —Winifred Holtby, *Poor Caroline*

> We, whom the storm-winds battered, come again
> Like strangers to the places we have known.
>
> —Vera Brittain,
> "The War Generation: Vale," *Testament of Youth*

AFTER DRAFTING COMMENTS "about the war" for "Professions for Women," the speech she had agreed to give in January 1931, Woolf chose to exclude them (*Pargiters,* 164). Reporting on the speech in "A Woman's Notebook," a column she wrote each week for the *Nation,* Vera Brittain, who had been in the Voluntary Aid Detachment during World War I and was then writing her war memoir, *Testament of Youth* (1933), made special mention of Woolf's "honest [book] reviews" (*Pargiters,* xxxv, n). This must have taken Woolf aback and brought to mind the excluded comment that were she, in 1931, given a second chance to review books about the war, she would decry the war as a "stupid and violent and hateful and idiotic and trifling and ignoble and mean display" and declare she was "bored by war books," at least those that encouraged romantic notions of it (*Pargiters,* 164).

For Vera Brittain, who had, like returning servicemen, seen the effects of the war on the front, there were no romanticized memories of combat. For Virginia Woolf, who experienced the war on the blacked-out streets of London, reading Brittain's *Testament of Youth* on 2 September 1933 "lit up a long passage." What Woolf found of special note was that Brittain "told in detail, without reserve, of the war" and that "[s]he feels . . . these facts must be made known" (*Diary* 4, 177). As with *We That Were Young* (1932), a war novel (albeit an autobiographical one[1]) written by Irene Rathbone, a V.A.D. as well, Brittain's book must have suggested to Woolf that there was light becoming visible at the end of the dark passage surrounding the history of the war because of what she had called in the "masculine state of mind" ("Professions for Women," 287). Although she did not review it, Woolf read Brittain's war book with great eagerness ("extreme greed," she said in her diary) and found it so "moving" that she neglected other reading, including the reading of Turgenev that she was doing in preparation for a review that she had promised to Bruce Richmond (see *Diary* 4, 194).

Woolf may well have seen Brittain's war story as a natural precursor to what she was about in the book that was growing out of "Professions for Women."[2] Brittain identified the war as central to her generation and to her book, yet, as she explained in her foreword, because she found the memory of the war was so painful, she had struggled with the book's form: moving from "a history in terms of personal life" in a "long novel"; to fictionalizing the diary she kept from 1913 to 1918; finally to, writing "an autobiographical study" that included a wide range of personal writings and historical documents from the years preceding the war until 1925 (*Testament of Youth*, 11–13). Woolf's own struggles with the form of her book are widely acknowledged and it is thought that her first idea, for a sequel to *A Room of One's Own*, occurred to Woolf the day before she delivered her speech; this in 1932 became the idea for an essay-novel and then a "novel of fact"; and then, in 1933, something that, reminiscent of her plan for *Mrs. Dalloway*, would "give the whole of the present society—nothing less: facts, as well as vision," now somehow combining *Night and Day*, her first novel of fact, which was written during the Great War, with *The Waves*, her novel of vision (*Diary* 4, 6, 129, 151–52; *Pargiters*, xv).

On 2 November 1932 she called the essay-novel "The Pargiters" and envisaged it as wide in scope (rather like a one-volume roman-fleuve) and quasi-biographical and/or historical in method, extending "from 1880 to here & now." On 2 September 1933 she "thought of 'Here & Now' as a title for The Pargiters" as it might obviate comparisons with other family sagas,

1. Published the year before Vera Brittain's *Testament of Youth,* Irene Rathbone's *We That Were Young* (according to Lynn Knight's "Introduction") "may have received fewer accolades owing to its fictional standing." Its reception improved when it was acknowledged to be autobiographical (xxi).

2. Mitchell Leaska discusses the provenance in his "Introduction" to *The Pargiters*. See also Middleton and Cramer for other readings.

such as the *Forsyte Saga* and the *Herries Chronicle,* the first a fiction that all but omitted the war altogether (although it covered the years 1886 to 1920), the other a fictional sequence based on the experiences of the author, Hugh Walpole (*Diary* 4, 129, 176).[3] In all, she had ten titles for what became *The Years* in 1935. After trying on a dozen titles, including "The Next War" for what began as a "sequel" to *A Room of One's Own* and became an epistolary "war book" (*Diary* 4, 361), she decided upon "Three Guineas" in November 1936.[4]

As Woolf was reading Brittain's *Testament of Youth,* written and published somewhat *after* the "war-books boom," she began to prepare for writing what would be the most difficult and strenuous section of her novel, "1917." Brittain's experience in writing her book anticipated Woolf's in that the pain caused by the war seemed not to be assuaged despite the passage of years and led to pain in writing about it, a circumstance that may explain why it took Woolf herself so long to confront her own experience of the war and

3. Galsworthy's *The Forsyte Saga* is a novel sequence published between 1906 and 1921; in 1922 the novels were published together. Hugh Walpole's *Herries Chronicle* is a historical novel sequence published in 1930, 1931, 1932, and 1933, and based on his life in Cumberland.

4. Madeline Hummel finds evidence that as late as 3 June 1938 Woolf still conceived of *Three Guineas* and *The Years* as a "unit" (152). The titles Woolf tried on for *The Years,* as noted in her diaries, were: "The Pargiters"; "Here & Now," or "Music" or "Dawn" on 17 August 1934; "Dawn" on 2 September 1934; "Sons & Daughters" or "Daughters & Sons" on 2 October 1934; "Ordinary People" on 30 December 1934; "the Caravan" on 11 January 1935; "Other People's Houses" on 22 August 1935; and, finally, "The Years" on 5 September 1935. Titles considered for *Three Guineas* were: "Professions for Women" on 20 January 1931; "The Open Door" on 23 January 1931; "Opening the Door" or "Open Door" on 26 January 1931; "A Knock on the door" on 28 May 1931; "the Tap on the Door" on 13 January 1932; "'Men Are Like That'" on 16 February 1932; "On Being Despised" on 14 April 1935; "P. & P." on 29 August 1935; "The Next War" on 15 October 1935; "The Next War" or "The War" on 27 October; "What Are We to Do" on 30 October 1935; "Answers to Correspondents" on 3 January 1936; "Letter to an Englishman" on 18 March 1936; "Two Guineas" on 24 March 1936; and, "3 Guineas" on 3 November 1936. The Berg Collection holding, "The Pargiters: a novel-essay based upon a paper read to the London National Society for Women's Service" (holograph; unsigned; dated Oct. 11, 1932–Nov. 15, 1934; 8 vols.) varies significantly from the published novel. The earliest material in volume 1 has been removed but is dated on a remaining stub: July 20, 1931. Beginning with "Notes for the knock on the door, July 21, 1931," the manuscripts include the following alternate titles: "Time Passes," "Here & Now," "In the Flesh," "The Dawn," "Uncles and Aunts," "Ordinary People," and "Sons and Daughters." See New York—New York Public Library—The Research Libraries, *The Dictionary Catalog of the Henry W. and Albert A. Berg Collection of English and American Literature,* 4 (1969), 449. References to this eight-volume handwritten text will be indicated in the body of the chapter by "Holograph" followed by volume and page number.

to transform it to the stuff of fiction. Unlike *Jacob's Room,* where the un-knowableness of a future enlistee is central to the narrative, and *Mrs. Dalloway,* where a former serviceman's experience is central, and *To the Lighthouse,* where the unknowableness of the war itself is central, *The Years* very much involves actual civilian experience.

The writing forced Woolf to confront not only her experience of the war, as she recorded it, but also her memories, and these in a way that had not been necessary heretofore. On Sunday, 17 December 1933, Virginia Woolf wrote that, having completed the fourth "part" of "Here & Now," she was "freshening [her] memory of the war" for the fifth part by reading "old diaries."[5] Presumably, she began by perusing those of January–February 1915. And, presumably, effecting a Bergsonian memory chain, they moved Woolf, "again & again," to the verge of tears (*Diary* 4, 193).[6]

Like Irene Rathbone, Woolf obviously felt more comfortable fictionaliz-ing her experience of the war: "What urgency is there on [Vera Brittain] to stand bare in public?" she had wondered (*Diary* 4, 177). Part of her discom-fort over agreeing to write Roger Fry's biography (in October 1934) had to do with her "dread" of "plung[ing] into the past" without the veil of fiction (*Diary* 4, 254). One could argue that "standing bare" was not Woolf's style, but her unease suggests more than an aesthetic disagreement. Woolf was seeking to repress her memories of the war by not writing about them directly.

We see this possibility more dramatically encoded in the diary entry made on 17 December 1933 when Woolf does not dwell on the several memories recalled directly in the war diaries or the memories elicited by them. Instead, she abandons discourse on the war and writes in hyperbolic terms (but with-out any suggestion of ironic intent) of "being very happy," of "liv[ing] fully, freely, & adventurously" in the present day, a shift that seems more a denial

5. Woolf's "war diaries" consist of daily entries for January 1915, an entry for 1 Feb-ruary, an interrupted entry for 2 February, and until 3 August 1917, three entries are for 13, 14, and 15 February; this suggests that if entries were made elsewhere, they have been lost or are no longer extant. After 3 August, there are daily entries for the rest of the month and for September; entries for all but eight days in October; fourteen entries for No-vember; and twelve entries for December. In 1918 there are twenty entries for January; five for February; fourteen for March; twelve for April; six for May; five for June; twelve for July; nine for August; five for September; ten for October; eight for November; and five for December. "Fifth part" refers to volume 5 (dated 23 November 1933) of the eight-vol-ume Holograph at the Berg Collection (see note 4, above).

6. Bergson says "our memories form a chain" that links the past and the present and thus define our "character," which is in turn responsible for our actions and, indeed, our reactions (145–46).

of memories of the war than a sincere description of living in 1933. Only ten days earlier, for example, she had been greatly affected by the death of Stella Benson, which was announced on a newspaper placard; Woolf had felt "some sort of reproach to [herself] in [Benson's] death, as in K[atherine] M[ansfield']s. . . . A curious feeling: when a writer like S. B. dies, that one's response is diminished. Here & Now wont be lit up by her: its life lessened" (*Diary* 4, 192–93). Yet, in the entry of 17 December, as if to explain or to compensate for the emotional outpouring her own living might further elicit, Woolf obliquely records that she sees her present life as growing out of "that strange prelude," the war. Woolf shifts her attention back to the safer territory of the novel, stating abruptly, but with authority and control: "The question that now fronts me as a writer is the war chapter" (*Diary* 4, 193). Yet, as if to put off confronting the chain of memories reflection on the war chapter might elicit, she resolves to allow them "to simmer" rather longer; she was clearly hoping to effect the distance necessary to aesthetic control and fictional transfiguration. She continues in the interim to read her war diaries, particularly the one she began for 1917, the year in which civilian endurance was most severely tested.

Unlike Rathbone, who, according to Jane Marcus, applied an "aesthetic of anaesthesia" as an "anodyne" to memory in *We That Were Young*, based largely on her own war service, Woolf was herself seemingly affected the more in remembering than she had been in experiencing what Husserl calls the "primal impression."[7] We may surmise that Woolf had so well repressed the actual memory of specific events during the war that when she was reminded of them, they affected her with such force that they may very well have led to her headaches. The inferred causality becomes more likely when we consider that "the Raid scene" is the only extended section of her writings involving the war drawn directly from her own experience, as reproduced in her own diaries, and from latent and perhaps repressed memories of the war.

Although she seemed to be making good progress in the writing of "1917," which was begun on 16 January 1934, by 30 January she was getting

---

7. In other words, although Husserl maintains that the actual experience (which leads to the "primal impression") undergoes modification and is usually more intense than the "primary remembrance" that follows it, it is entirely possible for a "secondary memory," not based on a consciousness of the impression, to emerge later. See Husserl, 50–57. Marcus, in "Afterword: The Nurse's Text: Acting Out an Anaesthetic Aesthetic," about Irene Rathbone's *We That Were Young*, says that the novel "operates under an *aesthetic of anaesthesia*, choosing to numb consciousness rather than to prick the conscience," 476, 477.

headaches over what she then saw as the never-ending "Raid Scene"; on 18 February she said she had had to stop the writing for three weeks and by 4 March she was on to another section (*Diary* 4, 200–5). The section, "1917," in which the raid scene figures prominently, is widely acknowledged to have caused Woolf the most anguish and to have undergone the most extensive revision, leading each time she worked on it to what she called as late as 21 March 1935 "the usual headache" (*Diary* 4, 289).[8] Although Woolf had declared that there would be "no preaching" in the novel (*Diary* 4, 152], she did not employ an aesthetic of anaesthesia that numbs feelings; in effect, if not by design, she was involved in creating an aesthetic of remembering that transfigured her own memories into the stuff of fiction, whatever feelings they aroused. While Woolf's headaches doubtlessly had multiple causes, it becomes increasingly apparent that they had more than a little to do with "that strange prelude," the Great War. She was coming to terms with how the war was perceived and experienced at the time, how it was remembered, and, as news of disturbances abroad continued to be reported in the newspapers, whether such memories mattered in the present day.

Woolf had involved latent memory of the war in *Mrs. Dalloway*, as, for example, when Clarissa, following a memory chain beginning with a June day, becomes conscious that "it [the war] was over; thank heaven—over" (*MrsD*, 5)—this some four years after the war officially ended. In the "Present Day" of *The Years* Woolf forges a chain of memory involving the Great War that again seems only as strong as its weakest links. From "1917" as the war is in progress, through the "Present Day" of the postwar world, the novel is overlaid with reminders of the war that are ignored, avoided, or denied by civilian characters. Unlike *Mrs. Dalloway* where the explicit dating

8. For example, in "'I Am Not a Hero'" Radin says that the "strain" caused in writing the novel "became unbearable" and refers to "five years of painful revision." She suggests that this anguish came as "Virginia Woolf, whose temperament and aesthetic sensibilities had always led her to express herself in a prose that was suggestive and impressionistic, was attempting to write an explicitly political, ideological novel" (195). Clearly, we all owe Grace Radin a debt of gratitude for the important work she has done on *The Years,* and on the base of her early work this is and, I am sure, later studies of *The Years* will be built. As Radin acknowledges in the introduction to *Virginia Woolf's "The Years": The Evolution of a Novel,* her work is not the final word on construction of the novel, but follows "certain trends, such as deletion of sexual and ideological material and the changes in the depiction of one character" (xxiv). Radin does not seriously consider the war, however. Besides references made in the text, we may see the relation of the war to the headaches in her diary entry of 30 January 1934: "Today, writing Here & Now, longing to end the Raid Scene, which draws out—hence my headache" (*Diary* 4, 200–1).

of the novel is a clue to the importance of the war in history, if not to the civilian characters, in *The Years* Woolf, with brilliant narrative ingenuity, suggests the importance of the war in memory, partly through the ambiguous dating of the last, longest, and most discussed section, "Present Day," and the explicit dating of the shortest chapter, which precedes it, "1918."

Woolf thus implies that the place of the war in dated history is insignificant when compared with experience of the war and how it is remembered. This is made more obvious through the seemingly disinterested, omniscient narrator, who combines the offices of a historian such as Gibbon and a biographer like Strachey: the one whose "quality of permanence [was that] it still excites abuse"[9] and the other who abused those who had seemingly achieved a quality of permanence. Woolf must have smiled when she wrote in 1937 of Gibbon's belief that the past is connected to the present by an "'indissoluble chain'" ("Historian," 118); in *The Years*, which has been called a historical novel,[10] Woolf shows the past connected to the present by a chain of memories, which will in turn form a link to the future. Where the anxiety and pain caused by the war is forgotten, the chain is broken and the security it might have afforded is lost. It may be that the novel does not "run ahead of history," as Joanna Lipking suggests (142), so much as seek to be a counterweight to "historians' histories," such as Woolf spoke of in "The War from the Street." *The Years*, then, becomes Woolf's own history of the war, written from a civilian vantage and out of her own civilian memories, a history that extends into a future that could very well repeat the threat of the past with even more frightening consequences.

Reviewing her war diaries, Woolf was reminded that during the war life had been at risk on the streets and in the villages as well as at the front. Yet, until 1917, the risks to civilian life were minimized. In a diary entry she made on 5 January 1915, five months after the start of the war, Woolf noted that in an editorial involving deaths and injuries caused by a train crash, the *Times* minimized their importance: "[I]t says that the war has taught us a proper sense

9. Virginia Woolf, "The Historian and the Gibbon," 115.

10. For example, James Naremore, "Nature and History in *The Years*," 244. Joanne Lipking calls the novel a "family chronicle" but says it "seems less historical than ideological" (141, 142), and Avrom Fleishman does not include it in his study of the historical novel *The English Historical Novel: Walter Scott to Virginia Woolf* (244), but he does say elsewhere that the "narrative point of view" in *The Years* is "in keeping with a historical perspective" (*Virginia Woolf,* 174).

of proportion in respect to human life."[11] The editorial in question, "The Loss of the Formidable," justifies the minimizing of civilian death over the death of those "who have laid down their lives for their country" (9). Just what "proper sense of proportion" was effected by the war is not explicitly stated in the *Times,* but the implication is obvious. In gauging deaths, some are more worthy than others: "In normal times [the Ilford crash in which eleven were killed and thirty-one injured] would have produced intense excitement, but just now it arouses little interest."

In Woolf's diary entry, however, the comments of the *Times* are preceded by a reference to three other and, apparently, accidental deaths, followed by Woolf's question, "Does the weather prompt suicide?" (*Diary* 1, 7). This seemingly random question, presumably an ironic non sequitur, sandwiched between the reports of death, on the one hand anticipates the importance of the weather in "news from the front," a staple of "eyewitness accounts"; an apparent rise in the number of home front suicides *reported* in the newspaper during the war; and Woolf's manner of beginning each section in *The Years.*[12] It would also seem to suggest that Virginia Woolf, a fortnight before the first zeppelin raid on 19 January 1915, was not convinced of a connection between civilian death and the war.

Having survived zeppelin attacks in 1915 and seen Leonard escape military service in 1916, Woolf had assumed that they would continue relatively unscathed. Until 1917, restrictions imposed by the Defence of the Realm Act (DORA) seemed not to affect them directly and, shuttling between London

11. The date of the *Times* leader in question is mistakenly identified as appearing on 5 January 1915 in *Diary* 1, 7n. In fact, the leader appears on page 9 on 2 January 1915, the day after the train accident in Ilford. If the published diary entry for 5 January is correctly dated, it could well be that Woolf was reading the Saturday paper (2 January) on Tuesday (5 January).

12. The article Woolf refers to is headed "Ilford Collision Inquiry. How the Signals Were Set. Great Speed of the Express." It appears at the top of column 1, page five, of the *Times* on Tuesday, 5 January 1915. I have discovered no official statistics on suicide. My research suggests that reports of suicides, particularly of residents and citizens of German ancestry, and "accidental deaths" increased during the war. On 19 January 1915, for example, one such incident was reported under the heading "Rumour and Suicide/A Sad Story of Village Life" (5). Fedden's findings suggest that war causes an immediate decline in the number of civilian suicides (339), but, as Peter Sainsbury observes, studies by psychologists and sociologists disagree as to why (11–29). Knightly also observes that "eyewitness" weather reports from the front were printed in lieu of reports of "what was really happening" (89–94); this seems an especially sound inference during the first two years and before the United States entered the war in April 1917.

and Sussex with little impediment, the Woolfs assumed themselves immune—or, at least, very lucky. The zeppelin raids against England, the first
of which occurred the night of 19 January 1915 (the first against London May
31–June 1) affected them less than repeated "false alarms." The Woolfs seemed
to enjoy access to rumors at the highest level—or, at least, having second-
hand access to the Admiralty and Whitehall. Yet, their main source of news
was reports in the newspapers, which, regulated by DORA, were confined
to ambiguous accounts of battles, with impersonal lists of combat deaths
and casualties sometimes offered days afterward.

Reports of zeppelin attacks at home were also censored, and their precise
targets were at first left unspecified.[13] Until 1917 Woolf found herself vaguely
amused both by the ironic bravado of the upper classes chasing their first
zeppelin in London and the "panic" that sent her servants running and hid-
ing in Sussex during a daylight raid (*Letters* 2, 64, 112). Moreover, although
there were fifty-one zeppelin attacks (the last of which was in 1918), by late
1916, according to Lee Kennett, zeppelin raids had "virtually ended" (23). In
part because of this respite; in part because of Woolf's daily reading of newspapers, which, complying with the first amendment to DORA, did little to
cause any "disaffection or alarm"; and, in part because rumors were becoming more and more suspect, Woolf was clearly not prepared for the more immediate and frightening risk facing civilians: what the military would, years
later, euphemistically label "strategic bombing."[14]

When on 25 May 1917 a German Gotha bombed Folkestone, in the south
of England, some fifty-five miles east of Lewes, the Woolfs in London seem
not to have noticed. Yet, this was just the beginning; German aeroplanes
raided England twenty-seven times between 25 May 1917 and 20 May 1918,

13. The passing of DORA was announced in the newspapers four days after the start
of the war. By my count, from 28 August 1914 to 31 March 1920 it was amended or extended ten times. In the first amendment to DORA (28 August 1914) it was forbidden
to "spread . . . reports likely to cause disaffection or alarm" (*Law Reports*, vol. 52, 378).
Fredette says that the press was "not permitted to mention the places hit or details of the
damage" to "inconvenience German intelligence." However, ambiguous reports of attacks
on "a coastal town to the south-east" jammed up telephone and telegraph lines at home,
as people sought news of casualties. Fredette says that after "one or two such raids, the
places bombed were reported without delay" (27–28). However, casualties were not immediately reported.

14. "Defence of the Realm Act, 1914 (No. 2)," *Law Reports*, vol. 52, 378; Lee Kennett uses
the following definition of strategic bombing, offered by Sir Charles Webster and Noble
Frankland in 1962: "The strategic air offensive is a means of direct attack on the enemy state
with the object of depriving it of the means or the will to continue the war" (ix).

including seventeen raids on London alone (Fredette, 263–66).[15] After the Woolfs' printing press was delivered at the end of April 1917, as Leonard remembers in his autobiography, "[t]he routine of our life became pretty regular" (*BgA*, 231). His sense of the "routine"—or, perhaps, his memory—differed from that of his wife. More than one entry in her war diaries resembles her letter of 6 October 1917, her account of having "sat in the cellar and listened to [aeroplanes pass overhead]." By then aeroplanes passing overhead had become so routine that she writes rather casually of having compared her account of sixteen German aeroplanes to the thirty-five "over Gordon Square" that Carrington had "just rung up" to report (*Letters* 2, 185). There was no doubt as to their origin; civilians could easily identify the distinctive sound of German Gothas.[16]

No bombs had been dropped, but both Woolf and Carrington might have been thinking of the massive bombing attacks of 1–2 October. However, the specific details of the attacks, that 3,705 kilograms (8,151 pounds) of bombs had been dropped on London, Kent, and Essex, leaving eleven killed and forty-one injured and countless others homeless had not been reported. On 2 October the *Times* reported "Last Night's Air Raid/London Again Attacked/Enemy in Four Groups/51 Casualties on Sunday" (7); on 3 October the *Times* reported forty-eight casualties; there were no civilian deaths reported (7). The planes seen by Carrington and Woolf were undoubtedly doing reconnaissance for the German raid on London, Ramsgate, and Dover on the night of 31 October–1 November 1917, when twenty-two Gothas dropped 5,815 kilograms (12,793 pounds) of bombs, killing ten civilians and injuring twenty-two.

Nearly twenty years later, in March 1936, at the same time as Virginia Woolf was "re-reading" *The Years* before sending manuscript to be printed in galleys, she recorded finding it "odd, how near the guns have got to our private life *again*. I can quite distinctly see them & hear a roar, even though

15. There were twelve bombings by airships and nineteen aeroplane attacks on London in all (Joseph Morris, v, 265–72). Besides raids, which are usually recorded in diary entries of some length, Woolf also refers to the absence of raids, as on 28 October and 7 December 1917 (*Diary* 1, 68, 85–89) and sightings of aeroplanes and zeppelins (airships), as on 11 September 1917 (*Diary* 1, 49).

16. According to Fredette, "For lack of a better name at first, many people referred to the strange machines as 'wong-wongs', a label which approximated their sonorous, double hum. However expressive, the term more accurately reflected British naïveté of the dangers of attack by the aeroplane. But before the summer was over, the word 'Gotha' was a familiar one in every British home within striking range of the new German bombers" (21).

I go on, like a doomed mouse, nibbling at my daily page" (emphasis added; *Diary* 5, 17). Echoes from the Great War were becoming deafening, the more so as they merged with portents of World War II. To Virginia Woolf, the more she lived in the present day, the less she could forget the Great War, while for Leonard "[o]nly a few incidents emerge from the fog [of the last year of the war] into my memory" (*BgA*, 255). Recalling the war in general and 1917 in particular, Leonard, modifying a comment made by the male presence in "A Mark on the Wall" (with "Three Jews," the first publication of the Hogarth Press 1917), recalls that "nothing seemed to happen" (197). The press would be destroyed in a strategic bombing raid on London during those months between September 1939 and May 1940 known as "the phony war" (Wheal, 370).

Unlike the routine of civilian life during World War II, where, as Leonard recalled it, "things moved and happened," during World War I one did not feel "the danger of death continually hanging over one's head." Nevertheless (and without significant elaboration), Leonard remembered the years 1914 to 1918 as "the most horrible period of my life" (*BgA*, 197).[17] That many civilians may indeed have been spared the constant terror of the blitz in the Great War is certain. But until the Great War civilians did not expect to be involved at all and the psychological impact of the bombing of civilian sites was certainly profound. As R. P. Hearne saw the situation in 1916, when most of the fifty-one zeppelin attacks on Great Britain, killing 557 people, occurred: "It is particularly humiliating to allow an enemy to come over your capital city and hurl bombs upon it. His aim may be very bad, the casualties may be few, but the moral effect is wholly undesirable. When the zeppelins came to London [as they did twelve times], they could have scored a falling technical triumph over us if they had showered us with confetti."[18]

When Freud wrote his "Reflections upon War and Death" in 1915, the ongoing effects of the strategic bombing of sites in Germany and England had not been felt.[19] In September 1932, when he published his letter in response

17. In Freud's *The Psychopathology of Everyday Life*, which Leonard read in 1918 [*Diary* 1, 110n], the distinction is made between "simple forgetting" and "forgetting motivated by repression" [17].

18. The statistical information is published: in H. A. Jones, *The War in the Air*, vol. 5, Appendix 1 (1831) and cited in Hilton P. Goss, *Civilian Morale under Aerial Bombardment, 1914–1939*, 11–12; and in Joseph Morris, *The German Air Raids on Great Britain, 1914–1918*, iii and 265–68. R. P. Hearne, *Zeppelins and Super-Zeppelins* 2, is quoted in Kennett, 24.

19. Peter Gay believes that "Freud's papers on war and death [of which "Reflections" is the first] show him coming to terms with these harrowing events" (*Freud*, 355).

to Albert Einstein's question "Why War?" Freud answers the question of how we might prevent the next war (as Woolf would do in *Three Guineas* in 1938) by first referring to the "starving and homeless victims of World War I" (135), in which category he may well have included himself and his family (Gay, 381–82). Yet, in writing about experience of the war in 1920, Freud singled out anxiety as a possible response to uncertainty, sharing with fear the element of passivity. Anxiety, like fear, involves anticipation, but it differs from fear in lacking a definite object; we might understand it as expectation, or dread. It is the passivity and indefiniteness implicit in the experience that increases anxiety, which may, in turn, lead to trauma or repression or both.[20]

During air raids the Woolfs seemed to escape trauma, an incapacitating feeling of helplessness, even as they waited for the bugles to sound, announcing the all clear.[21] But it would seem that for Virginia Woolf, the possibility of death, now part of what Husserl terms a "secondary remembrance" (57) could not be safely restored to the unconscious, even after being used in writing *The Years.* According to George Panichas, editor of *Promise of Greatness,* "of all the experiences of war, what remains unwavering in the survivors' recollections is the omnipresence of death" (xxiv). Panichas speaks mainly of the experience of the war on the front. But notwithstanding the absence of civilian deaths from newspaper accounts, the routine of civilian life from the first included news of death on the front, and the telephone could offer more immediate and more personal notification. For Woolf, the ringing of a telephone came to represent something ominous, sometimes signaling news of the death of a friend or relative, as it had in the death of Rupert Brooke and as it would in the death of Cecil Woolf in early December 1917.[22]

20. See Freud, *BPP,* 11, 24, and *Inhibitions, Symptoms, and Anxiety,* 11. See also Ernest Jones, 463–64, on Freud's sense of the possibility of repression set in motion by anxiety rather than anxiety by repression.

21. Fredette says that after trying whistles and car horns to signal "All Clear" in London, officials tried the "Paris system of bugle calls" using several hundred Boy Scouts who had volunteered for service. "Blowing cheerfully, they undoubtedly roused anyone who managed to sleep up to this point" (164–65). Virginia Woolf included a rendition of Kitty Maxse's comments on raids in her diary entry for 7 December 1917: "[W]hen the raids come we go & sit . . . on the ground floor. But they ought to tell one about the Bugles. Why, when they first blew, I thought it might be the Germans themselves" (*Diary* 1, 88–89).

22. See Spotts, 411, and Levenback, "Virginia Woolf and Rupert Brooke," 6.

To Montaigne, whom Woolf was again reading as she wrote *The Years,* the anxiety of not knowing may be worse than grief over the death of a loved one.[23] During the war, anxiety both on the front and at home accompanied not the fact of death, but its possibility or its likelihood. In the days preceding the September 30–October 1 air raid, Woolf noted that Roger Fry was "[a]nxious about raids," adding that despite listening, neither Woolf had seen or heard anything (*Diary* 1, 54). By the end of January 1918, as possibility seemed to become certainty, during the height of the Gotha raids, Woolf was not sure what she was feeling: "Home I went, & there was a raid of course. The night made it inevitable. From 8 to 1.15 we roamed about, between coal hole kitchen bedroom & drawing room. I don't know how much is fear, how much is boredom; but the result is uncomfortable" (*Diary* 1, 116). Freud believed that what is first manifest as a "signal" of "unpleasure" may later become manifest as "anxiety" (*Inhibitions,* xxxiii, 10ff).

In choosing 1917 Woolf implicitly brought to mind her memories of the very real threat that existed not only on the street and in the drawing room but also under the Military Service Acts. The question of personal safety, avoided for so long, seemed more and more to demand acknowledgment. Two months after the first Military Service Act of January 1916, which introduced conscription for single men aged eighteen to forty-one, the second one widened the net and for the first time in British history mandated general conscription. Eventually, as Alfred Havighurst says, "some six million out of ten million within the prescribed age limits, went into uniform" (133).[24] The possibility of air raids are routinely acknowledged in Woolf's journal, particularly after the six raids on England from 24 September to 1–2 October 1917. On 9 October Leonard was called up before the tribunal a second time, despite what Woolf had called in June his "complete exempt[ion]," owing to his tremor (*Letters* 2, 102).

23. Woolf refers to Montaigne in her diary entry of 2 September 1933 (*Diary* 4, 176). In describing anxiety bred of uncertainty, Montaigne quotes Seneca ("A soul anxious about the future is most vulnerable" [8]) and in describing anxiety bred of anticipating the future, he quotes Cicero ("[T]here is no use in knowing what is to be; for it is wretched to be tormented to no purpose" [27]). That Montaigne and Freud should agree on anxiety and its source is not surprising. Peter Burke, for example, asserts, "It is not difficult to see why Sigmund Freud should have read Montaigne with attention. They agreed about dreams and about the importance of the earliest years. . . . Like Freud, Montaigne saw himself as a lone explorer of the self" (39).

24. Havighurst estimates that there were sixteen thousand conscientious objectors and "thirteen hundred went to prison." Some of their individual accounts, he notes, are published in Julian Bell's *We Did Not Fight* (133).

Her diary entry for 9 October suggests a divided response: "We had a horrid shock. L. came in so unreasonably cheerful that I guessed a disaster. He has been called up. Though rather dashed for 20 minutes, my spirits mounted to a certainty that, save the nuisance, we have nothing to fear" (*Diary* 1, 56). The language does itself suggest what Woolf was feeling behind the ostensible bravado, and the anxiety caused by acknowledging the very real threat to safety the recall suggested. That Woolf references the "horrid shock" and "disaster" while subsequently referring to the entire affair as a "nuisance" offering "nothing to fear" certainly suggests repression, especially in the light of the fact that conscription had been extended to include married men back in May 1916 and that the heavy losses on the front led to what Leonard called "the great comb out of 1917." Leonard does not recall it as a "nuisance," and he was neither sanguine nor certain of the outcome. He recalls finding it almost incredible that he received exemption for a second time: "I . . . thought that I should inevitably be sent to scrub floors and tables, at the very least, [but] I was again given the same complete exemption" (*BgA*, 179).[25] Leonard must have understood just how fortunate he was in his examining officer; according to J. W. Winter, the army found that the number of medical deferments depended on the judgment of the examining doctor and in 1916–17 doctors were instructed to reject fewer men.[26]

Neither the threat of conscription nor bombing raids was ever truly routine, though they might have seemed so retrospectively. Among the seeming routines Woolf explores in *The Years*, the air raid, clearly, is the one she must

25. George Spater and Ian Parsons, in *A Marriage of True Minds*, refer to the first time Leonard was called up, but ignore the second: 84, 90. Leon Edel, in *Bloomsbury*, pays scant attention to Leonard's potential induction, though he comments (parenthetically) that Leonard's "nerves of steel and capacity for endurance would have made him a good soldier" (223). In the one letter (from "[Early May 1916]") involving conscription that is included by Frederic Spotts in *Letters of Leonard Woolf*, Leonard says, "I am in great trouble about conscription. I shall of course apply for exemption on grounds of health (shaking hands) & domestic hardship. Craig ought to give me a pretty strong letter about V—but I am not hopeful of the results. I feel I am a conscientious objector—for I loathe the thought of taking any part in this war—& yet I feel very much the difficulty, from the point of view of reason, of the position. I go to see Craig on Wednesday to hear what he says about V." In a note, Spotts explains, "Craig thought that VW would probably have a breakdown. Both he and Maurice Wright wrote letters declaring LW unfit to serve on the grounds both of VW's medical condition and of his trembling hands. LW was formally exempted on June 30 and again the following year" (214–15 and note).

26. *Great War and the British People*, 52. See also Adrian Stephen, "The Tribunals," in Julian Bell's *We Did Not Fight*, 377–92.

have thought most representative of the civilian experience, both because it was the one immediately life-threatening phenomenon that confronted civilians during the war years proper and because it is the one that demonstrates most dramatically the pattern of denial in their lives. In the novel the disinterested tone of the narrative reports suggests that whatever activity goes on outside the cellar (where the dinner party is finally held) is of as little consequence as it was at Abercorn Terrace in the years before the war. The weather reports, which begin each section of the novel, involve, until "1917," a few hours of one day in a seemingly randomly chosen season of a randomly chosen year, as if one year is pretty much like the last and one day is like another. In January 1933, the year before she began to write "1917," Woolf "visualise[d] this book . . . as a curiously uneven time sequence—a series of great balloons, linked by straight narrow passages of narrative" (*Diary* 4, 142).

The balloons, or significant events, are, ironically, until the war, associated with deaths and the passages that connect them are straight and narrow, beginning in the first chapter, "1880," with the death of Colonel Pargiter's wife, the mother of his children Eleanor, Edward, Martin, Morris, Milly, Delia, and Rose. In the prewar years the deaths occur at irregular intervals: Parnell, the Irish patriot, and Delia's hero (1891); King Edward (1910); Colonel Pargiter (1912); and, in 1914, the death of an age: "The nineteenth century going to bed" (*Years,* 266). In the hours Woolf chooses to represent 1917, there are no deaths, not even a mention of death, even though Morris's son, Eleanor's nephew North, leaves for the front and there is an air raid in London as Eleanor joins her first cousin Maggie and her husband, Renny (René, his given name, is sometimes used in the holograph); Maggie's sister Sara (Elvira in the holograph); and Sara's friend Nicholas for a dinner party.

The section "1917" not only demonstrates that there was more than one routine of war but also that civilian victims of the war were not only those killed or wounded in the raids. The section suggests Woolf's concern for the long-term effects of the war, not only to adults but to children. By 19 December 1932, when Woolf had completed a draft of what would eventually become "1880" in *The Years,* she was aware of the increasingly threatening situation in Germany. In her account of a party the Woolfs attended on 1 June 1932, for example, after referring to the talk "about the German youth movement: about bad people," she breaks off, as if to deny what she heard, and ends the entry with an abrupt "oh damn, oh damn—not an idea in my head or a wish to be brilliant," as if to suggest the futility of effort against "bad people" (*Diary* 4, 106). As she continued with "the second chapter" of what was then the essay-novel, Hitler was on his way to becoming German Chancellor, and the Woolfs learned of the danger signals from reading newspapers. Virginia Woolf, in particular, was clearly the more affected by reports she heard from friends and acquaintances, reports in newspapers being suspect since the Great War. On 28 April 1933, at a dinner party, the Woolfs had learned firsthand of the increasingly threatening conditions in Germany through Bruno Walter.

> "You must not think of the Jews" he kept on saying. "You must think of this awful reign of intolerance. You must think of the whole state of the world. It is terrible—terrible." Then he told us how you can't talk above a whisper. There are spies everywhere. . . . All the time soldiers were marching. They never stop marching. And on the wireless, between the turns, they play military music. . . . We must make them feel themselves outcasts—not by fighting them; by ignoring them. (*Diary* 4, 153)

Although this is not the only diary entry from the thirties to be echoed in the novel or one of its versions, it does suggest the extent to which the portents of the second war called to Woolf's mind her experience (or blurred with her memory) of the first. In one of what Leonard Woolf called the "two enormous chunks" (*Downhill*, 156) deleted from the novel, Crosby's young charges "gap[e] . . . at the soldiers . . . [who] were marching down Richmond High Street [as a] drum beat a regular tick, tick, tick." Then she reflects on their unnatural obedience and regularity: "The children . . . could be trusted to walk alone"; unlike her prewar charges, Rose and Martin Pargiter, "Alf and Gladys were sober, straight-haired children, with no spirit in them."[27] Such, it is suggested, is something that happens when the country is infected with war. Children aspiring to become clones of soldiers may well become what Susan Squier calls adult civilians: "vital machines and deathly human automata" (155).

Woolf must have been thinking of the effect of the war on her nephews Julian (born in 1908) and Quentin Bell (born in 1910) as she was reviewing her war diaries in preparation for "1917." Julian was undoubtedly on her mind as well when she considered the relation between education and war, particularly the Great War, in *The Years* and in her "war book," *Three Guineas* (1938). As much as she lamented Vanessa's absence from London, Woolf

27. This is from the final proof sheets of *The Years* reproduced as part of Grace Radin's "'Two Enormous Chunks'" 228. The proof sheets are also included in her *Virginia Woolf's "The Years,"* 160.

clearly thought it fortunate that her sister and particularly her nephews, based at Charleston in Sussex, were spared not only reminders of the war in London, which included bombardment from German aircraft, but also the bombardment of the war mentality in public schools.[28] During the war years, rather than send Julian and Quentin to public schools, Vanessa had hired a governess and undertook herself some of the educational regimen (Spalding 162). Nevertheless, as Woolf wrote "1917," Vanessa must have recalled that despite a "war-time boyhood" spent mostly in the country, the educational "advantages" Julian had enjoyed were an ironic counterpoint to what he referred to as his "passion for war and war games."[29] That the war bug got to Julian, despite what Peter Stansky sees as the Bloomsbury influence and eventually led to his participation in the Spanish Civil War, must have made obvious to Woolf the effect of the public-school experience on more malleable minds with either a predisposition to war or an ignorance of it.

Despite the preoccupation with "the next war" in *Three Guineas,* Woolf hearkens back to the lived history of the Great War to frame her concerns with an educational system that "does not teach people to hate force, but to use it" (*3G,* 29). It is clear in *Three Guineas* that the first responsibility for the deaths of such public-school boys as the poet Wilfred Owen fell to the patriarchal educational system that gained popularity in the late nineteenth century, as Lytton Strachey made clear in *Eminent Victorians* (1918), which Woolf read in draft throughout the war. As Woolf takes the position in her war book that such an education invites the repetition of the Great War experience, it is not to be wondered that in *The Years* Woolf places North Pargiter, in whom we may find traces of Julian Bell, in a position of entering his country's service only during the final call-up. At one point in her writing, Woolf considered the possibility of having North visit Sara during

---

28. It seems that the war mentality played some part in Vanessa's decision to take her sons to live at Charleston in Sussex from 1916 to 1918 (see Spalding, 155). Affecting her decision also was a change in the farming venue of conscientious objectors Duncan Grant and David Garnett.

29. Julian Bell enclosed the poem "Autobiography" in a letter to his mother in 1935; it was subsequently published in his posthumous *Essays, Poems & Letters,* edited by his brother Quentin and published by the Hogarth Press in 1938; it is reprinted in Stansky, *Journey to the Frontier* (126–28). In the autobiographical essay that introduces *Essays,* Julian Bell makes the cited comment about his passion for war and war games (13). In *Journey* Stansky says that Julian Bell was sent to Leighton Park School in Reading in January 1922 because of its Quaker conscientious objection to war; Stansky notes that "25 old Leightonians lost their lives in World War I" (30–31).

home leave from the front, as was common during the war, rather than to say good-bye before shipping out. However, it seems that having him join up in 1917 better suited her ultimate vision of the novel and of North Pargiter.

North's Uncle Martin, in the nineteenth century, had apparently been "tracked" for the military (in an early holograph he is said to have attended the equivalent of Sandhurst), a military career having been the honorable route to follow not only for the aristocracy but also for the middle class.[30] That his nephew leaves for the war over three years *after* it began suggests that North's enthusiasm for "war and war games" was neither that of his forebears, nor that of Kitchener's "first hundred thousand," nor that of the nearly 2.5 million volunteers who enlisted in 1914 and 1915, including Rupert Brooke, Siegfried Sassoon, and thousands of other public-school boys. North did not "join up" in fact until 1917, a year when, according to Peter Parker in *The Old Lie: The Great War and the Public School Ethos,* "if there was rebellion in the air, there was also complacency" (25). The year 1917 was significant in a number of ways. It was the year after the battle of the Somme and the year of the Battles of Ypres and Passchendale, leaving massive death on the front; the year Alec Waugh finally saw the publication of his *The Loom of Youth,* an autobiographical novel that is antagonistically critical of public-school (and particularly Sandhurst's) "social training" that led to the high rate of volunteerism and death among educated youth; and the year Siegfried Sassoon was brought before the Medical Board and went to a hospital to be cured of the disease of opposition to the war; it was the year Cecil Woolf was killed in the trenches and Philip Woolf returned, wounded and broken; in 1917, Leonard Woolf was called up for a second time, and, perhaps significantly, by 1917, when North goes to the war, the United States had joined in and allied victory became more likely.

30. See Mitchell Leaska's edition of *The Pargiters* by Virginia Woolf: "Bobby was sent off to Mr Hurst's at Folkestone to be prepared for the Army" (56). Peter Parker, in *The Old Lie: The Great War and the Public School Ethos,* identifies Sandhurst as a leading public school "with a military bias" (56). Thomas Seccombe, in the preface to Alec Waugh's *The Loom of Youth* (1917), identifies the Royal Military College as Sandhurst (9). David Cannandine, *The Decline and Fall of the British Aristocracy,* writes that "as the last quarter of the nineteenth century opened, it was still generally agreed that war is the occupation of the nobility and gentry" (264), in part because to enter the military one needed a private income (270). This may partly explain why Woolf, the writer with a need for a room of her own and five hundred pounds a year, felt she shared common ground with both soldiers and officers. Cannandine notes that the percentage of middle-class officers rose steadily, from 50 percent in 1875 to 65 percent in 1913 to 73 percent in 1926 (273).

North, it would seem, was not originally intended to be a flat representation of Woolf's view of education as set forth in *Three Guineas,* but a rounded character whose experience of the war, however short (compared to Philip Woolf), had left him (like Philip) broken and not eager to face what Leed calls "reintegration" into postwar London. In the version Woolf was writing in 1934, Elvira pointedly tells the guests at the dinner party news of having just been visited by "Eleanor's nephew," an identification that, Grace Radin believes, suggests that Eleanor and North share the same attitude to the war (*Virginia Woolf's,* 68). North was on his way to the front, having become a lieutenant in what Elvira tauntingly calls "His Majesty's Royal Regiment of Rat-catchers," a reference that perhaps came to Woolf's mind after she had seen the Royal Sussex Regiment parade in Lewes. "Not an inspiring sight," Woolf observed in her diary on 27 August 1933 (*Diary* 4, 175). She also could have been thinking of Siegfried Sassoon, who had also left, albeit in 1915, a lieutenant in the Royal Welch Fusiliers. Apparently, being "a cricketing boy" (as Eleanor recalls him) was by 1917 qualification enough to become an officer.[31] When North is confronted by his cousin Sara, with whom he presumably shares a close relationship (much closer than with Eleanor, who is more than twenty-five years his senior), his stated reasons for joining are more abstract than those of Septimus Warren Smith, and may be seen to reflect his public-school training, as much as his military forebears (in which group is included his grandfather, Col. Abel Pargiter, who lost two fingers in the Indian Mutiny of 1857).

In the version Woolf was writing from 1933–34, when Elvira sneeringly asks, "Do you think this is the act of a brave man? What did you do it for?" North (or George or John, in earlier versions) "stand[s] to attention," and answers "My King, my country." As bells begin to ring, Elvira explains, "I pelted him with dead rose leaves," clearly an ironically aggressive act and one that, howsoever intended, is deleted from the published novel (Holograph V, 78).[32] Elvira's antagonism to North in the holograph seems to be blurred, to involve more than opposition to the war; certainly, perhaps suggesting denial, such opposition to the war is not directly stated. Nicholas, her friend, believes her behavior hostile and her attitude unfair. His com-

31. Peter Parker offers anecdotal evidence of the discretionary selection of officers in the case of Peter Davies, who was accepted as an officer upon enlistment because the colonel in charge had (like Davies) himself played cricket at Eton: "So easy was it, in August 1914, to obtain the King's commission in the Special Reserve of the 60th Rifles" (39–40).

32. This part of Holograph V is dated "1 Jan 1934." See Woolf's diary entry for 22 May 1934, in which she refers to "Elvira & George, or John, talking in her room" (*Diary* 4, 221).

ments in the holograph express the view taken by Woolf herself in *Three Guineas* that it is unreasonable to expect anyone brought up in the military tradition and schooled at Eton to resist the constant appeals to patriotism and courage—although they are measured by a different standard and according to a different definition: "How can you expect a boy . . . who has been educated like that, who is in no way remarkable, who sees his friends go to the war who is rather bored by his profession . . . to take an attitude that requires a great deal of courage?" (Holograph V, 79). In the holograph, North responds to the arguments of *Three Guineas* that are expressed, humorlessly and without irony, by Elvira, who berates him for not having thought of them himself—and before he left to fight in the war [Holograph VI, 67–68]. In the holograph, North admits "'You were right. It was Hell,'" (Holograph VI, 72).

In *The Years*, while the division between the civilian and the combatant appears rigid, like so much of the war in progress, it is blurred, though less obviously than it is in the holograph. When Stephen Spender, who had something of the literary sensibility Woolf remembered of Rupert Brooke, observed the absence of combat action in the published novel, Woolf responded:

> I couldnt bring in the Front as you say partly because fighting isnt within my experience, as a woman; partly because I think action generally unreal. Its the thing we do in the dark that is more real; the thing we do because peoples eyes are on us seems to me histrionic. (*Letters* 6, 122)

Grace Radin suggests that the changes and deletions Woolf made to the holograph may have been owing to Leonard's concern about her being subject to "adverse criticism for belittling patriotism" while the country prepared for another war (*Virginia Woolf's*, 140). In writing the novel, Woolf found blurring pervasive and on 25 March 1933 thought it an "odd coincidence! that real life should provide precisely the situation I was writing about! I hardly know who I am, or where: Virginia or Elvira; in the Pargiters or outside" (*Diary* 4, 148).[33] To Woolf's mind, Elvira and Eleanor, rather than distinct and separate characters were also blurred; even their names suggest this blurring.[34]

33. Longenbach discusses rhetorical blurring during the Great War in the pervasive use of military metaphors: 98ff. The "odd coincident" may have been related to Woolf's refusal of an honorary degree at Manchester University.

34. On 17 August 1934, Woolf could "see the end of Here & Now (or Music, or Dawn, or whatever I shall call it). Its to end with Elvira going out of the house & saying What did I make this knot in my handkerchief for? & all the coppers rolling about—" (*Diary* 4,

What polarity and distinction existed before the war, Woolf suggests, became indistinct and fused during it, finally becoming more apparent than real in 1917. It may be understandable that Eleanor, the oldest (having been born before 1860), rather than the others, "sees" the blurring; Woolf explains in her letter to Spender that though she considered Maggie and Sara in the published novel among the walking wounded, "Eleanor . . . was meant to be all right; sound and rooted." At the dinner party, Eleanor notices that Elvira's childhood disability had all but disappeared: "She too had changed, Eleanor thought. As a child she had looked so queer; now she was scarcely crooked" (Holograph V, 75). Before the war, in "1914," it was all "clear-cut" and "there was no blur, no indecision" (*Years*, 254).

A month or so after the declaration of war, in September 1914, the blurring begins and Eleanor feels "guilty" because she had forgotten the war while watching a play.[35] In "1917," shortly after Eleanor begins drinking wine at the dinner party, "She was feeling already a little blurred; a little light-headed. It was the light after the dark; talk after silence; the war, perhaps, removing barriers" (*Years,* 284) and then "A little blur had come round the edges of things. It was the wine; it was the war" (287). René is a chemist but in the published novel he merely says "I help them to make shells" (286). In the holograph, he finds the blurring more disturbing and he calls himself "one of the hypocrites" (Holograph V, 79).

───────────

237). Eleanor does this in the published novel. The names Eleanor and Elvira themselves are confusing and tend to blur—something Woolf realized would be difficult for the reader, which may be why she chose to change Elvira to Sara. Woolf had confused (or blurred) Elvira and Eleanor on 23 January 1935, in referring, parenthetically, to "Sarah & Elvira," which suggests that they are two separate characters (*Diary* 4, 276). On 17 April 1935, Woolf writes of "E's soliloquy," and the editors believe she refers to Elvira; but the full reference seems to me ambiguous, and might also refer to Eleanor: "In E's soliloquy I think I have tapped a new method of argument—very short & compact: but then this is spun out with description" (*Diary* 4, 302).

35. Grace Radin misidentifies the placement of the "two enormous chunks" Woolf deleted in proof. Although this and an earlier section is identified by Radin as preceding the dinner party, my reading reveals that this section was intended to be placed at the end of "1914." Page 179 of the proofs refers to the "sultry September" sunshine," which is far removed from the cold night in December 1917 on which the dinner party takes place. On page 188, Eleanor reckons that ten years from yesterday would be 1924, which also points to a 1914 dating. And, it is clear that war has been declared, because of the soldiers on the streets as Crosby walks with her two young charges and later as Miriam Parrish is on the omnibus. It may also seem unlikely for the sixty-plus-year-old Eleanor to go to the theater, plan to walk home and take the omnibus because it was there, read the paper and her mail, and then go to the dinner party in Deans Walk. For a fuller explanation of the issues raised by Woolf's exclusions, see Levenback, "Placing the First 'Enormous Chunk.'"

In the holograph, even the line between wartime patriotism and what Nicholas sees as "self interest" is blurred. In the published novel, the issue is barely raised. By consulting the earliest version of "1917" we discover, through the recollections of Elvira and Eleanor, that Eleanor's youngest sister, forty-seven-year-old Rose Pargiter, prudently chose military service rather than go to prison for hitting the prime minister with a brick during a suffragist demonstration and that she is neither war resister nor (in the usual sense) volunteer. Though Eleanor says "I don't know anybody who is more patriotic," Nicholas disputes the existence of patriotism, believing it a euphemism for self-interest (Holograph V, 101, 104–5). Woolf chose to all but delete from the final version of the novel Rose's participation in the war as an ambulance driver in France, not unlike the women of the Field Ambulance Corps in Belgium observed by May Sinclair in *A Journal of Impressions from Belgium* (1915) or like R. J. Tennent, who was herself an ambulance driver for the Red Cross in France, or like Hugh Walpole who served in Russia with the Red Cross during the war, or, perhaps, like Julian Bell, who would die while driving an ambulance in Spain four months after *The Years* was published.[36]

The number of women in the Voluntary Aid Detachment grew from 47,196 at the start of the war to 82,857 in April 1920. Woolf might have thought of Rose as part of the Red Cross, like E. M. Forster, who had been a "searcher" (see appendix) in Alexandria, or like R. J. Tennent, who was a "F.A.N.Y." (a member of the First Aid Nursing Yeomanry of the British Red Cross) in France. To do service as a V.A.D. for the Red Cross in any capacity, as E. M. Forster learned, was no easy task, and the red tape was enormous, which may suggest that Rose had served with one of the other volunteer organizations or ambulance corps.[37] In any case, unlike Sinclair, who paints a realistic picture of her impressions, thus suggesting the courage and self-sacrifice of the ambulance drivers, Elvira imagines Rose as rather ridicu-

36. Holograph V, 101, 104. See May Sinclair's *A Journal of Impressions in Belgium* [1915] and Rebecca West's review of it, "Miss Sinclair's Genius." The review is reprinted in *The Young Rebecca,* ed. Jane Marcus, 304–7. See also the fascinating *Red Herrings of 1918* by R. J. Tennent; A. G. S. Enser's *A Subject Bibliography for the First World War* lists twenty-one studies by and about ambulance drivers, including Sinclair. *The Dark Forest* (1916) is based on Walpole's experience in the Russian Red Cross during the war. *The Years* was published 11 March 1937; Julian Bell died on 18 July 1937.

37. *Statistics of the Military Effort of the British Empire During the Great War,* 192–194. Between 1 August 1914 and 1 April 1920, the voluntary aid detachments grew from 70,243 to 122,766 (193). According to the statistical index of Laurence Binyon, in *For Dauntless France: An Account of Britain's Aid to the French Wounded and Victims of War* (1918), which is admittedly incomplete, there were eighty-five committees, benevolent societies, and

lous and, in lines deleted from the final novel, finds her driving more note-worthy than her service; she drives "to the amazement of the natives," Elvira says [Holograph V, 104]. It may also be related to Elvira's French brother-in-law René that Woolf deletes this gratuitous reference; the Indian "natives" confronted by the original "Pargiter of Pargiter's horse" in the Mutiny of 1857 are not the French "natives" who get out of the way "when they see Rose coming." Notwithstanding the ridicule of Sara and later that of Martin and even her niece Peggy, Rose had offered service formidable enough to have been presented a medal for her work during the war, which was only awarded to women "for devotion under fire."[38]

In "1917" we see evidence that the traditional roles of combatants and civilians have become fused, confused, or interdependent, albeit more emphatically in the version Woolf was writing in 1934. More important is that to Woolf's mind, it seems clear that this curious transference takes place not when combatants return home for a two-week leave, as so many of them did,[39] but when civilians are being threatened, like soldiers in the trenches, not only with shortages but with guns and bombs. Yet, it was commonly assumed that only the combatant understood the horror of war. Arthur Marwick says that "a chasm opened between the society of the trenches and society at home" (*Britain,* 40). Samuel Hynes, in citing "Some Reflections

hospitals in France, and no fewer than ten ambulance corps. The British Ambulance Committee, for example, included five convoys, each consisting of twenty motor ambulances, traveling workshop, two lorries, staff cars, etc.; one motorcycle section consisting of ten motorcycle sidecars with stretchers; there was a personnel of about three hundred always maintained in France (324). See *Red Herrings of 1918* by R. J. Tennent, M.M., whose epigraph is "F.A.N.Y.s—Not Fish Flesh nor Fowl but dam' good Red Herrings"—General Plumer, 2d Army. See also Lyn Macdonald, *The Roses of No Man's Land.*

38. This was probably a "M.M." (Military Medal), such as R. J. Tennent received. The M.M. is No. 29 among 33 medals given; No. 1, the Victoria Cross, is the most honorable. The M.M. was established in March 1916, and given to men in the army who "show themselves to the fore in action, and set an example of bravery and resource under fire, but without performing acts of such pre-eminent bravery as would render them eligible for the Conspicuous Gallantry Medal." According to Wyllie, "It may be awarded to women for devotion under fire." A total of 114,529 Military Medals were awarded in the Great War (118, 117). According to *Statistics of the Military Effort of the British Empire During the Great War* (1922), between August 1914 and May 1920 there were 15,399 "honours conferred for services in connection with the war" and 229,434 "honours conferred for services in the field" (554–55).

39. See Fussell, *The Great War,* 64–69.

of a Soldier," R. H. Tawney's 1916 essay, suggests that the soldier maintained illusions about war to survive the unprecedented ordeal of trench warfare, and that those at home became disillusioned.[40]

"We were thinking you were dead," René says to Elvira when she arrives late to the party in lines Woolf had written and crossed out in the early version of "1917" (Holograph V, 75). And, in the published version, Woolf includes only one specific memory of the combatant North, and that involves not a comrade's death, but that of a civilian, his mother, and the night of the dinner party, the night he left for the front:

> It was the night of the raid, he remembered. He remembered the dark night; the searchlights that slowly swept over the sky; here and there they stopped to ponder a fleecy patch; little pellets of shot fell; and people scudded along the empty blue-shrouded streets. He had been to Kensington to dine with his family; he had said good-bye to his mother; he had never seen her again. (*Years*, 314)

Woolf does not sketch a picture of the combatant under attack, as Rose Macaulay had done in *Non-combatants and Others* or like Siegfried Sassoon, whose third war memoir, *Sherton's Progress*, was released in 1936, or even like Vera Brittain in *Testament of Youth*. Instead, Woolf focuses on civilians who exhibit the stoic resolve and calmness that some authors of thinly disguised war fiction reserve for those under fire on the front line.

To all appearances, the Pargiters, true to their name, not only whitewash the danger to North, who is leaving for the front, but to themselves.[41] Even the challenge brought by the war to life itself has been minimized. If 1917 was, as Arthur Marwick suggests, the final stage of the war at home, which included increasingly rigorous "State control, and, for the people as a whole, the time when serious shortages began to be felt for the first time" (*Deluge*, 12), the Pargiters, excepting Sara, appear not to have noticed. Eleanor wears a shabby coat and has had to cut back on her wine, but she has not had to do without; neither has Maggie, as Renny's family is in the wine business. Maggie has to do without new clothes and dishes, but Sara has to live on her ration of sugar, a condition reduced in the published novel

40. In *A War Imagined*, (116–19), Hynes identifies R.H. Tawney as the author of "Some Reflections of a Soldier," which is published unsigned in the *Nation* 20 (Oct 21, 1916), 104–6.

41. See Mitchell Leaska's "Virginia Woolf, the Pargeter: A Reading of *The Years*," for a brilliant etymological analysis of "Pargiter/Pargeter."

to the question "How many lumps of sugar does a lieutenant in the Royal Rat-catchers require? . . . One. Two. Three. Four. . . ." (*Years,* 285). In recalling the visit from North, Sara is called "bitter," though in an early version Eleanor says that Rose always had "a curious bitterness" (Holograph V, 102). Rationing of sugar had begun in December 1917, having only been identified as a source of concern in October; but, although sacrifices had been asked of all, the less well-to-do had felt the pinch and routinely queued up at the grocery while the well-to-do seem not to have noticed.[42] It is not to be wondered that in "1917" an air raid is perceived as routine and the threat to personal safety is seen as inconsequential. Analogously, in "1918," as Crosby queues up to buy food, "the guns went on booming and the sirens wailed" and she would not have known that the war was over if someone had not told her so (*Years,* 305).

In the published novel, perhaps because Woolf believed as she said in 1935 that "this fiction is dangerously near propaganda" (*Diary* 4, 300), she used the offices of her seemingly apersonal historian/biographer/narrator to represent her retrospective sense of the irony implicit in the civilian attitude toward the war. The narrative voice serves as a curious balance to the civilian attitude that minimizes danger at home and leaves unconsidered danger at the front. In the holograph, Eleanor walks to the dinner party in the Deans Yard section of London on "a bitter cold night in the middle of December" (Holograph V, 69);[43] in the published novel the date is never mentioned and we are told only that it is "[a] very cold winter's night" (*Years,* 279), which, with the deletion of "bitter," suggests that there is little to distinguish this night from any other. The street is described only as "dark" (279). In the holograph, Eleanor's uncertainty about the location of Maggie and René's house is complicated by the "shrouded lights. . . . The street lamps hooded with blue shed only a muffled twilight illumination. . . . Great fans of light,

42. Shortages of sugar had begun to be reported in the *Times of London* from January 1916, usually in small "items." In 1917 a major shortage of sugar was reported in the *Times* of 17 May (7e) and 18 May (6c). A ration scheme for sugar using cards is reported in the *Times* on 2 October 1917 (3a), and an article "Sugar cards: Last Days for Making Application" appears on October 3 (3a). See also Marwick, *The Deluge,* 191ff. On 7 December 1917, Woolf refers to shortages of coal and butter and says "sometimes we can't even get the nice kind of margarine"; on 15 December she refers to the queues for tea (*Diary* 1, 87, 93).

43. The notation "6th Jan" is in the margin of this page of the holograph. As the group toasts the new year after the raid, Elvira mistakenly identifies the date as "January 14th 1917" and is corrected by Renny, who says, "You can't even get the date right" [Holograph V, 109].

turning like the sail of a windmill, moved across the sky; revealing little and stopping sometimes as if to examine some patch of the sky more closely" (Holograph V, 69). This graphic and lyrical evocation of wartime London streets, which Woolf wrote on 6 January 1934, is altered in the novel published three years later; in the published novel, notwithstanding a final ironic edge, the narrative is starker and more direct, making the description less mysterious and more routine: "[T]he air seemed frozen, and, since there was no moon, congealed to the stillness of glass spread over England. . . . Darkness pressed on the windows. . . . No light shone, save when a searchlight rayed round the sky, stopped, here and there, as if to ponder some fleecy patch" (*Years*, 279). Although the possibility of an air raid is not mentioned in the final novel, in the holograph we are informed: "It was possible that there would be an air raid tonight. On the other hand, it was quite four or five nights where there had been none for there was no moon. But there was no raid this month so far: & next week the moon would be rising again." Although Woolf had at first intended to credit Eleanor with this reflection, "Eleanor reflected" is crossed out, suggesting that even in draft Woolf instinctively preferred this observation to remain in the province of the omniscient narrator (Holograph V, 69).[44]

In the published novel the *possibility* of a raid is not mentioned at all. "Another raid," Maggie comments, with seeming indifference, when a "fog horn" is confused with an air raid siren (*Years*, 288). In *The Years* Woolf suggests, sometimes ironically and through indirection, that though a raid is as routine as denial, in the long run, denial is not immunity. In 1917 Woolf was cognizant of the signs, and her diaries suggest a consciousness of the risk, whatever sangfroid she exhibited, particularly in her retrospective diary entries and especially when the threatened raid turned out to be a "false alarm," as it did on 3 November 1917.

> The raid didn't actually happen but with our nerves in the state they are (I should say Lottie's & Nelly's nerves) the dipping down of electric lights was taken as a sign of warning: finally the lights went out, & standing on the kitchen stairs I was deluged with certain knowledge that the extinction of light is in future our warning. I looked out of the hall door, however, heard the usual patter & voices of suburbans coming home; & then, to bear out my assurance, the lights suddenly came on again. (*Diary* I, 70).

44. Woolf made several other changes to this early version, apparently as she wrote, and also included another rendering of this section immediately afterward, something she did several times when writing "1917" in particular.

Anticipating "1918," which involves only a few moments on Armistice Day, the air raid scene in *The Years* also calls to mind the prewar experience of Rose being attacked by the man with a pocked face, though in 1917 the real threat of faceless aeroplanes offers a somber contrast; yet, in each case, nothing happens to the Pargiters. As the raid begins Nicholas asks Eleanor, "D' you mind air raids? People differ so much." "'Not at all,' she said. She would have crumbled a piece of bread to show him that she was at her ease; but as she was not afraid, the action seemed to her unnecessary" (*Years,* 289). Such shows of fearlessness (fearlessness suggesting ignorance of a threat) assert rationality in the face of war, or assert perhaps that, as Woolf says in *Three Guineas,* "men and women . . . can act, and think for themselves" (*3G,* 6). But Eleanor, who, like Woolf, is an avid reader of newspapers, takes a line from Woolf's own diary and explains, "The chances of being hit oneself are so small" (*Years,* 289; see *Diary* 1, 32).

Despite the appearance of pargeting, the civilian population had 835 deaths and 1,972 casualties as a result of raids by German airplanes between 25 May 1917 and 20 May 1918; between 22 August 1917 and 1 May 1918 there were nineteen raids, of which Woolf noted ten in her diaries. During the same period, Woolf sighted airships (two on 11 September) and noted four "false alarms"; most false alarms, Woolf wrote were "ignored by the press" (*Diary* 1, 144). After directly or vicariously experiencing massive raids throughout September (and until 31 October–1 November), it would seem natural that the civilian population, particularly that of London, was expectant and anxious. London was attacked on 6 and 18 December 1917 and again on 28–29 and 29–30 January 1918 (Fredette, 262–66). In the version Woolf wrote in 1934, Maggie brings the children to the kitchen, and her husband comments that it does not make any difference, as a bomb would kill them all anyway; later in the draft he says that "if a bomb drops, we shall all be killed at the same time" (Holograph V, 90, 91). What she intends, however, is to allow the children to sleep, something that is less emphatically suggested in the published novel.

It may well be that the greater the blurring, the less obvious the immunity. The sense of immunity is less emphatic in the holograph, and particularly in the raid scene, where

> Eleanor told herself that at any moment they might be killed. But she could not think of anything appropriate to say, even to herself. "It does seem so silly" she said as if she were apologising to the self which tried to stir her with a vision of sudden death. "It's unpleasant of course," she added (Holograph V, 93).

Until the "Present Day" section of the novel, the controlling narrative voice had become increasingly important as Woolf sought to "bring about proportion" in what she called in November 1934 "compacting the vast mass": "The thing is to contract: each scene to be a scene, much dramatised; contrasted; each to be carefully dominated by one interest; some generalised" (*Diary* 4, 261). The narrator heightens the incongruous, and thereby calls attention to "one interest," an expression that suggests participation in or responsibility for what Eleanor identifies after the raid as "immunity."

In the much-edited final version of *The Years*, Woolf's ironic intent can be seen in Eleanor's sense that "[l]ike *all* the French . . . [Renny] cares *passionately* for his country. But contradictorily, she felt" (*Years*, 284), a judgment that seems sustained in Renny's "*exaggerated* gesture of boredom" as "*[e]verything* seemed to be going past very quickly." The ironic juxtaposition is maintained and emphasized as booming guns come closer and closer and sound louder and louder until Nicholas "took out his watch. The silence was *profound. Nothing happened.* . . . Another gun boomed. . . . There was *profound silence. Nothing happened*" (*Years*, 288–90; emphasis added). Sara says "It didn't come to much, did it?" and Nicholas responds "Ah, but we were frightened." Then, as if to support such an inference, he says "Look—how pale we all are." But Maggie denies even this: "It's partly the light" she says (292). In *Beyond the Pleasure Principle*, Freud says that "'[f]right' . . . is the name we give to the state a person gets into when he has run into danger *without being prepared for it;* it emphasizes the factor of surprise. There is something about anxiety that protects its subject against fright and so against fright-neuroses" (emphasis added; 11).

Unlike courage, which depends on conscious recognition of danger, a sense of immunity, ironically, gives rise to fearlessness, a distinction Woolf understood not only through reading her war diaries but through her reading of Montaigne, who (anticipating Roosevelt) said "The thing I fear most is fear" (*CW*, 53). The posture of fearlessness is as contradictory as the "masklike expression" of extreme patriotism that Eleanor recognizes in Renny (*Years*, 284), who demonstrates its contradictions rather more overtly than the Britons, though, curiously, with the same vigorous "tendency to denunciation" that Woolf had noted during the war in her husband, Leonard, and his family (*Diary* 1, 124). It is the absence of responsiveness to or even recognition of the threat of sudden death when the raid is over that Woolf shows to be the more curious and, ultimately, the more damaging. Woolf seems to suggest here that although Renny reacts impotently and *after* the planes have passed, what is significant is that he, like his wife, *does* react:

"'They're only killing other people,' said Renny savagely. He kicked the wooden box" (*Years*, 293). As fearlessness is impossible to maintain *during* a raid, Nicholas, who is Polish, reverts to a dismissive attitude toward the war (and his own risk) when the guns fire "far away in the distance": "'[W]hat nonsense Renny talks,' said Nicholas, turning to [Eleanor] privately. 'Only children letting off fireworks in the back garden'" (293).

Through the vision of the narrator we see what Woolf called in 1935 "the movement (that is the change of feeling as the raid goes on)" (*Diary* 4, 347). Importantly, we see that only Eleanor, who "looked like an abbess" after the raid, comes to see the connection between the risk of personal death and a sense of immunity.

> Everything seemed to become quiet and natural again. A feeling of great calm possessed her. It was as if another space of time had been issued to her, but, *robbed by the presence of death of something personal, she felt*—she hesitated for a word—"*immune?*" Was that what she meant? Immune, she said. . . . Immune, she repeated. . . . (emphasis added; *Years*, 293–94)

Woolf seems to suggest that for Eleanor it is the *recognition* of her own proximity to death that had released a consciousness of the *illusion* of immunity: war is *not* a pyrotechnic display. Anticipating the family reunion some ten years later in the "Present Day," Woolf shows the characters forgetting the air raid almost as soon as it ends. Only Eleanor demonstrates a consciousness of the sense of immunity that seemingly nullified the immediate threat to life represented by the air raid. This consciousness is signaled several hours later, as the party breaks up: "The raid! [Eleanor] said to herself. I'd forgotten the raid! . . . 'I'd forgotten the raid!' she said aloud. . . . She was surprised but it was true" (*Years*, 300).

Bergson says that a sorting process goes on in memory that involves not only what he calls "the recall of useful recollection" but also "the provisional banishment of all the others" (*Matter and Memory*, 177). "Useful memory," as Bergson defines it "may complete and illuminate the present situation with a view to ultimate action" (179). This function of memory leads not only to Renny's actions, however futile, but to Eleanor's "provisional" banishing of the primal impression of the air raid as well. When Eleanor "forgets" the *war* in what Woolf calls "the first war scene" in "1914," there is no perceived civilian risk (*Diary* 4, 286); when Eleanor "forgets" the *raid* in "1917," she denies the possibility of death or injury; but, when she is afraid to walk in the park in 1921, in the postwar world, Eleanor may be finding secondary memory the more "useful." After all, she was, Woolf said, "meant to be all right; sound and rooted; the others were crippled in one way or another" (*Letters* 6, 122). But, perhaps because Eleanor finds in "1921" that her sense of immunity from personal risk has not lasted beyond the war, Woolf chose to delete this section. In so doing, Woolf avoided "propaganda" (by which she meant a set of ideas propagated with an action in mind, a practice she found objectionable in the thirties poets, and which she had long found objectionable in Edwardian novelists) and offered only a rather blurred message of hope in the "Present Day," thus leading the way for the antiwar polemic of *Three Guineas*.

Between 30 September 1934, when she claimed to have written the "last words of the nameless book," and 30 December 1936, when she finished correcting the final proofs of *The Years,* Woolf deleted hundreds of pages of text, including "two enormous chunks" in proof, in part to make the novel more manageable, but also, and I think more importantly, to intensify the issue of civilian immunity and lay the foundation for *Three Guineas.* She was firm, however, about avoiding "the Aldous [Huxley] novel" (*Diary* 4, 281), that is, a novel that propagated ideas, at the expense of form and character.[45] When Woolf sent final corrections to the proofs on 30 December 1936, she had deleted what she called "the first war scene," made extensive cuts to what she called "the raid scene," and eliminated "1921" altogether. What these changes make clear is that by the time of the publication of *The Years* on 11 March 1937, Woolf was concerned with exploring the illusion of civilian immunity that existed during the Great War and that more and more seemed part of the present day in which the novel was being written; much of the blurring in the published novel seems related to Woolf's own secondary remembrance of the Great War and events in the present day. From 22 April 1935, when Woolf noted the "complete reversal to pre-war days"; to 29 August, when she wrote that "war seems inevitable"; to 4 September 1935, which "the papers" called "the most critical day since August 4th 1914," the march toward a second Great War seemed unstoppable (*Diary* 4, 304, 336, 337).

45. Clearly, the word *propaganda* did not have the derogatory connotations of the cold war years and meant, as the *OED* says, a tenet or doctrine of a particular party or sect. It was not commonly used during the Great War and Woolf does not use the word in her novels (Haule, *Concordance*). Aldous Huxley's *Brave New World* had been published in 1932, but Woolf was only just reading *Point Counterpoint* (1928) in 1935. "Not a good novel," she wrote, "all raw, uncooked, protesting . . . interest in ideas; makes people into ideas" (*Diary* 4, 276).

More and more, distinct echoes, conscious memories, and secondary remembrance from the Great War were blurring her daily experience, her reading, and her writing. It is not by coincidence, I think, that Woolf begins
Three Guineas by referring to a letter received in 1935 asking "how can we
prevent war?" Neither is it a surprise that Wilfred Owen is the only war poet
to figure prominently in *Three Guineas*. On 27 November 1935 Woolf wrote:
"I've reached the no man's land that I'm after" in what she had expected
would be her final review of the novel (*Diary* 4, 355). Yet, she continued revising well into 1936; on 4 March 1936 she was still "copying the raid scene,"
she estimated, "for the 13th time. . . . So I'm in sight . . . of the beginning of
the other book which keeps knocking unmercifully at the door" (*Diary* 5,
14). On 13 March 1936 Woolf called herself a pacifist (like Aldous Huxley),
the only time she ever did so in her writings, either public or private (*Diary* 5,
17]. On 11 November, the Woolfs "completely forgot" Armistice Day and on
17 November, Lord Cecil called Bertrand Russell "insane" for proposing sub-
mission to Hitler before telling the Woolfs of his own visit to see Mussolini
(*Diary* 5, 32, 33–34). By 30 November, Woolf seemed satisfied with *The Years*,
calling it "[a] full packed book" with "more 'real' life in it; more blood &
bone" (*Diary* 5, 38). She must have realized how much of 'real' life is clotted
blood and broken bones; on 23 November, she had begun *Three Guineas* and
on 14 December, "Why Art To-day Follows Politics" was published in the
Daily Worker.

Taken apart from other exclusions, the elimination of the "two enormous
chunks" makes more emphatic the sense of immunity, and presents dramatically the irony implicit in a *wartime* sense of immunity—denial by another name. Taken with them, we see that changes thereby effected in the
characters of Eleanor and North Pargiter in particular intentionally lead to
Three Guineas and the "Society of Outsiders." Although widely accepted as
taking place "in 1917, just before Maggie's dinner party" as Grace Radin asserts, the "first war scene" seems clearly intended to have been part of "1914,"
a month or so after the beginning of the Great War, in the "sultry September sunshine." The year is identified by Eleanor as she reckons children "born
yesterday" at ten years old in 1924;[46] what Woolf consistently calls "the raid
scene" occurs in December 1917. In crossing out on the earliest holographic
version the comment Eleanor makes after the raid, that "[s]everal millions

46. Radin, "Two Enormous Chunks": 227, 228, 233. As in the proof sheets for 1918 and
1921, the proof sheets for the excluded "episodes" involving Crosby and Eleanor are more
reasonably placed with "1914," which precedes them, than with "1917," which follows. See
also note 34 above.

are being killed [in the war]," Woolf must have seen that a civilian could not have made such a comment; certainly, Woolf must have realized that such a surmise would have implied an understanding that civilians were deprived of (even if they, like Eleanor, read newspapers assiduously) and, importantly, would have presupposed the ignorance that led to the illusion of immunity (Holograph V, 97). In the section deleted in proof from "1914," Eleanor notices the name of a young sailor who, like Jacob Flanders, had been reported killed, and, perhaps anticipating too obviously the question raised in *Three Guineas,* asks herself: "[H]ow could I have stopped him?" (Radin, "'Two Enormous Chunks,'" 233). Woolf had intended, at first, to go even further: "If she as a girl had always read the papers; if she had followed the course of politics; if she had twenty years ago formed a society & headed a procession & gone to Whitehall, & said, if you don't stop what you're doing" (Holograph V, 55).[47] But in *The Years* Woolf was not seeking to anticipate the argument—or to propagate the ideas or "propaganda"—of *Three Guineas,* but to embody the history that made it necessary.

In making "1918" the shortest section of the novel, Woolf suggests that civilians, regardless of class, recognized little that separated the war itself from the peace. The only character in "1918" is the aging nurse, Crosby. In a version dated February 27 [1934], Woolf emphasizes character, and makes clear that just as there was little to separate war from peace, Crosby finds little to distinguish Armistice Day from the war just ended: "Crosby hobbled across the green out to do her morning shopping. It was a still November morning" (Holograph V, 143). In the published novel, references to the day and the scene begin the section and Crosby is not introduced until the second paragraph: "A veil of mist covered the November sky. . . . Sounds coming through the veil—the bleat of sheep, the croak of rooks—were deadened" (*Years,* 302). On 11 November 1918 Woolf had herself noted the rooks and their silent circling, a seeming symbol of "creatures performing some ceremony, partly of thanksgiving, partly of valediction over the grave" (*Diary* 1, 216). But what Woolf and her circle noticed most of all was an "unsettling" restlessness, as she wrote to Vanessa at 11.30: "I, on the whole though rather emotional . . . feel also immensely melancholy" (*Letters* 2, 290).

The Woolfs, restless for some activity, went to London, where they found "in everyone's mind the same restlessness & inability to settle down, & yet discontent with whatever it was possible to do." In the novel, it is not the

47. Radin also includes these lines in the commentary section of "'Two Enormous Chunks'": 235.

restlessness that Woolf exploits, but the indifference, the lack of respon-siveness. Peering from windows at their neighbors on Armistice Day, the Woolfs "saw the housepainter give one look at the sky & go on with his job; the old man toddling along the street carrying a bag out [of] which a large loaf protruded, closely followed by his mongrel dog" (*Diary* 1, 216). There was little to call attention to the day, which was cloudy and, because of the guns now "announcing peace," smoky.

What change came with peace was more apparent than real, or so it may have seemed. James Strachey, Woolf reported on 19 November, "didn't seem to have noticed much difference" (*Letters* 2: 298). Business as usual remained the definitive slogan although rationing as usual should have reminded the population that the effects of the war did not end with the signing of a treaty. But, four days after the armistice, Woolf noted, "Peace is rapidly dis-solving into the light of common day"; a month later, she said that "the war already seems an unimportant incident" and news of preparations for war in Russia, was met with indifference (*Diary* 1, 217, 229). Civilians went on as if nothing had happened. Woolf's descriptions of Peace Day, 19 July 1919, suggest that celebrations were worse than perfunctory. She reflected ironi-cally that "with the Zeppelin raid [the parade] will play a great part in the history of the Boxall [a servant] family" (*Diary* 1, 292), as if zeppelin raids, which had made the civilian a victim of war, could be equated with libera-tion from such victimization, as if the war had been as transient and as memorable as a parade. Leonard Woolf recalls being able to find Belgium chocolates in Richmond "some months after the Armistice" and declaring "the war was finally over," even as rationing of some products continued (ra-tioning of sugar, for example, continued well into 1920), and if returning soldiers were not recovering in a hospital, they were often unemployed (*BgA*, 256–57; Mowat, *Britain*, 125–29). As a returning V.A.D., Vera Brittain, explains, in the chapter of her war memoir entitled "Survivors Not Wanted," "1919 seems a horrid year, dominated by a thoroughly nasty Peace. But when it came in, it appeared to an exhausted world as divine normality, the spring of life after the winter of death, the stepping-stone to a new era, the gateway to an infinite future" (*Testament of Youth*, 467).

Woolf had written "1921" to include evidence of the apparent changes that peace brought and civilian unconsciousness of them. One way Woolf sug-gested the blurring of the war and the peace was by moving from 11 Novem-ber 1918 to May 1921 without a section break; another, and less subtle method, is seen in her characters' responses to the peace. For Edward Pargiter, one of Eleanor's brothers and an Oxford don (many of [whose] pupils had been "killed in the War" [Radin, "'Two Enormous Chunks,'" 239]), driving with Kitty Lasswade, a cousin and a widow (though not a war widow), the war had almost no effect. Although he intends to repeat an observation on postwar England made by a diplomat who had been at the Hague since 1916, he leaves Kitty's company before he even begins (Radin, "'Two Enormous Chunks,'" 240). Kitty is affected by the war and the peace only indirectly; her son, who has been left the title to her husband's estate, "[wi]ll be forced to sell sooner or later," she says, "like everybody else" (Radin, "'Two Enormous Chunks,'" 239). In fact, the breakup of large estates that began before the war was accelerated, particularly in the depressed economic conditions of the early twenties.[48] For Eleanor, who had been intimidated by her more worldly and wealthy cousin since before the war, the gloves she needs to overcome her "fear" in visiting the sixty-year-old Kitty are now available in the shops, though not in the right shade (Radin, "'Two Enormous Chunks,'" 242–43). But, while Kitty sees Eleanor and her "patriotism" as naive (as Nicholas had done in the air raid scene), Eleanor is the one who has been changed by the war and who recognizes changes in the postwar world. Eleanor, who had not admitted to being afraid during the air raid in "1917," recognizes that "fear" in the outside world cannot be assuaged by buying a new pair of gloves or by walking on well-lit streets.

In the postwar world the only thing that is not blurred is danger on the streets: "She [Eleanor] was afraid—even now, even I, she thought . . . afraid. Afraid to walk through the Park alone" (Radin, "'Two Enormous Chunks,'" 249). In the postwar world, though fear takes on a reality unacknowledged during the Great War, what remains blurred is the relation between combatants and civilians. In "1917," North Pargiter says good-bye to Sara before he leaves London for the front; in "1921," Eleanor receives a letter from North Pargiter, who had gone to Africa after the war, but she ignores it: "She used to like North, but he had been abroad so long she scarcely knew him now, she thought, as she pushed the letter back into its envelope" (Radin, "'Two Enormous Chunks,'" 247).

By canceling "1921" from *The Years*, Woolf made more dramatic both the return of North Pargiter to London in the "Present Day," and her picture of a postwar world that had removed barriers between civilians and non-

48. Cannadine, who describes the situation in *Decline and Fall* (110–12), quotes Edward Wood, who said in a speech before the House of Commons in December 1924: "We are, unless I mistake it, witnessing in England the gradual disappearance of the old landed classes." Cannadine adds, "In the years immediately before and after the First World War, some six to eight million acres, one-quarter the land of England, was sold" (111).

combatants by refusing to admit they existed. By making North the only combatant-character other than Septimus Warren Smith to return from the war, Woolf calls attention to their shared experiences as outsiders.[49] North's return in the "Present Day," which, although undated in the final novel presumably takes place in 1927,[50] is greeted with ignorance and indifference, as his leaving for the front had been met critically, and with morbid foreboding. During the dinner party held in the basement during an air raid, the same night North leaves for the front, Eleanor notes that Nicholas speaks of North as if he were already one of the honored dead: "it struck her that Nicholas spoke of him as if he were dead" (Holograph V, 79).

Although much of the published novel involves memory, Woolf chose to delete Sara's renewed attack on North's enlistment during his visit in "Present Day," before Delia's party and family reunion, which is part of her 1934 holograph, a deletion effectively suggesting North's isolation and the short-term memory of civilians (Holograph VI, 54). There is little evidence to suggest that North's relatives remember either his experience of the war or their own. His return to England in 1927 appears not to have raised many eyebrows: "It's so nice to see you. . . . And you haven't changed," says Eleanor (*Years*, 307), as if he had not seen combat, as if he had been away for a short time, rather than for ten years. When he goes to visit Sara, she does not even break off her telephone conversation to greet him when he appears (312). Unlike the training poster and like the postwar experience of Septimus, no one asks him "What did you do in the Great War?" "'You can talk to Eleanor,'" North observes in an early holograph (Holograph VI, 47), but *not* about his experience of the war. In fact, when North returns to London he does not want to talk about it to anyone: "'Oh the war—that's over' he sighed," to Sara in an early holograph; then "he broke off, as if to change the conversation" (Holograph VI, 54).

49. See Levenback, "Virginia Woolf and Returning Soldiers."

50. In the context of the novel, this seems to me to be a reasonable assumption. The section "1921," the last of the "two enormous chunks" deleted in proof, suggests 1927 as reasonable in sequence, and in context. In 1931, when Woolf was thinking of the years as a novel-essay, she considered extending the sequence into the future, to the year 2032, but she subsequently modified the plan. See Charles G. Hoffman, "Virginia Woolf's Manuscript Revisions of *The Years*," *PMLA* 84 (Jan. 1969), 79–89, and Grace Radin, *Virginia Woolf's "The Years": The Evolution of a Novel*, 92. On the other hand, Howard Harper, in *Between Language and Silence*, believes "the topical references . . . clearly point to the mid-1930s, the time of the book's composition" (252). Mark Hussey agrees with Harper, pointing to a reference to "Fascist propaganda" (*Diary* 4, 337), which is echoed in *The Years* (310) (letter to author, 27 July 1994).

Woolf echoes "1917" in "Present Day," in part, I think, to fill the gap left by deleting "1921."[51] As they had in 1917, North and the family seem to deny the war altogether. Concerned with North's future, the Pargiters remember only the immediate past: "He's just back from Africa," Delia explains at her party (*Years*, 400). It is equally curious that though North is critical of his relatives for talking only "money and politics," he is himself concerned with seeking employment, but more obviously in early drafts. It is not be wondered that in the "Present Day" of the novel, North's family questions him repeatedly about his plans and his prospects for employment in the tight postwar economy, Eleanor going so far as proposing to make out a budget for him when he admits to having saved "four or five thousand" (381–82). Farming, or, more specifically, raising sheep, had led to his having acquired enough profit to live on; in early drafts Sara speaks of his having spun gold out of wool (Holograph VI, 103, 104),[52] but Woolf deleted the passages involving the length to which he goes to secure employment in the published novel, perhaps to increase the unknowableness of a former soldier who had experienced the war from the front. Grace Radin observes that Woolf originally intended to have North go to Australia, but it would seem that greater resonance was achieved by having North live in an unidentified country in Africa (although Jimmy, his cousin, has been in Uganda, specifically), which demonstrates yet again the English ignorance of that which is outside their experience.[53] Although Woolf deletes Sara's naive question involving "tigers howl[ing] in the jungle" (Holograph VI, 58) in the published novel, the family repeatedly ask North whether he intends to return to "the wilds of Africa" (*Years*, 319), to that "horrid farm" (307).

North's experiences, in the war and in Africa after the war, are all but unknown. When he remembers the war, he says nothing and quickly brushes it aside: "The idea of dynamite, exploding dumps of heavy earth, shooting earth up in a tree-shaped cloud, came to his mind, from the War. But that's all poppy-cock, he thought" (375). What is key is that the war was *not* pop-

51. Compare Radin, *Virginia Woolf's "The Years,"* xxii, and Allen McLaurin, *Echoes Enslaved*, 158–65.

52. In "Pargeting 'The Pargiters': Notes of an Apprentice Plasterer," Marcus says: "The sheep marks the scene of sexual initiation as, later, in the bloody sacrifice North and Sara share [at dinner] it marks North's initiation into London society and community responsibility after his African exile and his fears as a warrior" (424).

53. Both Leonard Woolf and his wife were continually reminded of this and very much aware of this tendency among those of their own class in particular. See Chapman and Manson, "Carte and Tierce."

pycock, and both North and most of his noncombatant relatives naively overlook the reality of the war, the death and suffering it caused, the changes it brought about, and its ongoing effects. Despite his front experience and the unspeakable conditions in the trenches, he "shivers" in disgust at Sara's description of the Jew's hair in the bathtub: "Hairs in food, hairs on basins, other people's hairs made him feel physically sick" (340). War in the trenches may be Hell, but in the published novel Sara remembers that she had described her own situation after the war in that way (321), and thereby draws attention in the "Present Day" to the problem of employment.

It is clear that the economic hardships that began with and followed the war are on the minds of the Pargiters in 1927. "What's the War done for us, eh? Ruined me for one," complains Delia's husband, Patrick (401). No one in the novel explicitly mentions the General Strike of 1926, which had been short-lived and had been followed by an apparent return to "business as usual," but Hugh Gibbs, Milly's husband, comments on "the paucity of jobs" (376) and Woolf herself had said at the time that the strike was "minded . . . more than the war" (*Diary* 3, 80). Kingsley Martin, in *The British Public and the General Strike*, said, "The War, and still more the Peace, have accelerated a decline already noticeable before 1914" (19). This assertion is sustained by postwar unemployment figures which reached 14 percent in 1922 and 10 percent or higher from 1923 to 1929, representing over a million workers, a number that increased to 2.5 million unemployed in December 1930 (Hirst, 283; Mowat, *Britain,* 357).[54]

Certainly, as Woolf was writing the novel, she was aware of the problem; six months after she attended the Labour Party Conference of October 1933, "the argument blazed: how the Labour party would come in: what it would do. . . . What is it going to do about unemployment, about agriculture?" What is even more suggestive is Woolf's next observation, "All these questions were put from the view of here & now," a resonant expression, as it was the working title of her novel at the time (*Diary* 4, 182 and n. 3, 230–31). It is telling that Woolf chose, in the published novel, to delete North's comment that employment was a sign of manhood, that "the unpardonable sin—in a man—[is] not having a job" (Holograph VI, 75). In August 1934, at a gathering hosted by the Keyneses, discussion involved the unemployment at the Lancashire cotton mills and the "financial crisis," which one guest claimed was because there was "no Treasury control of the soldiers"

54. Hirst's figures (the first quoted) are based on the *registered* unemployed, those receiving unemployment compensation from the government; Mowat cites *Statistical Abstract of U.K. 1930,* 97.

(*Diary* 4, 236). Woolf's concern for returning soldiers in 1927 was, to her mind, part of her present-day concern with the economic conditions of the postwar world, and not with conditions of manhood that might have motivated a former soldier.

The ambiguities surrounding North are more pronounced than those of the other major character, particularly in "Present Day." Although some ambiguities are clarified in early holographs, the deletion of what detail appears there offers insight into Woolf's perception of the returning soldier. For example, while North reckons that his sister Peggy is thirty-seven or thirty-eight in "Present Day" (*Years,* 394), we know only that North is some years younger; in the novel Eleanor observes that North is graying, and when he speaks to Sara, he implies that they are near the same age (322). Though he had been a "cricketing boy" in 1911, when he smoked his first cigar (202), he did not become part of the military until 1917. But then, having experienced the war, what he appreciated in Africa was "peace" and "solitude"; what he notices in postwar London is that it is crowded and noisy and, perhaps remembering the rationing during the war, he believes "[e]verything" to be "profusion [and] plenty" (308), and observes how "prosperous" his relatives seem to be (392). In an early holograph, however, Sara (Elvira) counterpoints this with "We've all come down in the world" (Holograph 6, 49), a condition less apparent in the published novel. Although his farming in "Africa" (the only geographic reference being to the continent) was probably done in Tanganyika, which was acquired by the British under the Treaty of Versailles in 1919, he offers no reason for not returning to England after the war, We know only that, far from going to Africa as a governor, like his Uncle Martin, North, in an early holograph, says he lived "miles from anywhere" (Holograph VI, 58). He was not affiliated with a government office, though former servicemen employed in government offices were counted as part of the "official statistics." But, it is clear that North, like Septimus, is not counted in official statistics.

Unlike the portrait of Septimus Warren Smith, the portrait of North Pargiter does not include his experience of the war, and deliberately so.[55] Whatever changes the war might have effected are shown to be short-lived, even to soldiers, or denied by them altogether, which may explain why North does not remember his brother Charles. Yet, in the published novel it is not only suggested that he was killed in the war but that this may be a reason why North does not return immediately afterward to England and

55. Victoria Middleton notes that the ambiguities in the novel are deliberate, but does not attempt to understand North Pargiter and his experience of the Great War.

cannot enjoy friendly relations with his sister Peggy in 1927. What we may infer is that North, unlike Siegfried Sassoon, seeks to forget about the war and gives up both letter writing and poetry while he is in Africa, where he enjoys the solitude of sitting on the verandah, listening to his sheep.

That "his comprehension of people is limited," as Victoria Middleton notes (168), would seem to me somehow linked to Woolf's attitude about returning soldiers, whose experience of the war left them in the postwar world ambiguous and solitary. Even if he had spoken of his experience of the war, it is clear that he, like Septimus, would have lacked a receptive audience. This also may suggest a reason why "Present Day" is not explicitly dated, as if, particularly for returning soldiers, every day were the only day. For Siegfried Sassoon, the war never ended, but he, unlike North and Septimus, had an audience. This point is made more clear if we consider that it was North's speech and not Nicholas's that, as late as 18 July 1935, Woolf had intended to make the focus of the "Present Day" (*Diary* 4, 332). But the plan was abandoned. Finally, North does not answer the call and does not articulate his vision of "another world, a new world" (*Years*, 422, 424).

North, like Septimus, returns to an England different from the one he left. Having himself observed "brand new villas" for the well-to-do amid a housing shortage for the poor and the less well-to-do, North says, "[T]hat's what strikes me . . . how you've spoilt England while I've been away" (376). North, as much as Peter Walsh, seems to avoid seeing the connection between the "new" England and the war. Yet, North, like Eleanor and like Woolf herself, recognizes the need "to connect" with other human beings, realizes that "we who make idols of other people, who endow this man, that woman, with power to lead us, only add to the deformity, and stoop ourselves" (380) and internally echoes the concern expressed in Woolf's 1934 essay, "Why?": "Why not create a new form of society founded on . . . equality? Why not bring together people of all ages and both sexes and all shades of fame and obscurity so they can talk without mounting platforms?" Finally, "Why not invent human intercourse? Why not try?" (281). But, the chance to communicate this eludes North, although he seems to seek understanding, like Woolf herself, of what she called in 1935 one's "duty as a human being" (*Diary* 4, 345). For North, and perhaps for Woolf as well, this may be related to having lost the solidity of the prewar world.

In postwar England, where North feels himself "an outsider" and where he "do[es]n't fit in anywhere," he realizes that the contribution he will be able to make is problematic "unless [he] know[s] what's solid, what's true;

in [his] life, in other people's lives" (317, 403; 409–10). Though Septimus tried his best to become "reintegrated" into the postwar world, four years after he returns from the war, the task proves too much for him. North has been back only ten days, as "Present Day" ends, and his future in postwar England is not assured, especially as portents of the next war are visible: "On every placard at every street corner was Death; or worse—tyranny; brutality; torture; the fall of civilisation; the end of freedom" (388). In the end, Septimus cannot become part of the postwar world, while North seeks to understand it. What neither death nor life in postwar London has assured, however, is the end to war and the end of the need for soldiers, many of whom had not returned.

Woolf's postwar experience had taught her that being an outsider was an advantage, what she herself called a "natural distinction" in 1938, the year *Three Guineas* was published and the Society of Outsiders was put forth to answer the question of how to prevent war (*Letters* 6, 236). This may be why she felt drawn to returning soldiers, whom she implicitly or explicitly saw as outsiders to the civilian population and victims of a postwar world that all but ignored them—and the reality of war. By 1936, the year before the novel was published, Woolf declared that she had "never known such a time of foreboding" (*Letters* 6, 35). A year later, and two days before *The Years* was published, the Woolfs had dinner with Julian Bell, just back from China. Four days later she wrote to Ethel Smyth: "I'm so rushed I cant write even my usual scrawl. We've been bothered about Julian, Nessa's boy, wanting to fight in Spain: and have to stop him, which means seeing people—politicians. But this by the way is confidential" (*Letters* 6, 113). This time, however, wire-pulling did no good.

By 1937, sons of soldiers who had returned from the Great War were fighting on another front, in the Spanish Civil War. On 7 June 1937 Julian Bell, her nephew, reported to a British medical unit near Madrid to serve as an ambulance driver. He did not return. He was fatally wounded near the village of Villanueva de la Canada and died on 18 July.

EPILOGUE

FINALLY, WOOLF DENIED seeing much connection between the Great War and World War II. The reality of the first year, 1939–40, seemed in prospect more like what Woolf herself called "a non-war" than a renewal of the Great War, for which the entire country had been preparing long before gas masks were distributed in 1938 (*Diary* 5, 240). And she was not the only one. At the front, the fighting lacked anywhere near either the predicted intensity or the expected number of casualties, and the only trenches that sappers dug were in England. So misleading were newspaper reports and popular wisdom that before the German offensive began on 10 May 1940, the press dubbed it the phony war; Churchill called it the Twilight War; and, on the street, it was called the Bore War (Turner, 180). Extending from this apparently false alarm was a confidence in regaining the powers (reading, writing) that Woolf had theretofore found flagging and which would allow her to get on with her work (journalism; *Roger Fry;* "Pointz Hall"; and, eventually, a "running commentary on the External" to prepare for "Anon"). So "obsess[ed]" was she with "ideas for articles" that she even took up Freud, "to enlarge the circumference, to give my brain a wider scope: to make it objective; to get outside" (*Diary* 5, 241, 248). Yet, by the time she was contacted by the *Forum* to write an article on women and war (which was eventually published in the *New Republic*[1]), Woolf was not sure of what to include and asked Sheena Simon for assistance (*Letters* 6, 375). She felt that what she wanted to say had less to do with the realities of the new war on the streets, than of coping with the fact that "nothing happens," a phrase that, ironically, recalls the Great War (*Diary* 5, 240).

1. The magazine suggests as much in footnote 1 (549), but Woolf may have refused the *Women's Forum* because they had not been prepared to pay her enough (*Diary* 5, 250 and n.6).

By stating that having survived the Great War, he and his generation were prepared for World War II ("my generation knew now exactly what war is" [*Journey*, 9]), Leonard Woolf was recalling the psychology of civilian life not only in wartime but during the interwar years. Yet, as we have seen, Virginia Woolf's writings *of* the time suggest that in the interwar years the lived experience of war in the trenches as well as on the streets had been deconstructed and reconfigured in disturbing ways. Several ways examined in this book come to mind: abnormal conditions had become "business as usual"; general insecurity had become general acquiescence; illusions of immunity had become belief in fate; death in war had been depersonalized, spiritualized, memorialized; survival had been scrutinized and questioned, or ignored and forgotten. Suggesting that such displacements are not legacies of the Great War, but reflect innate tendencies in the British character (as some historians are wont to do), does not explain the context surrounding the emergence of ignorance, a condition defined by Mrs. Swithin in the version of *Between the Acts* that Woolf was writing in 1938–39: the ignorant: those who ignore (*Pointz Hall*, 87). Beyond the psychological effects of war with which both Leonard and Virginia Woolf were concerned are a number of questions that were never asked directly. Whatever the quandary, it followed from the categorical breakdown of peace and war; life and death; civilians and combatants. When the Great War began, the lines had been clearly drawn. Blurring occurred rarely, and then only when death was involved, during strategic bombing, for example. War could be seen as acceptable—or unacceptable—only as long as its realities and its experience were fixed.

This sense of certainty was a casualty of the Great War, although its demise was largely ignored. We have seen, however, how often Woolf connected the Great War with problems of the interwar years, albeit indirectly, suggesting finally that not even language had been immune. Her war-consciousness can be seen to justify her ironic treatment of postwar denial, but it did not prepare her for how far the domestication and normalization of war itself would extend. When she admits to uncertainty about the "influence of the [Great] War" in the memoir she began writing on 18 April 1939 ("Sketch of the Past," 81), she is revealing an ambivalence toward both its dismembered and re-membered realities. Yet, the tension she thematized in her postwar novels survived into the thirties, even as long-term projections and preparations for the next war continued at home (appointment of air raid wardens, evacuation of children). The populace, historians agree, was "prepared for war," but, the realities described in Woolf's writings were themselves more and more ironic—or, in the context of World War II, tragic.

Even before the publication of *Three Guineas* in 1938, Woolf nurtured a renewed confidence in her own ability to meet the challenge of survival, a resolve sustained in the face of the personal losses suffered in the thirties (Roger Fry, Lytton Strachey, Julian Bell) and the increasing likelihood of a second world war. Yet, we see suggestions that there was an effort to distance herself from the realities of preparation, even in her diary. "Now I must ward off the old depression," she recorded eighteen months before the start of the war and as "the public world" was increasingly filled with soldiers, suicides, and refugees (*Diary* 5, 131). Nor did she abandon this project once the declaration of war had been issued, although suicide was being discussed as an option immediately thereafter, briefly interfering with the progress of her writing of *Roger Fry:* "[I]f one cant write, as Duncan [Grant] said yesterday, one may as well kill oneself. . . . But I intend to work" (239). Such resolve conflicted with the hopeless spirit not only of her husband (who also saw suicide as a reasonable alternative) but of her friends and intimates, inside and outside Bloomsbury (Vita Sackville-West, for example, felt physically and spiritually drained, and Vanessa Bell was fearful of losing another son—at least until Quentin was exempted from military service in September 1939). It must have been inconceivable to Woolf that the realities (which sometimes seemed quite exciting—sometimes merely dull) would ever move her to a state of desperation. By January 1940 much of the popular sense of anxiety had abated as well, replaced with a sense of impatience and annoyance at the calls for sacrifice and discomfort, rather like a collective death wish—or denial. But on another level, Woolf knew that however constant the climate seemed, change was coming, and one of these days life itself would go from bad to worse. Perhaps then, when the realties proved too immediate to ignore, suicide could be considered. Perhaps, as Kierkegaard said, suicide *was* the ultimate irony, because death prevents the actor from being a spectator—or a victim.

Woolf's relative composure rested on the certainty that there was a way out. What anxiety she experienced did not surface as the phony war ended and the Battle of Britain began, but when death itself became problematic. Her antiwar message in *Three Guineas* exploited (ironically) the very distance that should have assured immunity (but did not), and, by the beginning of the Blitz on 9 September 1940, it was clear that categorical distinctions in gender, class, and age, as well as in military status, howsoever represented, had become irrelevant. The distinction that counted was that the Woolfs were well-known intellectuals (Leonard a Jewish intellectual), a category putting them at risk in ways unimaginable during the Great War.[2] In *Three Guineas* Woolf remarks not only of the conditions that lead to war (including "Hitlerism" and militarism) but also of the fact of war; yet, she seemed oblivious to how they would touch her. In looking beyond the present moment, what she did know was that "we live without a future" (*Diary* 5, 355). This may explain why she finished "Pointz Hall"—even fulfilling the promise she made in June 1940 and renaming it *Between the Acts*—"by way of an end" (*Diary* 5, 298, 356). Yet, by the end of 1940 Woolf was not immune to but showed no sign of feeling an immediate peril (a shortsightedness that would run counter to "the public mood") and was persuaded that not even the risk of invasion was real—at least until the weather improved.[3]

By the beginning of 1941 the realities of the war (like daily bombings) had been so reduced that even for the most astute of the civilian population it took a leap of faith to regard them as threatening and resist the temptation to protest increased rationing and preventative measures. Woolf herself writes of the "lull in the war" with a renewed sense of possibility (*Diary* 5, 354), and there was little in the atmosphere at Rodmell or in the real world outside to cause anything like the desperation that is often imputed to her.[4] Even the article published by the *New Republic* in October (and dated "August, 1940," during an air raid) begins and ends with "Thoughts on Peace," howsoever it implores assistance of the Americans, because Woolf, like her husband, knew that before Hitlerism and militarism could be stopped, Hitler must be stopped. This was the reality. Woolf's last works, including the posthumously published *Between the Acts,* reach back to the Great War, not as a measure of war, but as a touchstone to its reality. And whatever theories of life and death she may have held to that point required continual revision thereafter. What I have tried to show is that her work, and particularly the novels that have the most direct relation to the Great War, reveal a persistence of memory; a consciousness of life and death; and an understanding of the public mood, in the war, after the war, and under threat

2. A list of "enemies" to the Nazis was discovered after the war; the names of Leonard and Virginia Woolf were on it. The list, *"Die Sonderfahndungsliste G.B."* [Gestapo arrest list for England], is headed *"Zur Beachtung!"* [Attention!]. The list is dated 1940 and includes the names of those who are to be arrested. Hoover Institution Archives.

3. This point is made in M. W. Fodor's "Rehearsal on the Channel" (551), the article that followed Woolf's "Thoughts on Peace in an Air Raid" in the *New Republic,* 21 October 1941.

4. See, for example, Zwerdling (327–28) and Silver ("'Anon'" 359). Compare Susan M. Kenney ("Two Endings").

of war. At the same time, these works, and particularly those written in the prospect of World War II, suggest an inability for individuals (even those around her) to resist the herd instinct, a reality that finally not even she can resist.

Constant in the years between the wars was a survival instinct: soldiers returned from the Great War and reentered civilian life; civilians (most of whom had survived the war) went on with the business of living. Woolf as well confronted the challenge affirmatively. And there is every reason to think that whatever "the association of the 1914 War" to which her friend and doctor, Octavia Wilberforce, refers after Woolf's death (quoted in Zwerdling 289), it gave Woolf the strength to survive into the second year of World War II. In planning a "running commentary on the External" for a projected cultural history, she decided to "Skip present day" and move to "A Chapter on the future," perhaps as a testament to a second postwar world that she would not live to see (Silver, "'Anon,'" 360).[5] What is significant to Woolf studies and indeed to the study of war has less to do with why she died than how she lived. Our own historical moment suggests that a reading of Woolf must take to account not only how the context of war informs her life and her work but also how her life and her work inform our understanding of war. The blurring that was part of Woolf's project in the years between the wars has taken over our vision of the world today, now that war itself has been deconstructed in the media and its horror integrated into the pattern of our lives. Perhaps her program for survival will do the same.

5. Zwerdling relates this to her "longer historical sense" (327) and Silver to her loss of hope in "the radical transformation of feminine and masculine identity" ("'Anon,'" 359)

APPENDIX

WORKS CITED

INDEX

APPENDIX

Selected Biographical Notes

Baganel, Barbara (née Hiles) (1891–1984): An art student in Paris, and then at the Slade School in London before and during the first year of the war (1913–14). During the war years, she helped at the Omega Workshops and on one occasion "toiled day and night to finish . . . costumes" for a pantomime given to benefit the Lena Ashwell Concerts for the Troops (Hill, 39); was apprenticed at the Hogarth Press in November 1917; and, met and was engaged to Nicholas Bagenal, whom she married in 1918. On Armistice Day she was in a hospital, having given birth to their first child, Judith, on 8 November (Gadd, 132).

Baganel, Nicholas ("Nick") Beauchamp (1891–1974): Before the war, a student at King's College, Cambridge (1910–13). In 1914 he served in France as a commissioned officer in the Suffolk Regiment and, wounded, he returned to England in 1916 and transferred to the Irish Guards. After marrying Barbara Hiles in February 1918, he returned to France and was seriously wounded in April. After demobilization (1919–20), he studied horticulture at the South-East Agricultural College at Wye in Kent (*Diary* 1, 299, n.5).

Bell, (Arthur) Clive (Heward) (1881–1964): An undergraduate student at Trinity College, Cambridge (1899–1902), Clive Bell subsequently was a member of the Bloomsbury Group and married Vanessa Stephen in 1907. By the time he had written and published *Art* (1914), where the phrase "significant form" was first used, he was convinced that the war meant that civilization was at an end. He was "ineligible for active [military] service because of an unhealed rupture that he had had since his teens" and "considered seeking employment as an interpreter in the Army Service or Medical Corps" (Spalding, 132). In 1915, he put together *Peace at Once,* a pamphlet encouraging a negotiated settlement of the war. By order of the lord mayor of London, the "pamphlet was publicly burned by the Common Hangman" (Q. Bell, *Bloomsbury Recalled*, 32). During the last years of the war, between 1916 and 1918, while working as a farm laborer at Garsington Manor (see Ottoline Morrell, below), he also wrote *Ad Familiares* (1917) and *Pot-Boilers* (1918).

Bell, Julian Heward (1908–37): Eldest son of Clive and Vanessa Bell, during the first two years of the war (1914–15), with his younger brother, Quentin, went to school and stayed with their nurse in London. Subsequently, Julian and Quentin lived first in Eleanor House, near their mother, who was residing at Wissett Lodge in the neighborhood of West Wittering, Sussex; and then with Vanessa Bell and Duncan Grant in the recently purchased Charleston Farmhouse, four miles from the Woolf home, Asheham. After the war, Julian went to King's College, Cambridge (1927) and was elected to the Apostles in 1929. In 1935 he edited *We Did Not Fight,* a collection of autobiographical writing from "war resisters" in World War I. Julian was killed in 1937 while driving an ambulance in the Spanish Civil War.

Bell, Quentin (Claudian Stephen) (1910–96): Second son of Clive and Vanessa Bell (see Julian Heward Bell, above, and Vanessa Bell, below), Quentin was exempted from service in World War II because of "pulmonary illness" (Hussey, *A to Z*, 20).

Bell, Vanessa (née Stephen) (1879–1961): Elder sister of Virginia Woolf, married Clive Bell in 1907. First exhibition of her paintings in 1907–8 and in 1912 at the second Post-Impressionist Exhibition. In 1913, with Roger Fry and Duncan Grant, founded the Omega Workshops "to produce decorative art from a background of painting rather than crafts" (Hussey, *A to Z*, 195). From 1914 until the Military Service Act of 1916, she saw the war from behind a "carapace of ignorance" (Spalding, 149), living with Duncan Grant at Wissett Lodge, Sussex. In 1916, the same year that she, Duncan, and the children moved to Charleston, four miles from the Woolf home at Asheham, Bell did some volunteer work for the No Conscription Fellowship and the Council for Civil Liberties. In 1917, she began educating her sons at a small school she set up at Charleston. On 11 November 1918, she was at Charleston when she heard of the armistice. On Christmas Day 1918 she gave birth to Duncan Grant's daughter, Angelica Bell.

Brenan, Gerald (1894–1987): Attended Sandhurst, and intended to have a career in the army, though he preferred poetry to guns (Panichas, 38). Yet, he enlisted with a commission in the local Territorials, then to the 48th Divisional Cyclists' Company (where he met Ralph Partridge [below]), and served in France (Gathorne-Hardy, 99–100). He was shot while on patrol in France in June 1918, and returned to England to recover. During the war he was awarded the Croix de Guerre. He was not officially demobilized until May 1919 and he left for Spain in September, arriving in Madrid on 4 October and Granada on 10 October (Gathorne-Hardy, 125, 141–42).

Brittain, Vera (Mary) (1893–1970): Entered Somerville College, Oxford, before the war (March 1914), leaving in 1915 to join the Voluntary Aid Detachment (V.A.D.) as a nurse in London, and then in Malta and France. During the war, her fiancé, her brother, and two of her friends were killed on the western front (one, Victor Richardson, whom she was to marry, had been blinded and later died [see Gorham]). During the war Brittain also wrote poetry (published as *Verses of a VAD* [1918]) and in 1933 she published her memoir of the Great War, *Testament of Youth.*

Brooke, Rupert Chawner (1887–1915): Having gone to King's College, Cambridge (1906), Brooke published his first book, *Poems,* in 1911, the year he completed the first version of his dissertation, *John Webster and the Elizabethan Drama.* He enlisted in the Royal Naval Division as a sublieutenant in September 1914 and died of blood poisoning en route to Gallipoli in April 1915. His second book of poetry, *"1914" and Other Poems,* was published posthumously in 1915.

Carrington, Dora de Houghton ("Carrington") (1893–1932): Like her friend Barbara Bagenal (above), a student at the Slade School of Art (1910–14). Carrington sold her first drawing in 1914 and became a member of the "Omega Club" in 1917, the same year that she cut the woodblocks for the third Omega book, *Lucretius on Death,* and the first publication of the Hogarth Press, *Two Stories,* by Leonard Woolf and Virginia Woolf (Hill 25, 38). Carrington met Lytton Strachey during the war (1915), and began living with him at Tidmarsh in 1917, an attachment that lasted through her marriage in 1921 to "Ralph" Partridge (below) and beyond Strachey's death in 1931.

Cecil, Lady Robert ("Nelly") (née Lady Eleanor Lambton) (1868–1956): A friend to Virginia Woolf since the beginning of the century, she married Lord Robert in 1889. Her brother-in-law was James Cecil, fourth Marquis of Salisbury, and chairman of the Central Tribunal. Woolf wrote to her during the war, and in June 1916 let her know "about the case of Duncan Grant the painter, who is a conscientious objector and will be coming before the Central Tribunal in a week or two." She went on: "If you didnt mind, and felt that you could possibly say

anything on his behalf to Lord Salisbury . . . I would send you details"
(*Letters* 2, 98). Lord Robert Cecil was head of the League of Nations Section of the British Delegation to the Versailles Conference (*BgA*, 189).

Cox, Katherine ("Ka") Laird (1887–1938): Graduate of Newnham College,
Cambridge (1910), she had an intense physical and emotionally drain-
ing relationship with Rupert Brooke before the war (see Laskowski,
12–16), which remained a mainstay of her life until her death. In 1918 Ka
Cox married William Arnold-Forster (V. Woolf, *Letters* 3, 415; Hussey,
A to Z, 63).

Craig, Dr. Maurice (1865–1936): An authority in "mental disorders" before
and after the war, he published a textbook, *Psychological Medicine,* in 1905
(Trombley, 185ff). The Woolfs' "nerve specialist" before and during the
war, he wrote a letter in support of Leonard's appeal for exemption from
military service in 1916. (Dr. Maurice Wright wrote another.) After the
war, Craig was a member of the War Office Committee of Enquiry into
"Shell Shock."

Fisher, Herbert Albert Laurens (H.A.L.) (1865–1940): Maternal cousin
of Virginia Woolf, before the war he was made vice-chancellor of
Sheffield University (1914). A historian, during the war he served as a
cabinet minister to Lloyd George and was appointed by him president
of the Board of Education in 1916, a position he held until October 1922.
On a visit to Asheham in October 1918, he announced news from the
secretary of state for war that "we've won the war today" and "we shall
have peace by Christmas" (*Diary* 1, 203 and n. 16).

Forster, E(dward) M(organ) (1879–1970): Attended King's College, Cambridge (1897–1901) where he was elected a member of the Cambridge
Conversazione Society (the "Apostles"). A member of the Bloomsbury
Group, Forster had published four novels by 1910. When war was declared, Forster was cataloging paintings at the National Gallery, and in
1915 was accepted by the Red Cross as a "searcher" (responsible for dis-
covering the fate of those reported missing by talking to the wounded
in hospitals) and sent to Alexandria. In January 1919, Forster returned
to England. Forster wrote *Alexandria: A History and a Guide* (1922) during the war. During the war years he also wrote for the local press, particularly the *Egyptian Mail,* writings that were later collected in *Pharos
& Pharillion: An Evocation of Alexandria* (Hogarth Press, 1923).

Fry, Roger (Elliot) (1866–1934): Art critic and painter, the eldest member
of the Bloomsbury Group and organizer of the first and second Post-
Impressionist exhibitions (1910, 1912). After working (with his sisters)

in France organizing a Quaker relief fund for victims of the war (1915), on 9 November 1915 he exhibited war images in his one-man show at the Alpine Club Gallery, including "a large oil and *papier collé* composition called *German General Staff*," in which the German generals are literally, as Fry said, "men without feet." Fry is thought to have used this painting in an (unsuccessful) effort to win appointment as an official war artist (Cork, 79–80; Collins, 122–24). During the war years he struggled to keep alive the Omega Workshops (which he had founded with Vanessa Bell [above] and Duncan Grant [below] before the war) and sought to find work for artists and conscientious objectors (Woolf, *RF*, 202, 213).

Garnett, David ("Bunny") (1892–1981): Before the war, friend of Adrian Stephen, Virginia Woolf's younger brother. During the first year of the war (June 1915), he went to France to join the Friends' War Victims Relief Fund (see Roger Fry, above). In 1916, he and Duncan Grant were called before the Blything Tribunal to defend their status as conscientious objectors. After intervention by Maynard Keynes at the Appeal Tribunal, both were granted exemption from combative service and lived at Charleston and worked at Newhouse Farm, Firle (Spalding, 152). In 1942 Garnett married Angelica Bell, Vanessa Bell and Duncan Grant's daughter, after having declared his intention to do so shortly after Angelica's birth in December 1918.

Grant, Duncan (James Corrowr) (1885–1978): A cousin of Lytton Strachey and the youngest member of prewar Bloomsbury, he began the Omega Workshops with Roger Fry and Vanessa Bell (1913). In 1915 Duncan and Vanessa lived at Wissett Lodge, where they painted and Duncan acted as a fruit farmer, raising apples and some livestock. After the death of Rupert Brooke (above), Duncan Grant worked on *In Memorium: Rupert Brooke 1915*, an oil and collage on panel (Cork, 79). After being called before the tribunal (see Vanessa Bell, David Garnett, above), Charleston became their permanent home and the two men secured work "of national importance" at a nearby farm (as Maynard Keynes advised [Skidelsky 327]).

Graves, Robert (von Ranke) (1895–1986): Educated at Charterhouse and a published poet at age eighteen; instead of entering Oxford in 1914, and although he "remained bitterly opposed to warfare," he became an officer in the Royal Welch Fusiliers (R. P. Graves, 110–11). Suffering from bronchitis and shell-shock in 1917, he was sent to a hospital at Somerville to recover, and regularly spent weekends at Garsington (see Ottoline

Morrell, below). He interceded on behalf of Siegfried Sassoon after the
publication of his antiwar declaration, and convinced the authorities of
"the mental collapse of a brother-in-arms" (R. Graves, *Goodbye*, 216).
After demobilization, Graves went to Oxford (October 1919). His autobiography, *Goodbye to All That*, which describes his life through the
Great War, was published in 1929, and in 1940 *The Long Week-End: A
Social History of Great Britain 1918–1939* by Graves and Alan Hodge was
published.

Gurney, Ivor (Bertie) (1890–1937): Born in Gloucester, won a scholarship
in composition at the Royal College of Music before the war (from
1911). He volunteered and served as a private on the western front with
the Gloucester Regiment (1915–17), where he was wounded and gassed.
During the war he wrote two volumes of poems: *Severn and Somme*
(1917) and *War's Embers* (1919). He was admitted to a mental institution
in 1922 and "continued to write 'war poetry,' convinced that the war was
still going on" until his death in the City of London Mental Hospital
(Fussell, *Great War*, 74; Drabble 424).

Hewlett, Maurice (Henry) (1861–1923): In 1898, published *The Forest Lover*,
his first novel, which signaled the beginning of his debt to the "costume
fiction of the nineteenth century" (Hynes, "Maurice Hewlett," 178). Before the war his wife, Hilda Hewlett, operated a flying school and is
thought to have trained the first six British officers to become pilots
(182). Hewlett was working on "his most ambitious effort to write a last-
ing poem" (*The Song of the Plow*) when war was declared and continued working on it until March 1916 (185–86). Virginia Woolf reviewed
his poem *The Village Wife's Lament* on 12 September 1918 in the *TLS*.

Keynes, John Maynard (1883–1946): Entered King's College, Cambridge
in 1902, and in February 1903 was elected an Apostle. Was a member of
the Bloomsbury Group, sharing rooms in 1909 with Duncan Grant and
in 1911 with Virginia Woolf, Duncan Grant, Adrian Stephen, and, later,
Leonard Woolf. On 2 August 1914, as England prepared for war, Keynes
was invited to the Treasury, but as he was not offered a post in Whitehall until January 1915, he spent the fall term teaching economics at a
"Cambridge depopulated of undergraduates" (Skidelsky, 294). Although
he had secured from the Treasury a six-month certificate of exemption
from military service in February 1916, he also claimed exemption as a
conscientious objector and assisted David Garnett and Duncan Grant
in their efforts (see David Garnett, Duncan (James Corrowr) Grant,
above), as well as Gerald Shove and several others. Ten days after the

armistice, he was, as he wrote to his mother, "put in principal charge of financial matters for the Peace Conference" (353). Keynes resigned from the Treasury in 1919 in "misery and rage," over the terms of the Treaty of Versailles and wrote *The Economic Consequences of the Peace,* which was published on 12 December 1919 (378, 384).

Lawrence, D(avid) H(erbert) (1885–1930): Born in Nottinghamshire, a poet, short-story writer, and published novelist before the war, he spent the war years in England with his German-born wife, Frieda von Richthofen Weekley. His fourth novel, *The Rainbow* (1915), was declared obscene and seized. He was declared unfit for service in 1916. In 1916 he finished writing *Women in Love,* which was not published until after the war (1920 in New York, 1921 in London). While he and his wife were living in Cornwall in 1917, they were suspected of being German agents, and his volume of poems *Look! We Have Come Through!* was published. In 1919 he and his wife left England for Italy and while in Australia in 1922, he wrote *Kangaroo* (1923).

Macaulay, Dame (Emilie) Rose (1881–1958): Attended Somerville College, Oxford (1900–3) and published six novels and one book of poetry before the war. After Rupert Brooke's death in 1915, Macaulay joined the V.A.D. and worked as a "scrubber" in a convalescent hospital at Mount Blow near Great Shelford (Emery, 152), leaving the V.A.D. after her father's death (6 July). In 1916 she published the antiwar novel *Non-Combatants and Others,* and in 1917 she worked as a clerk in the Exemptions Bureau of the Ministry of War in London and published a second volume of poems; in 1918 she was placed in the Department of Propaganda; and in 1918–19 she was moved to the Ministry of Information and was a reader for Constable, a publishing house. In 1919 she published *What Not,* which was written during the war, and in 1920 *Potterism: A Tragi-Farcical Tract,* her "newspaper novel," whose "theme is the debasement of language and thought by the popular press" (Emery, 185), controlled during the war by Lords Northcliffe and Beaverbrook "in conjunction with the political maneuvering of Lloyd George" (Bensen, 68).

MacCarthy, Sir (Charles Otto) Desmond (1877–1952): Attended Trinity College, Cambridge (1894–98), an Apostle and member of the Bloomsbury Group. Joined the staff of the *New Statesman* as dramatic critic in 1913. During the first winter of the Great War, he was an ambulance driver and stretcher bearer with the Red Cross, assigned to serve with the French Army (1914–15). He returned to London the following spring and rejoined the *New Statesman. Remnants,* a collection of his articles, was published in April 1918 and seven memoirs of his experiences of the war are included in the sixty-two published in *Experience* (1935).

MacCarthy, Mary Josefa ("Molly") (née Warre-Cornish) (1882–1953): Married Desmond MacCarthy in 1906. In January 1915 she "took Desmond" to the Porch, Freshwater, Isle of Wright, "to live cheaply & write a novel" (*Diary* 1, 27 and n.78). Her only novel, *A Pier and a Band,* was sent to Chatto & Windus in January 1918 and was published. According to Miranda Seymour, "Among the Bloomsbury women, only Molly MacCarthy was unexpectedly warlike" (202). After the war, she wrote *A Nineteenth-Century Childhood* (1924), a memoir.

Mansfield, Katherine (Beauchamp) (1888–1923): Moved from New Zealand to London in 1903, married George Bowden in March 1909, and published Bavarian sketches in the *New Age* (1910). In 1911 she published "In a German Pension" and met John Middleton Murry, whom she married in May 1918, shortly after her divorce became final and seven months before the armistice. During the war, she traveled to Paris several times (see Mortelier; Bardolph). In 1915 her only brother, Leslie Heron Beauchamp, was killed in a hand grenade accident in France. In 1916 she first visited Garsington (see Ottoline Morrell, below); began work as a translator at the War Office; and met Virginia Woolf.

Matthaei, Louise Ernestine (1880–1969): Classical scholar and then fellow and director of studies at Newnham College, Cambridge (1909–16). Said to have left "under a cloud" during the war, allegedly owing to her father's German origins (*Diary* 1, 135–36 and n.14).

Morrell, Lady Ottoline (Violet Anne) (née Cavendish-Bentinck) (1873–1938): Literary hostess and friend to a large circle of literary and political figures (including Bertrand Russell [below], with whom she maintained a long-term relationship, through the war years and his brief imprisonment in 1918 for an article published in the newspaper of the No Conscription Fellowship), had married Philip Morrell (below) in 1902. Before the war (March 1913), Ottoline Morrell and her husband bought Garsington Manor, which served as a refuge for refugees, pacifists, and conscientious objectors during the war. During the first year of war, O. Morrell also became part of "Friends of Foreigners," a relief organization to help those "whose lives had been destroyed by the war" (Seymour, 203).

Morrell, Philip Edward (1870–1943): Married in 1902 (see Ottoline Morrell, above), Liberal member of Parliament, his first seat was in 1906 (representing South Oxfordshire) and in 1910 (representing Burnley). On 3 August 1914, two days after Germany declared war on Russia, P. Morrell addressed a hostile House of Commons on staying out of the war. Later, having voted against the first and second Conscription Bills (1916), P. Morell advised the Burnley Liberals that he would not stand at the next election (Darroch, 167–68). Yet, he did not lose his seat until the general election of 1918 (Seymour, 283n).

Murry, John Middleton (1889–1957): Before the war, while an undergraduate at Brasenose College, Oxford, he was editor of *Rhythm* (later *The Blue Review*) (1911–13), through which he met Katherine Mansfield (above), whom he married on 3 May 1918. He joined the staff of the *Westminster Gazette* before the war (1912) and from 1914 served as a full-time reviewer and art critic. In September 1916 he was hired as a translator at the War Office; his *Fyodor Dostoyevsky: A Critical Study* and *Still Life,* a novel, were published in 1916 as well. After the armistice (December 1918), Murry published his *Poems 1917–1918.* Early in 1919, after becoming editor of the *Athenaeum* and resigning from his position as chief censor, his poem *The Critic in Judgment* was published by the Hogarth Press (*Letters of John Middleton Murry to Katherine Mansfield,* ed. C. A. Hankin).

Northcliffe, Lord (Alfred Charles William Harmsworth, 1st Viscount Northcliffe) (1865–1922): Born in Dublin, "largely self-educated, rejecting Cambridge and the bar for journalism" (Drabble, 435), an acknowledged "press lord" in England before the war (Chisholm and Davie, 92), owning the *Evening News* (with his brothers); the *Daily Mail;* the *Daily Mirror* (which was "devoted exclusively to women's interests" [Drabble]), and the *Times of London.* During the war, he led a war mission to the United States (1917) and was the director of British propaganda in enemy nations (1918). In 1917 *At the War* by Lord Northcliffe was "published for the Joint War Committee of the British Red Cross Society, and the Order of St. John of Jerusalem in England" (i).

Owen, Wilfred (1893–1918): Educated in Liverpool and at Shrewsbury Technical College, before the war he taught English in Bordeaux (1913–15). Returned to England in September 1915, intending to join the Artists' Rifles. Commissioned into the Manchester Regiment in June 1916 and sailed to France in December, attached to Lancashire Fusiliers. His first experience in the trenches was in January 1917, and "he was in and out of the line half a dozen times during the first four months of 1917" (Fussell, *Great War,* 289). Suffering from "neurasthenia" (or shell-shock), he was removed to Craiglockhart War Hospital, Edinburgh, in June 1917 where he met Siegfried Sassoon (below). Owen was released in fall 1917 and assigned to light duty at a Scarborough facility in November. He returned to France in September 1918 and, "already the winner of the Military Cross, was leading his men in an attack on the Western Front when he was machine-gunned to death," a week before the armistice (Fussell, *Norton*, 163). Only five of his poems were published during the Great War; the first edition of his poems (edited and with a memoir by Edmund Blunden) was published in 1931.

Partridge, (Reginald) "Ralph" Sherring (1894–1960): Passed the examination for Sandhurst, but never attended. Before the war, entered Christ Church, Oxford (1913), to which he returned after the war (Gadd, 136). Served in the army, in the 48th Divisional Cyclists' Company where he met Gerald Brenan (above). In the summer of 1918, he met Dora Carrington (above), to whom he was married after the war (1921), during his tenure at the Hogarth Press (1920–23).

Rathbone, Irene (1892–1980): Before the war, sought a career on the stage. A V.A.D. during the war, she worked at YMCA camps in France. Rathbone's experiences are the basis for *We That Were Young* (1932) (see Knight, "Introduction").

Richmond, Sir Bruce (Lyttelton) (1871–1964): Joined the *Times of London* in 1899 and was editor of the *Times Literary Supplement* from its founding in 1902, through the Great War and until 1938.

Russell, Bertrand (Arthur William) (1872–1970): Attended Trinity College, Cambridge, an Apostle and friends with members of the Bloomsbury Group. Before the war, he had invented the Theory of Descriptions, written *The Principles of Mathematics* (1903) and (in collaboration with A. N. Whitehead) *Principia Mathematica* (1910). Russell was with Ottoline Morrell (above) when war was declared and "at Christmas time in 1914, by Ottoline's advice . . . I took to visiting destitute Germans on behalf of a charitable committee to investigate their circumstances and to relieve their distress if they deserved it" (Russell, *Autobiography* 2, 8). In 1915 he wrote *Principles of Social Reconstruction* (published as *Why Men Fight* in the United States). With the coming of conscription, Russell devoted himself to the affairs of conscientious objectors and the No Conscription Fellowship. Russell lost his position at Cambridge because of his opposition to the Great War and was sent to Brixton Prison because of an article published in *The Tribunal,* the newspaper of the No Conscription Fellowship, in January 1918. While he was incarcerated, the military age was raised. Russell became liable to military service, and was called up for a medical examination, "but the Government with its utmost efforts was unable to find out where I was, having forgotten that it had put me in prison" (127).

Sackville-West, Victoria Mary ("Vita") (1892–1962): In 1913 she married Harold Nicolson (a diplomat in Foreign Service, who played a role in the Peace Conference in Paris after the war) and two days after the beginning of the war, their first son, Benedict Nicolson, was born. In 1915 they bought Long Barn, near Knole, and in 1916 Harold was exempted from military service because of his work in the Foreign Office. Vita's *Poems of the West and East* was published in 1917, the same year as the birth of her second son, Nigel Nicolson. After her first novel, *Heritage* (1919), was accepted for publication early in 1918, she began to write her novel *Challenge* (1923, United States), which would not be published in England until 1974. She met Virginia Woolf in 1922, and the Hogarth Press began publishing her books in 1924.

Sassoon, Siegfried (Loraine) (1886–1967): Educated at Clare College, Cambridge, he volunteered for military service several days before England declared war on 4 August 1914. His arrival at the front was delayed owing to a riding accident in January 1915, and, according to Robert Wohl, it was a "series of lucky accidents, illnesses, and nonfatal wounds between 1915 and 1918 that kept Sassoon from the front and thus helped to save his life" (*Generation*, 96–97). He finally went to France as a Royal Welch Fusilier in November 1915, and in June 1916 won the Military Cross. In September 1916 he spent a week at Garsington (see Ottoline Morrell, above) and returned to France in February 1917. In June 1917 his antiwar statement ("Finished with the War: A Soldier's Declaration") was published and, thanks to the intervention of Robert Graves (above), he was pronounced "neurasthenic" and sent to Craiglockhart War Hospital where he met Wilfred Owen (above). Woolf reviewed his *The Old Huntsman and Other Poems* for the *TLS* in May 1917 and *Counter-attack and Other Poems* in July 1918. After the war, Sassoon wrote the largely autobiographical trilogy *Memoirs of a Fox-Hunting Man* (1928), *Memoirs of an Infantry Officer* (1930), and *Sherston's Progress* (1936) (see also Sternlicht).

Simon, Lady Shena Dorothy (née Potter) (1883–1972): Educated at Newnham College, Cambridge (1904–7), married Sir Ernest Simon. During the war, she lost her only brother in 1916 and worked for the League of Nations Union. When she met Virginia Woolf in June 1933, she was a city councillor in Manchester. Before World War II, she trained as an air raid warden.

Sinclair, May (Mary Amelia St Clair) (1863–1946): Educated at home, save for one year at Cheltenham Ladies' College (Drabble, 905). A well-known novelist and poet before the war, she published *Journal of Impressions in Belgium* in 1915, based on her experiences as secretary and publicist to a Motor Ambulance Unit (Tylee, 27). In the last years of the war, she published two war novels, *Tasker Jevons* (1916) and *The Tree of Heaven* (1917). After the war, in 1920, she won the first Femina-Vie Heureuse prize for *William—An Englishman* (1919), which involves how "an ordinary little man is affected by his experience of the German invasion of Belgium" (Tylee, 134).

Spearing, E[velyn] M[ary] (Simpson) (1885–1963): Research on Elizabethan drama at Cambridge was interrupted by the war, during which she was a V.A.D., first in Cambridge at a Red Cross Hospital and then in France.

Stephen, Adrian Leslie (1883–1948): Younger brother of Virginia Woolf, read law at Trinity College, Cambridge. Although he had "announced his intention of enlisting" during the first weeks after the declaration of war (Spalding, 132), he remained a "committed pacifist," and served as secretary of the No Conscription Fellowship and treasurer of the National Council for Civil Liberties during the war (Hussey, *A to Z,* 263–64). In 1916 Adrian participated in the military exemption hearings of Duncan Grant and David Garnett, along with Philip Morrell and John Maynard Keynes. And, to maintain his own status as a conscientious objector, he worked on a farm, but because of a strain to his heart, he received a doctor's order to cease in October 1917. Adrian married Karen Costelloe two months after the start of the war; the first of their children (Ann) was born two years later and their second (Karin Judith) nine days after the armistice. After the war, Adrian and his wife studied medicine, planning to become psychoanalysts.

Strachey, (Giles) Lytton (1880–1932): Went to Trinity College, Cambridge, in 1899, and in 1902 was elected a member of the Apostles. Was writing *Eminent Victorians* (1918) when the war began. Had been involved with the No Conscription Fellowship and the National Council Against Conscription, and when called for military service in March 1916, he claimed exemption on the grounds of being a conscientious objector, although, as Michael Holroyd points out, he was an "invalid" who would not have been accepted on the grounds of health alone (569). He was declared unfit for service of any kind in June 1916. By 1917 he completed *Eminent Victorians,* and was living with Carrington (above) at Tidmarsh.

Tennent, R.J[osephine]. (née Pennell) (1898–?): In 1918, accepted as a V.A.D. ambulance driver for a convoy organized by the British Red Cross to replace an Army Service convoy (see Knightley, 94, and Macdonald). She was awarded a military medal for heroism during an air raid in France, and in 1978 wrote *Red Herrings of 1918,* a memoir of her experiences, drawn mainly from letters to her family.

Walpole, Sir Hugh Seymour (1884–1941): Born in New Zealand, he attended Emmanuel College, Cambridge, and had published three novels before the war. During the war, he worked with the Russian Red Cross and wrote *The Dark Forest* (1916), based on his experience. Woolf reviewed his novel *The Green Mirror* in the *Times Literary Supplement* (24 January 1918). After the war Walpole published a historical sequence (four books) called the *Herries Chronicle* (1930–33).

Webb, Beatrice (née Potter) (1858–1943): Before the war, with her husband, **Sidney Webb,** (1859–1947), founded the *New Statesman* (1913). Met the Woolfs when they asked Leonard to write a supplement to "International Government," published by Allen and Unwin and the Fabian Society (1915), of which they were founding members. During the war, B. Webb lectured on "the War and the Spirit of Revolt" until she became ill (with cancer, it was thought). During her convalescence, she knit socks for soldiers and began to edit her diaries and write an autobiography. She also worked with her husband on a pamphlet involving the war aims of the Labour Party (Muggeridge and Adam, 208–12).

Wells, H(erbert) G(eorge) (1866–1946): Before the war, an established author and (since 1903) a member of the Fabian Society (see Beatrice Webb, above). The day after England entered the war, Rebecca West gave birth to Wells's son, Anthony West. In his memoir, A. West claims that his father had "been predicting the big war as far back as 1908" (23). During the war, H. G. Wells's output included *Boon* (1915); a series of articles for the *Daily Express,* "The War That Will End War," a slogan he would also use in *Mr Britling Sees It Through* (1916), a novel about the advent of the war; and *The Elements of Reconstruction* (1916), called a "turning point in journalism, from focus on England to world affairs" (Smith, xvi). In February 1918 he was asked to chair the Policy Committee for Propaganda in Enemy Countries, a post he resigned in June (A. West, 62–64). Between mid-July and September 1918, he began to plan his *Outline of History* (1920). He also worked with Leonard Woolf on establishing the League of Nations, and had met Virginia Woolf during the war, in 1917 (Hussey, *A to Z,* 363–64).

West, Dame Rebecca (Cecily Isabel Fairfield) (1892–1983): Educated at George Watson's Ladies College in Edinburgh and the Academy of Dramatic Arts, she found employment on the staff of *The Freewoman* (1911), which became *The New Freewoman* and finally the *Egoist,* and was called at the time "a technical trade journal on Womanhood." She wrote for *The Clarion* (1912–13) and six weeks before the war, she published a story in the first issue of *Blast* (Marcus, ed., *Young Rebecca,* 1–17). Her son, Anthony West (see H. G. Wells, above), was born the day after the war began and during the first two years of the war, West worked at the *Daily News* and wrote *Henry James* (1916). Her first novel, *The Return of the Soldier,* was published in 1918.

Woolf, Cecil Nathan Sidney (1887–1917): Younger brother of Leonard Woolf, educated at Trinity College, Cambridge. Cecil and brother Philip (below) "joined up from the first day of the war," and were commissioned in the Hussars (*BgA,* 177). Sent to France, Cecil was killed in the Battle of Cambrai on 29 November 1917. He was buried in a cemetery in France. A commemorative volume of his poems ("*Poems* by C. N. Sidney Woolf/Late 20th Hussars . . . /Fellow of Trinity College, Cambridge") was printed at the Hogarth Press (1918).

Woolf, Leonard Sidney (1890–1969): Educated at Trinity College, Cambridge (1899–1904), the first Jew elected to the Apostles. A member of prewar Bloomsbury, he married Virginia Stephen on 10 August 1912. Published his second (and last) novel (*The Wise Virgins*) and two pamphlets (on trade unionism and on education and trade unionism) before the war in 1914, the year after meeting Beatrice and Sidney Webb and becoming involved with the Fabian Society. After the war began, Leonard did some reviewing, published a supplement on the League of Nations ("International Government") in the *New Statesman* (1915) (see Beatrice Webb, above), and began a book about the Co-operative Movement. Was twice called up for military duty and was twice exempted by the Tribunal (1916 and 1917) (see Dr. Maurice Craig, above). In 1917 Leonard Woolf organized the 1917 Club (to provide the Labour Party with "some equivalent" to the "society salons" where much of the "business of the Conservative and Liberal Parties was conducted" [quoted in Hussey, *A to Z,* 192]); and the Woolfs purchased the Hogarth Press. In the last year of the war, Leonard became "entangle[d]" with the Labour Party (*BgA,* 226), and in 1918 he published *After the War* and *A Durable Settlement after the War by Means of a League of Nations* and was appointed secretary to the Labour Party Advisory Committee on International Questions (Hussey, *A to Z,* 373). After the war, he was a candidate for Parliament and political editor of the *Nation.*

Woolf, Philip Sidney (1889–1962): Youngest brother of Leonard Woolf, before the war he studied painting. Joined up with brother Cecil (above) after both brothers had served in the Territorial Army (the Inns of Court Regiment) (1912–14). In the Battle of Cambrai (November 1917) Philip was wounded by the same shell as the one that killed Cecil. Philip was sent to recuperate at Fishmongers Hall, London, and was returned to France in July 1918. Demobilized in 1919, he trained as a farmer and eventually secured a position as estate manager of Waddeson Manor in Buckinghamshire.

Woolf, (Adeline) Virginia (née Stephen) (1882–1941): Educated at home, before the war she had married Leonard Woolf (1912) and completed her first novel, *The Voyage Out,* which was accepted for publication in April 1913. She and Leonard Woolf (above) were at Asheham when the declaration of war was issued on 4 August 1914, and when *The Voyage Out* was published on 26 March 1915, she was at a nursing home and her husband organized their move to Hogarth House in London. During the last three years of the war (1916–18), Woolf wrote more than eighty review and periodical articles and her second novel (*Night and Day,* 1919), and in 1916–17, when her husband and friends in Bloomsbury were being called before the tribunal, she wrote letters on behalf of their petitions for conscientious objector status. Her story "A Mark on the Wall" and Leonard's "Three Jews" were the first publication of the Hogarth Press in 1917: *Two Stories.* (See also Leonard Woolf, above).

WORKS CITED

Abel, Elizabeth. *Virginia Woolf and the Fiction of Psychoanalysis*. Chicago: Univ. of Chicago Press, 1989.

Alvarez, A. *The Savage God: A Study of Suicide*. 1971. New York: W. W. Norton, 1990.

Ariès, Philippe. *The Hour of Our Death*. Translated by Helen Weaver. New York: Alfred A. Knopf, 1981.

Asquith, Lady Cynthia. *Diaries: 1915–1918*. London: Hutchinson, 1968.

Banks, Joanne Trautmann. "Some Woolf Letters." *Modern Fiction Studies*. 30, no. 2 (Summer 1984): 175–202.

Bardolph, Jacqueline. "The French Connection: Bandol." In *Katherine Mansfield*, edited by Roger Robinson, 158–72. Baton Rouge: Louisiana State Univ. Press, 1994.

Barker, Pat. *The Eye in the Door*. 1993. New York: Dutton, 1994.

———. *The Ghost Road*. New York: William Abrahams/Dutton, 1995.

———. *Regeneration*. 1991. New York: Plume, 1993.

Barthes, Roland. *Writing Degree Zero*. Translated by Annette Lavers and Colin Smith. New York: Hill and Wang, 1977.

Bazin, Nancy Topping, and Jane Hamovit Lauter. "Virginia Woolf's Keen Sensitivity to War: Its Roots and Its Impact on Her Novels." In *Virginia Woolf and War*, edited by Mark Hussey, 14–39. Syracuse: Syracuse Univ. Press, 1991.

Becker, Ernest. *The Denial of Death*. New York: Free Press, 1973.

Beer, Gillian. "Hume, Stephen and Elegy in *To the Lighthouse*." *Essays in Criticism*. 34, no. 1 (Jan. 1984): 33–55. In *Virginia Woolf's "To the Lighthouse*," edited by Harold Bloom, 75–93.

Bell, Julian. *Essays, Poems, and Letters*. Edited by Quentin Bell. London: Hogarth Press, 1938.

———, ed. *We Did Not Fight: 1914–1918. Experiences of War Resisters*. London: Cobden-Sanderson, 1935.

Bell, Quentin. "The Biographer, the Critic, and the Lighthouse." *Ariel: A Review of International English Literature* 2, no. 1 (Jan. 1971): 94–101.

———. *Bloomsbury Recalled*. New York: Columbia Univ. Press, 1995.

———. *Virginia Woolf: A Biography.* New York: Harcourt Brace Jovanovich, 1972.

Bensen, Alice R. *Rose Macaulay.* New York: Twayne, 1969.

Bergson, Henri. *Matter and Memory.* Translated by N. M. Paul and W. S. Palmer. New York: Zone Books, 1991.

Binyon, Laurence. *For Dauntless France: An Account of Britain's Aid to the French Wounded and Victims of the War.* London: Hodder and Stoughton [1918].

Bishop, Edward (E. L.). "The Shaping of *Jacob's Room:* Woolf's Manuscript Revisions." *Twentieth Century Literature* 32 (Spring 1986): 115–35.

———. "The Subject in *Jacob's Room.*" *Modern Fiction Studies.* 38 (Spring 1992): 147–75.

Blackstone, Bernard. *Virginia Woolf: A Commentary.* N.Y.: Harcourt Brace Jovanovich, n.d.

Bloom, Harold, ed. *Clarissa Dalloway.* New York: Chelsea House, 1990.

———. *Virginia Woolf's "To the Lighthouse."* New York: Chelsea House, 1988.

Blunden, Edmund. "Infantry Passes By." In *Promise of Greatness,* edited by George A. Panichas, 23–37. New York: John Day, 1968.

———. *Undertones of War.* 1928. Harmondsworth, England: Penguin, 1987.

Blunden, Edmund, Cyril Falls, H. M. Tomlinson and R. Wright, comp. *The War, 1914–1918: A Booklist.* London: The Reader, 1929.

Boorman, Derek. *At the Going Down of the Sun: British First World War Memorials.* York, England: William Sessions: 1988.

Booth, Allyson. *Postcards from the Trenches: Negotiating the Space Between Modernism and the First World War.* New York: Oxford Univ. Press, 1996.

Booth, Wayne C. *A Rhetoric of Irony.* Chicago: Univ. of Chicago Press, 1974.

Borg, Alan. *War Memorials: From Antiquity to the Present.* London: Leo Cooper, 1991.

Bourke, Joanna. *Dismembering the Male: Men's Bodies, Britain, and the Great War.* London: Reaktion Books, 1996.

Brenan, Gerald. "A Survivor's Story." In *Promise of Greatness,* edited by George A. Panichas, 38–52. New York: John Day, 1968.

British Gazette. 8 issues. London: H. H. Stationary Office, 1926.

British Worker: Official Strike News Bulletin. 10 issues. London: General Council of the Trades Union Congress, 1926.

Brittain, Vera. *Testament of Experience: An Autobiographical Story of the Years 1925–1940.* 1957. London: Virago, 1979.

———. *Testament of Friendship: The Story of Winifred Holtby.* New York: Seaview Books, 1981.

———. *Testament of Youth: An Autobiographical Study of the Years 1900–1925.* 1933. New York: Penguin, 1989.

———. "War Service in Perspective." In *Promise of Greatness,* edited by George A. Panichas, 363–76.

———. *Women's Work in Modern England.* London: N. Douglas, 1928.

Brooke, Rupert. *The Letters of Rupert Brooke,* edited by Geoffrey Keynes. New York: Harcourt, Brace and World, 1968.

Brown, Malcolm. *The Imperial War Museum Book of the First World War: A Great Conflict Recalled in Previously Unpublished Letters, Diaries, Documents and Memoirs.* Norman: Univ. of Oklahoma Press, [1991] 1993.

Buber, Martin. *I and Thou.* Translated by Walter Kaufmann. New York: Charles Scribner's Sons, 1970.

Buckley, Jerome Hamilton. *Tennyson: The Growth of a Poet.* 1960. Cambridge, Mass.: Harvard Univ. Press, 1974.

Buitenhuis, Peter. *The Great War of Words: Literature as Propaganda 1914–18 and After.* London: B. T. Batsford, 1989.

Burke, Peter. *Montaigne.* 1981. New York: Hill and Wang, 1982.

Burt, John. "Irreconcilable Habits of Thought in *A Room of One's Own* and *To the Lighthouse.*" *ELH* 49, no. 4 (Winter 1982): 889–907.

Caine, Barbara. "Beatrice Webb and Her Diary." *Victorian Studies* 27, no. 1 (Autumn 1983): 81–89.

Cameron, Julia Margaret. *Victorian Photographs of Famous Men and Fair Women.* 1926. Boston: David R. Godine, 1973.

Cannadine, David. *The Decline and Fall of the British Aristocracy.* 1990. New York: Anchor Books, 1992.

———. "War and Death, Grief and Mourning in Modern Britain." In *Mirrors of Mortality: Studies in the Social History of Death,* edited Joachim Whaley, 187–242. New York: St Martin's, 1982.

Carrington, Charles Edmund. "Some Soldiers." In *Promise of Greatness,* edited by George A. Panichas, 155–66. New York: John Day, 1968.

Chapman, Wayne K., and Janet M. Manson. "Carte and Tierce: Leonard, Virginia Woolf, and War for Peace." In *Virginia Woolf and War,* edited by Mark Hussey, 58–78. Syracuse: Syracuse Univ. Press, 1991.

Chesler, Phyllis. *Women and Madness.* 1972. San Diego: Harcourt Brace Jovanovich, 1989.

Chisholm, Anne, and Michael Davie. *Lord Beaverbrook: A Life.* New York: Alfred A. Knopf, 1993.

Clausewitz, Carl von. *On War.* Translated by J. J. Graham. 1908. Edited by Anatol Rapoport. Harmondsworth, England: Penguin, 1968.

Cobley, Evelyn. *Representing War: Form and Ideology in First World War Narratives.* Toronto: Univ. of Toronto Press, 1993.

Cohn, Dorrit. "Narrated Monologue: Definition of a Fictional Style." *Comparative Literature* 18 (Spring 1966): 97–112.

Collins, Judith. *The Omega Workshops.* Chicago: Univ. of Chicago Press, 1984.

Compact Edition of the Oxford English Dictionary. 2 vols. 1971. New York: Oxford Univ. Press, 1979.

Cooke, Miriam, and Angela Woollacott, eds. *Gendering War Talk*. Princeton: Princeton Univ. Press, 1993.

Cooper, Helen M., Adrienne Auslander Munich, and Susan Merrill Squier, ed. *Arms and the Woman: War, Gender, and Literary Representation*. Chapel Hill: Univ. of North Carolina Press, 1989.

Cooper, J. C. *An Illustrated Encylopedia of Traditional Symbols*. London: Thames and Hudson, 1978.

Cork, Richard. *A Bitter Truth: Avant-Garde Art and the Great War*. New Haven: Yale Univ. Press, 1994.

Corsa, Helen Storm. "*To the Lighthouse*: Death, Mourning, and Transfiguration." *Literature and Psychology* 21, no. 3: 115–31.

Cramer, Patricia. "'Loving in the War Years': The War of Images in *The Years*." In *Virginia Woolf and War*, edited by Mark Hussey, 203–24. Syracuse Univ. Press, 1991.

Dangerfield, George. *The Strange Death of Liberal England 1910–1914*. 1935. New York: Capricorn, 1961.

Darroch, Sandra Jobson. *Ottoline: The Life of Lady Ottoline Morrell*. New York: Coward, McCann, and Geoghegan, 1975.

"Dean Inge at St. Paul's. Spirit of the Marty-Patriot." *Times of London*, 5 Apr. 1915, 8.

Death notice. "Rupert Brooke." *Times of London*, 26 Apr. 1915, 1.

DeSalvo, Louise. *Virginia Woolf: The Impact of Childhood Sexual Abuse on Her Life and Work*. Boston: Beacon Press, 1989.

Deutsch, Helene. *Neuroses and Character Types: Clinical Psychoanalytic Studies*. New York: International Universities Press, 1965.

Dick, Susan. "The Restless Searcher: A Discussion of the Evolution of 'Time Passes' in *To the Lighthouse*." *English Studies in Canada* 5, no. 3 (Autumn 1979): 311–29.

——, ed. *The Complete Shorter Fiction of Virginia Woolf*. (See Woolf, Virginia. *The Complete Shorter Fiction* below)

——. *To the Lighthouse*. (See Woolf, Virginia. *To the Lighthouse*.)

——. "*To the Lighthouse*": *The Original Holograph Draft*. Toronto: Univ. of Toronto Press, 1982.

Die Sonderfahndungsliste G.B. [Gestapo arrest list for England.] Berlin, 1940. Hoover Institution Archives.

Directory Catalogue of the Henry W. and Albert A. Berg Collection of English and American Literature. 6 vols. Boston: G. K. Hall, 1969.

Drabble, Margaret, ed. *The Oxford Companion to English Literature*. 5th ed. Oxford: Oxford Univ. Press, 1985.

Durkheim, Emile. *Suicide: A Study in Sociology*. Translated by John A. Spaulding and George Simpson. Edited by George Simpson. Glencoe, Ill: Free Press, 1966.

Edel, Leon. *Bloomsbury: A House of Lions*. Philadelphia:Lippincott, 1979.

Edwards, Lee R. "War and Roses: The Politics of *Mrs Dalloway*." In *The Authority of Experience: Essays in Feminist Criticism*, edited by Arlyn Diamond and Lee R.

Edwards, 161–77. Amherst: Univ. of Massachusetts Press, 1977: rpt., *Clarissa Dalloway*, edited by Harold Bloom, 99–112. New York: Chelsea House, 1990.

Ehrenreich, Barbara. *Blood Rites: Origins and History of the Passions of War.* New York: Henry Holt, 1997.

Eksteins, Modris. *Rites of Spring: The Great War and the Birth of the Modern Age.* 1989. New York: Doubleday, 1990.

Elshtain, Jean Bethke. *Women and War.* New York: Basic Books, 1987.

Emery, Jane D. *Rose Macaulay: A Writer's Life.* London: John Murray, 1991.

"England's Duty." *Times of London,* 1 Aug. 1914, 6.

Enser, A. G. S. *A Subject Bibliography of the First World War: Books in English, 1914–1978.* London: André Deutsch, 1979.

Evans, William A. *Virginia Woolf: Strategist of Language.* Lanham, Md.: Univ. Press of America, 1989.

Farwell, Byron. *The Great War in Africa: 1914–1918.* New York: W. W. Norton, 1986.

Fedden, Henry Romily. *Suicide: A Social and Historical Study.* London: Peter Davies, 1938.

Ferrer, Daniel. *Virginia Woolf and the Madness of Language.* Translated by Geoffrey Bennington and Rachel Bowlby. London: Routledge, 1990.

Ferro, Marc. *The Great War: 1914–1918.* 1973. London: Ark, 1987.

Field, Frank. *British and French Writers of the First World War.* Cambridge: Cambridge Univ. Press, 1991.

Fleishman, Avrom. *The English Historical Novel: Walter Scott to Virginia Woolf.* Baltimore: Johns Hopkins Univ. Press, 1971.

———. *Virginia Woolf: A Critical Reading.* Baltimore: Johns Hopkins Univ. Press, 1975.

Flint, Kate. "Revising *Jacob's Room*: Virginia Woolf, Women, and Language." *Review of English Studies* 42 (Aug. 1991): 361–79.

———. "Virginia Woolf and the General Strike." *Essays in Criticism* 36, no. 4 (Oct. 1986): 319–34.

Florey, R. A. *The General Strike of 1926.* London: John Calder, 1980.

Fodor, M. W. "Rehearsal on the Channel." *New Republic* 103 (21 Oct. 1940): 551–53.

Forster, E. M. *Aspects of a Novel.* 1927. New York: Harcourt, Brace, and World, 1954.

Foucault, Michel. *Language, Counter-Memory, Practice: Selected Essays and Interviews.* Edited by Donald F. Bouchard. Translated by Donald F. Bouchard and Sherry Simon. Ithaca, N.Y.: Cornell Univ. Press, 1977.

"Four Young Poets." Review of *Escape and Fantasy: Poems* by George Rostrevor, *Jones's Wedding and Other Poems* by A. H. Sedgwick, *Forlorn Adventures* by Arthur Lewis Jenkins, and *Poems* by S. N. Sidney Woolf. *The Times Literary Supplement,* 23 Jan. 1919, 40.

Fredette, Raymond. *The Sky on Fire: The First Battle of Britain 1917–1918.* 1966. Washington D.C.: Smithsonian Institution Press, 1991.

Freud, Sigmund. *Beyond the Pleasure Principle.* 1920. Translated and edited by James Strachey. New York: W. W. Norton, 1961.

———. *Character and Culture.* Edited by Philip Rieff. New York: Collier, 1963

———. *Inhibitions, Symptoms and Anxiety.* 1926. Translated by Alix Strachey. Revised and edited by James Strachey. New York: W. W. Norton, 1959.

———. "Mourning and Melancholia." 1917. In *The Freud Reader,* edited by Peter Gay, 584–89. New York: W. W. Norton, 1989.

———. "Psychoanalysis and War Neurosis." Translated by James Strachey. 1921. In *Character and Culture,* 215–19.

———. *The Psychopathology of Everyday Life.* 1901. Translated and edited by James Strachey. London: Ernest Benn, 1966.

———. "Reflections upon War and Death." 1915. Translated by E. Colburn Maynes. In *Character and Culture,* 107–33.

———. *Totem and Taboo.* 1913. Translated by A. A. Brill. 1918. New York: Vantage, 1946.

———. "Why War?" Translated by James Strachey. *Character and Culture,* 134–47.

Friedman, Melvin J. "Three Experiences of the War: A Triptych." In *Promise of Greatness,* edited by George A. Panichas, 541–55. New York: John Day, 1968.

Fromm, Gloria G. "Re-inscribing *The Years:* Virginia Woolf, Rose Macaulay, and the Critics." *Journal of Modern Literature* 13 (July 1986): 289–306.

Fry, Roger. *Letters of Roger Fry.* 2 vols. Edited by Denys Sutton. London: Chatto and Windus, 1972.

Fussell, Paul. *The Great War and Modern Memory.* New York: Oxford Univ. Press, 1975.

———, ed. *The Norton Book of Modern War.* New York: W. W. Norton, 1991.

Gadd, David. *The Loving Friends: A Portrait of Bloomsbury.* New York: Harcourt Brace Jovanovich, 1974.

Galsworthy, John. *The Forsyte Saga.* 1922. New York: Scribner, 1996.

Gathorne-Hardy, Jonathon. *Gerald Brenan: The Interior Castle.* New York: W. W. Norton, 1993.

Gay, Peter. *Freud: A Life for Our Time.* New York: W. W. Norton, 1988.

Gibbs, Philip. *More That Must Be Told.* New York: Harper and Bros., 1921.

———. *Now It Can Be Told.* N.Y. and London: Harper and Bros., 1920.

Gilbert, Martin. *The First World War: A Complete History.* New York: Henry Holt, 1994.

Gilbert, Sandra M. "Soldier's Heart: Literary Men, Literary Women, and the Great War." In *Behind the Lines: Gender and the Two World Wars,* edited by Margaret Randolph Higonnet, Jane Jenson, Sonya Michel, and Margaret Collins Weitz, 197–226. New Haven: Yale Univ. Press, 1987.

———, and Susan Gubar. *No Man's Land: The Place of the Woman Writer in the Twentieth Century.* 3 vols. New Haven: Yale Univ. Press, 1988, 1989, 1994.

Gorer, Geoffrey. *Death, Grief, and Mourning in Contemporary Britain.* London: Cresset Press, 1965.

Gorham, Deborah. *Vera Brittain: A Feminist Life*. Oxford, England: Blackwell, 1996.

Goss, Hilton P. *Civilian Morale under Aerial Bombardment, 1914–1939*. Maxwell Air Force Base, Ala.: Air University, 1948.

Graham, J. W. "Manuscript Revision and the Heroic Theme of *The Waves*." *Twentieth Century Literature* 29, no. 3 (Fall 1983): 312–32.

———, ed. *"The Waves": The Two Holograph Drafts*. Toronto: Univ. of Toronto Press, 1976.

Graham, Stephen. *A Private in the Guards*. London: Macmillan, 1919.

Graves, Richard Perceval. *Robert Graves: The Assault Heroic 1895–1926*. London: Papermac, 1987.

Graves, Robert. *Good-bye to All That*. 1929. Harmondsworth, England: Penguin, 1981.

———. "The Kaiser's War: A British Point of View." *Promise of Greatness*, edited by George A. Panichas, 3–11. New York: John Day, 1968.

———, and Alan Hodge. *The Long Week-end: A Social History of Great Britain, 1918–1939*. 1940. New York: W. W. Norton, 1963.

"A Great Naval Anniversary." *Times of London*, 1 Aug. 1914, 9.

Gregory, Adrian. *The Silence of Memory: Armistice Day 1919–1946*. Oxford, England: Berg, 1994.

Hafley, James. *The Glass Roof: Virginia Woolf as Novelist*. New York: Russell and Russell, 1954.

Hankin, C. A., ed. *The Letters of John Middleton Murry to Katherine Mansfield*. New York: Franklin Watts, 1983.

Hankins, Leslie Kathleen. "A Splice of Reel Life in Virginia Woolf's 'Time Passes': Censorship, Cinema, and 'the usual battlefield of emotions.'" *Criticism* 35 (Winter 1993): 91–114.

Hanley, Lynne. *Writing War: Fiction, Gender, and Memory*. Amherst: Univ. of Massachusetts Press, 1991.

Harrisson, Tom. *Living Through the Blitz*. New York: Schocken, 1976.

Harper, Howard. *Between Language and Silence: The Novels of Virginia Woolf*. Baton Rouge: Louisiana State Univ. Press, 1982.

Hassall, Christopher. *Rupert Brooke: A Biography*. London: Faber and Faber, 1964.

Haule, James. "'Le Temps passe' and the Original Typescript: An Early Version of the 'Time Passes' Section of *To the Lighthouse*." *Twentieth-Century Literature: A Scholarly and Critical Journal* 29 (Fall 1983): 267–311.

———. "*To the Lighthouse* and the Great War: The Evidence of Virginia Woolf's Revisions of 'Time Passes.'" In *Virginia Woolf and War*, edited by Mark Hussey, 164–79. Syracuse: Syracuse Univ. Press, 1991.

———, and Philip H. Smith, Jr., eds. *A Concordance to the Novels of Virginia Woolf*. 3 vols. New York: Garland, 1991.

———. *A Concordance to "To the Lighthouse" by Virginia Woolf*. Oxford, England: Oxford Microfilm, 1982.

Havighurst, Alfred F. *Twentieth-Century Britain.* 2d ed. New York: Harper and Row, 1962.

Hearne, R. P. *Zeppelins and Super-Zeppelins.* London: John Lane, 1916.

Heilbrun, Carolyn G. *Toward a Recognition of Androgyny.* New York: Harper and Row, 1973.

———. *Writing a Woman's Life.* New York: W. W. Norton, 1988.

Heine, Elizabeth. "Postscript to the Diary of Virginia Woolf, Vol. 1: 'Effie's story' and *Night and Day.*" *Virginia Woolf Miscellany* 9(Winter 1977): 10.

Henke, Suzette A. "*Mrs Dalloway:* The Communion of Saints." In *New Feminist Essays on Virginia Woolf,* edited by Jane Marcus, 125–47. Lincoln: Univ. of Nebraska Press, 1981.

Hessler, John G. "Moral Accountability in *Mrs. Dalloway.*" *Renascence* 30 (Spring 1978): 126–36; rpt., *Clarissa Dalloway,* edited by Harold Bloom, 126–36. New York: Chelsea House, 1990.

Hewlett, Maurice. *The Village Wife's Lament.* London: Martin Secker, 1918.

Higonnet, Margaret R. "Not So Quiet in No-Woman's-Land." In *Gendering War Talk,* edited by Miriam Cooke and Angela Woollacott, 205–26.

———, Jane Jenson, Sonya Michel, and Margaret C. Weitz, eds. *Behind the Lines: Gender and the Two World Wars.* New Haven: Yale Univ. Press, 1987.

Hill, Jane. *The Art of Dora Carrington.* New York: Thames and Hudson, 1995.

Hirst, Francis W. *The Consequences of the War to Great Britain.* London: Humphrey Milford/Oxford Univ. Press, 1934.

Hoffman, Charles G. "'From Lunch to Dinner': Virginia Woolf's Apprenticeship." *Texas Studies in Literature and Language: A Journal of the Humanities* 10, no. 4 (Winter 1969): 609–27.

———. "From Short Story to Novel: The Manuscript Revisions of Virginia Woolf's *Mrs. Dalloway.*" *Modern Fiction Studies* 14, no. 2 (Summer 1968): 171–86.

———. "Virginia Woolf's Manuscript Revisions of *The Years.*" *PMLA* 84 (Jan. 1969): 79–89.

Hollingsworth, Keith. "Freud and the Riddle of *Mrs. Dalloway.*" In *Studies in Honor of John Wilcox,* edited by A. Dayle Wallace, 239–50. Freeport: Books for Libraries, 1958.

Holroyd, Michael. *Lytton Strachey: A Biography.* 1971. Harmondsworth, England: Penguin, 1987.

Holtby, Winifred. *Poor Caroline.* 1931. New York: Penguin-Virago, 1986.

———. *Virginia Woolf: A Critical Memoir.* 1932. Chicago: Cassandra, 1978.

Homberger, Eric. "The Story of the Cenotaph." *Times Literary Supplement,* 12 Nov. 1976, 1429–30.

Hummel, Madeline M. "From the Common Reader to the Uncommon Critic: *Three Guineas* and the Epistolary Form." *Bulletin of the New York Public Library* 80 (Winter 1977): 151–57.

Hungerford, Edward A. "Mrs. Woolf, Freud, and J. D. Beresford." *Literature and Psychology* 5 (Aug. 1955): 49–51.

Husserl, Edmund. *The Phenomenology of Internal Time-Consciousness.* Edited by Martin Heidegger. Translated by James S. Churchill. Bloomington: Indiana Univ. Press, 1964.

Hussey, Mark. Letter to the author, 27 July 1994.

———. "Living in a War Zone: An Introduction to Virginia Woolf as a War Novelist." In *Virginia Woolf and War: Fiction, Reality, and Myth,* edited by Mark Hussey, 1–13. Syracuse: Syracuse Univ. Press, 1991.

———. *The Singing of the Real World: The Philosophy of Virginia Woolf's Fiction.* Columbus: Ohio State Univ. Press, 1986.

———. *Virginia Woolf A to Z: A Comprehensive Reference for Students, Teachers, and Common Readers to Her Life, Work, and Critical Reception.* New York: Facts on File, 1995.

———, ed. *Virginia Woolf and War: Fiction, Reality, and Myth.* Syracuse: Syracuse Univ. Press, 1991.

Hynes, Samuel. *A War Imagined: The First World War and English Culture.* New York: Atheneum, 1991.

———. "Maurice Hewlett: An Edwardian Career." In his *Edwardian Occasions: Essays on English Writing in the Early Twentieth Century,* 173–90. New York: Oxford Univ. Press, 1972.

"Ilford Collision Inquiry." *Times of London,* 2 Jan. 1915, 5.

"Ilford Accident." *Times of London,* 5 Jan. 1915, 5.

Inglis, K. S. "The Homecoming: The War Memorial Movement in Cambridge, England." *Journal of Contemporary History* 27, no. 4 (1992): 583–605.

Jay, Martin. *Force Fields: Between Intellectual History and Cultural Critique.* New York: Routledge, 1993.

Johnson, Donald F. Goold. *Poems . . . with a Prefatory Note by P. Giles.* Cambridge, England: Cambridge Univ. Press, 1919.

Johnstone, J. K. "World War I and the Novels of Virginia Woolf." *Promise of Greatness,* edited by George A. Panichas, 528–40. New York: John Day, 1968.

Jones, Ernest. *The Life and Works of Sigmund Freud.* Edited by Lionel Trilling and Steven Marcus. New York: Basic Books, 1961.

Jones, Henry A. *The War in the Air.* 7 vols. Oxford: Clarendon, 1922–1937.

Kavanagh, P. J., ed. *Collected Poems of Ivor Gurney.* Oxford: Oxford Univ. Press, 1982.

Keegan, John. *A History of Warfare.* New York: Alfred A. Knopf, 1993.

Kelley, Alice van Buren. *The Novels of Virginia Woolf: Fact and Vision.* Chicago: Univ. of Chicago Press, 1973.

Kennard, Jean E. *Vera Brittain and Winifred Holtby: A Working Partnership.* Hanover N.H.: Univ. Press of New England, 1989.

Kennett, Lee. *A History of Strategic Bombing.* New York: Scribner's, 1982.

Kenney, Susan M. "Two Endings: Virginia Woolf's Suicide and *Between the Acts*." *University of Toronto Quarterly* 44 (Summer 1975): 265–89.

Kierkegaard, Søren. *The Concept of Anxiety. A Simple Psychologically Orienting Deliberation on the Dogmatic Issue of Hereditary Sin.* 1844. Edited, and translated by Reidar Thomte. Princeton: Princeton Univ. Press, 1980.

——. *The Concept of Irony. With Continual Reference to Socrates.* 1840. Edited and translated by Howard V. Hong and Edna H. Hong. Princeton: Princeton Univ. Press, 1989.

——. *The Sickness unto Death. A Christian Psychological Exposition for Edification and Awakening by Anti-Climacus.* 1849. Translated by Alastair Hannay. London: Penguin, 1989.

"Killed in Action." *Times of London,* 26 Apr. 1915, 1.

Kirkpatrick, B. J. *A Bibliography of Virginia Woolf.* 3d ed. Oxford, England: Clarendon, 1980.

Knight, Lynn. "Introduction" to *We That Were Young,* by Irene Rathbone, ix–xxv. New York: Feminist Press, 1989.

Knightley, Phillip. *The First Casualty. From the Crimea to Vietnam: The War Correspondent as Hero, Propagandist, and Myth Maker.* New York: Harcourt Brace Jovanovich, 1975.

Knox-Shaw, Peter. "'To the Lighthouse': The Novel as Elegy." *English Studies in Africa: A Journal of the Humanities.* 29, no. 1 (1986): 31–52.

Laing, R. D. *The Divided Self: An Existential Study in Sanity and Madness.* 1959. London: Penguin, 1965.

Laskowski, William E. *Rupert Brooke.* New York: Twayne, 1994.

"Last Night's Air Raid." *Times of London,* 2 Oct. 1917, 7.

Laurence, Patricia Ondek. *The Reading of Silence: Virginia Woolf in the English Tradition.* Stanford: Stanford Univ. Press, 1991.

Lavin, J. A. "The First Editions of Virginia Woolf's *To the Lighthouse*." In *Proof: The Yearbook of American Bibliographical and Textual Studies,* vol. 2, edited by Joseph Katz, 185–211. Columbia, S.C.: Univ. of South Carolina Press, 1972.

Law Reports. *The Public General Statutes,* vols. 52–54, 56, 58. London: Eyre and Spottiswoode, 1915–16, 1919, 1921.

Leaska, Mitchell. "Virginia Woolf, the Pargeter: A Reading of *The Years*." *Bulletin of the New York Public Library* 80 (Winter 1977): 172–210.

——. *Virginia Woolf's Lighthouse: A Study in Critical Method.* New York: Columbia Univ. Press, 1970.

——, ed. *The Pargiters: The Novel-Essay Portion of "The Years."* (See Woolf, Virginia. *The Pargiters.*)

——. *Pointz Hall: The Earlier and Later Typescripts of Between the Acts.* (See "Woolf, Virginia. *Pointz Hall.*")

Lee, Hermione. *Virginia Woolf.* New York: Alfred A. Knopf, 1997.

Leed, Eric J. *No Man's Land: Combat and Identity in World War I*. Cambridge: Cambridge Univ. Press, 1979.

Lehmann, John. *Rupert Brooke: His Life and His Legend*. London: Weidenfeld and Nicolson, 1980.

Levenback, Karen L. "Placing the First 'Enormous Chunk' Deleted from *The Years*." *Virginia Woolf Miscellany* 42 (Spring 1994): 8–9.

———. "Tradition and Transition." Review of *Virginia Woolf and the Real World* by Alex Zwerdling. *Modern Age* 32 (Spring 1988): 169–72.

———. "Virginia Woolf and Returning Soldiers: The Great War and the Reality of Survival in *Mrs. Dalloway* and *The Years*." *Woolf Studies Annual* 2(1996): 71–88.

———. "Virginia Woolf and Rupert Brooke: Poised Between Olympus and the 'Real World.'" *Virginia Woolf Miscellany* 33 (Fall 1989): 5–6.

Levesque-Lopman, Louise. *Claiming Reality: Phenomemology and Women's Experience*. Totowa, N.J.: Rowman and Littlefield, 1988.

Liddington, Jill. *The Road to Greenham Common: Feminism and Anti-Militarism in Britain Since 1820*. New York: Syracuse Univ. Press, 1989.

Lifton, Robert Jay. *Death in Life. Survivors of Hiroshima*. New York: Random House, 1967.

———, and Eric Olson. *Living and Dying*. New York: Praeger, 1974.

Lilienfeld, Jane. "'The Deceptiveness of Beauty': Mother Love and Mother Hate in *To the Lighthouse*." *Twentieth Century Literature* 23, no. 3(1977): 345–76.

———. "Where the Spear Plants Grew: The Ramsays' Marriage in *To the Lighthouse*." In *New Feminist Essays on Virginia Woolf*, edited by Jane Marcus, 148–69. Lincoln: Univ. of Nebraska Press, 1981.

Lipking, Joanne. "Looking at Monuments: Woolf's Satiric Eye." *Bulletin of the New York Public Library* 80 (Winter 1977): 141–45.

Litman, Robert E. "Sigmund Freud on Suicide." *Essays in Self-Destruction*, edited by Edwin S. Shneidman, 324–44. New York: Science House, 1967.

Little, Judy. *Comedy and the Woman Writer: Woolf, Spark, and Feminism*. Lincoln: Univ. of Nebraska Press, 1983.

Longenbach, James. "The Women and Men of 1914." In *Arms and the Woman: War, Gender, and Literary Representation*, edited by Helen M. Cooper, Adrienne Auslander Munich, and Susan Merrill Squier, 97–123. Chapel Hill: Univ. of North Carolina Press, 1989.

"Loss of the Formidable." *Times of London*, 2 Jan. 1915, 9.

Macaulay, Rose. *Catchwords and Claptrap*. London: Hogarth Press, 1926.

———. "The New London since 1914." *Current History: A Monthly Magazine* 24(May 1926): 171–80.

———. *Non-Combatants and Others*. London: Methuen, 1916.

———. *Potterism: A Tragi-Farcical Tract*. London: W. Collins, 1920.

Macdonald, Lyn. *The Roses of No Man's Land*. 1980. New York: Atheneum, 1989.

Majumdar, Robin, and Allen McLaurin, eds. *Virginia Woolf: The Critical Heritage.* London: Routledge and Kegan Paul, 1975.

Malcolm, Norman. "Memory and the Past." In his *Knowledge and Certainty,* 187–221. Englewood Cliffs: Prentice-Hall, 1963.

Mallon, Thomas. *A Book of One's Own: People and Their Diaries.* New York: Ticknor and Fields, 1984.

Marcus, Jane. "Afterword: The Nurse's Text: Acting Out an Anaesthetic Aesthetic." In *We That Were Young,* by Irene Rathbone, 467–98. New York: Feminist Press, 1989.

——. "The Asylums of Antaeus: Women, War, and Madness—Is there a Feminist Fetishism?" In *The New Historicism,* edited by H. Aram Veeser, 132–51. New York: Routledge, 1989.

——. "Corpus/Corps/Corpse: Writing the Body in/at War." In *Arms and the Woman: War, Gender, and Literary Representation,* edited by Helen M. Cooper, Adrienne Auslander Munich, and Susan Merrill Squier, 124–67. Chapel Hill: Univ. of North Carolina Press, 1989.

——. "'No More Horses': Virginia Woolf on Art and Propaganda." *Women's Studies* 4 (1977): 265–89.

——. "Pargeting 'The Pargiters': Notes of an Apprentice Plasterer." *Bulletin of the New York Public Library* 80 (Spring 1977): 416–35.

——, *The Young Rebecca: Writings of Rebecca West 1911–17.* Bloomington: Indiana Univ. Press, 1982.

——, ed. *New Feminist Essays on Virginia Woolf.* Lincoln: Univ. of Nebraska Press, 1981.

Martin, Kingsley. *The British Public and the General Strike.* London: Hogarth Press, 1926.

Marwick, Arthur. *Britain in Our Century: Images and Controversies.* New York: Thames and Hudson, 1985.

——. *The Deluge: British Society and the First World War.* Boston: Little, Brown: 1965.

Massie, Robert K. *Dreadnought: Britain, Germany, and the Coming of the Great War.* 1991. New York: Ballantine, 1992.

Massis, Henri. "The War We Fought." Translated by Sally Abeles. In *Promise of Greatness,* edited by George A. Panichas, 273–84.

McIntyre, Colin. *Monuments of War: How to Read a War Memorial.* London: Robert Hale, 1990.

McLaurin, Allen. *Virginia Woolf: The Echoes Enslaved.* Cambridge, England: Cambridge Univ. Press, 1973.

Mellor, Adrian, Chris Pawling, and Colin Sparks. "Writers and the General Strike." In *The General Strike,* by Margaret Morris, 338–58. Harmondsworth, England: Penguin, 1976.

Metchim, D. Bridgman. *Our Own History of the War from a South London View.* London: Arthur H. Stockwell, 1918.

Middleton, Victoria S. *"The Years:* A Deliberate Failure." *Bulletin of the New York Public Library* 80 (Winter 1977): 158–71.

Miller, J. Hillis. "Virginia Woolf's All Souls' Day: The Omniscient Narrator in *Mrs. Dalloway.*" In *The Shaken Realist: Essays in Modern Literature in Honor of Frederick J. Hoffman,* edited by Melvin J. Friedman and John B. Vickery, 100–27. Baton Rouge: Louisiana State Univ. Press, 1970.

Ministry of Reconstruction. *Reconstruction Problems.* 38 pamphlets. Great Britain: H.M. Stationery Office, 1918–19.

Minow-Pinkney, Makiko. *Virginia Woolf and the Problem of the Subject.* New Brunswick, N.J.: Rutgers Univ. Press, 1987.

Mitchell, Major T. J., and Miss G. M. Smith. *Medical Services: Casualties and Medical Statistics of the Great War.* London: His Majesty's Stationery Office, 1931.

Montaigne, Michel de. *Complete Works.* Translated by Donald M. Frame. 1948. Stanford: Stanford Univ. Press, 1989.

Moon, Kenneth. "Where Is Clarissa? Doris Kilman in *Mrs. Dalloway.*" *CLA Journal* 23, no. 3 (Mar. 1980): 273–86; rpt., *Clarissa Dalloway,* edited by Harold Bloom, 147–57. New York: Chelsea House, 1990.

Morgenstern, Barry. "The Self-Conscious Narrator in Jacob's Room." *Modern Fiction Studies* 18 (Autumn 1972): 351–61.

Moriarty, Catherine. "The Absent Dead and Figurative First World War Memorials." *Transactions of the Ancient Monuments Society* 39 (1995): 1–40.

Morris, Joseph. *The German Air Raids on Great Britain, 1914–1918.* 1925. London: H. Pordes, 1969.

Morris, Margaret. *The General Strike.* Harmondsworth, England: Penguin, 1976.

Mortelier, Christiane. "The French Connection: Francis Carco." In *Katherine Mansfield,* edited by Roger Robinson, 137–57. Baton Rouge: Louisiana State Univ. Press, 1994.

Mosse, George L. *Fallen Soldiers: Reshaping the Memory of the World Wars.* New York: Oxford Univ. Press, 1991.

Mowat, Charles Loch. *Britain Between the Wars 1918–1940.* 1955. Boston: Beacon, 1971.

Muggeridge, Kitty, and Ruth Adam. *Beatrice Webb: A Life, 1858–1943.* New York: Alfred A. Knopf, 1967.

Mullen, John Douglas. *Kierkegaard's Philosophy: Self-Deception and Cowardice in the Present Age.* New York: Meridian, 1981.

Murry, Middleton. (See Hankin, C.A., ed. *Letters of John Middleton Murry to Katherine Mansfield.*)

Naremore, James. "Nature and History in *The Years.*" In *Virginia Woolf: Revaluation and Continuity,* edited by Ralph Freedman, 241–62. Berkeley: Univ. of California Press, 1980.

The National Inventory of War Memorials. London: Imperial War Museum, the Royal Commission on the Historical Monuments of England and the National Heritage Memorial Fund, 1998.

Niederland, William G. "Introductory Notes on the Concept, Definition, and Range of Psychic Trauma." In *Psychic Traumatization: Aftereffects in Individuals and Communities,* edited by Henry Krystal and William G. Niederland, 1–9. Boston: Little, Brown, 1971.

Northcliffe, Lord. *At the War.* London: Hodder and Stoughton, 1917.

Ouditt, Sharon. *Fighting Forces: Writing Women, Identity, and Ideology in the First World War.* London: Routledge, 1994.

"Our Booking Office." *Punch, or the London Charivari* 151 (20 Sept. 1916): 212.

Oxford English Dictionary. (See *Compact Edition of the Oxford English Dictionary.*)

Panichas, George A., ed. *Promise of Greatness: The War of 1914–1918.* New York: John Day, 1968.

Parker, Peter. *The Old Lie: The Great War and the Public School Ethos.* London: Constable, 1987.

Pelling, Henry. *A History of British Trade Unionism.* Baltimore: Penguin, 1963.

———. *A Short History of the Labour Party.* 2d ed. London: Macmillan, 1965.

Petrie, Sir Charles. "Fighting the First World War in London." In *Promise of Greatness,* edited by George A. Panichas, 259–70. New York: John Day, 1968.

Phillips, Kathy J. *Virginia Woolf Against Empire.* Knoxville: Univ. of Tennessee Press, 1994.

Pippett, Aileen. *The Moth and the Star: A Biography of Virginia Woolf.* 1953. Boston: Little, Brown, 1958.

Poole, Roger. "Indirect Communication 1. Hegel, Kierkegaard, and Sartre." *New Blackfriars* 47 (July 1966): 532–41.

———. "Kierkegaard on Irony." *New Blackfriars* 48 (Feb. 1967): 245–49.

———. *The Unknown Virginia Woolf.* 3d ed. Atlantic Highlands, N.J.: Humanities Press, 1990.

———. *The Unknown Virginia Woolf,* 4th ed. New York: Cambridge Univ. Press, 1995.

———. "'We All Put Up with You Virginia': Irreceivable Wisdom about War." *Virginia Woolf and War,* edited by Mark Hussey: 79–100. Syracuse: Syracuse University Press, 1991.

Radin, Grace. "'I Am Not a Hero': Virginia Woolf and the First Version of *The Years.*" *Massachusetts Review* 16 (Winter 1975): 195–208.

———. "'Two Enormous Chunks': Episodes Excluded during the Final Revisions of *The Years.*" *Bulletin of the New York Public Library* 80 (Winter 1977): 221–51.

———. *Virginia Woolf's "The Years": The Evolution of a Novel.* Knoxville: Univ. of Tennessee Press, 1981.

Raitt, Suzanne, and Trudi Tate, eds. *Women's Fiction and the Great War.* Oxford: Clarendon Press, 1997.

Rathbone, Irene. *We That Were Young.* 1932. New York: Feminist Press, 1989.

Ray, William. *Literary Meaning: From Phenomemology to Deconstruction.* 1984. New York: Blackwell, 1986.

Reconstruction Problems. (See Ministry of Reconstruction.)

Reid, Panthea. *Art and Affection: A Life of Virginia Woolf.* New York: Oxford Univ. Press, 1996.

———. "On Writing Yet Another Biography of Virginia Woolf." *Virginia Woolf Miscellany* 46 (Fall 1995): 6.

Remarque, Erich Maria. *All Quiet on the Western Front.* Translated by A. W. Wheen. 1928. New York: Fawcett Crest, 1958.

Report of the War Office Committee of Inquiry into "Shell-Shock." London: His Majesty's Stationery Office, 1922.

Richter, Harvena. *Virginia Woolf: The Inward Voyage.* Princeton: Princeton Univ. Press, 1970.

Ricks, Christopher, ed. *The Poems of Tennyson.* 3 vols. 1969. Essex, England: Longman, 1987.

Robinson, Roger, ed. *Katherine Mansfield: In From the Margin.* Baton Rouge: Louisiana State Univ. Press, 1994.

Roe, Sue, ed. *Jacob's Room.* (See Woolf, Virginia. *Jacob's Room.*)

Rose, Phyllis. *Woman of Letters: A Life of Virginia Woolf.* San Diego: Harcourt Brace Jovanovich, 1978.

Ruddick, Sara. "Notes Toward a Feminist Peace Politics." In *Gendering War Talk,* edited by Miriam Cooke and Angela Woollacott, 109–27. Princeton: Princeton Univ. Press, 1993.

"Rumour and Suicide/A Sad Story of Village Life." *Times of London,* 19 Jan. 1915: 5.

Ruotolo, Lucio P. *The Interrupted Moment: A View of Virginia Woolf's Novels.* Stanford: Stanford Univ. Press, 1986.

———, ed. *Freshwater: A Comedy.* (See Woolf, Virginia. *Freshwater.*)

Russell, Bertrand. *Analysis of Mind.* New York: Macmillan, 1921.

———. *The Autobiography of Bertrand Russell: The Middle Years—1914–1944.* Boston: Little, Brown, 1968.

Sainsbury, Peter. *Suicide in London: An Ecological Study.* London: Butler and Tanner, 1955.

Salmon, Thomas W. *The Care and Treatment of Mental Diseases and War Neuroses ("Shell Shock") in the British Army.* New York: War Work Committee of the National Committee for Mental Hygiene, 1917.

Sassoon, Siegfried. *Memoirs of a Fox-hunting Man.* 1928. London: Faber and Faber, 1960.

———. *Memoirs of an Infantry Officer.* 1930. London: Faber and Faber, 1965.

———. *Sherston's Progress.* 1936. London: Faber and Faber, 1983.

Scarry, Elaine. *The Body in Pain: The Making and Unmaking of the World.* 1985. New York: Oxford Univ. Press, 1987.

Schaefer, Josephine O'Brien. *The Three-fold Nature of Reality in the Novels of Virginia Woolf.* The Hague: Mouton, 1965.

Schlack, Beverly Ann. *Continuing Presences: Virginia Woolf's Use of Literary Allusion.* University Park: Pennsylvania State Univ. Press, 1979.

————. "A Freudian Look at *Mrs. Dalloway*." *Literature and Psychology* 22, no. 2 (1973): 49–58.

Schneider, Karen. "Of Two Minds: Woolf, the War, and *Between the Acts*." *Journal of Modern Literature* 16(Summer 1989): 93–112.

Seccombe, Thomas. "Preface" to *The Loom of Youth* by Alec Waugh. London: Grant Richards, 1917.

Seymour, Miranda, *Ottoline Morrell: Life on the Grand Scale*. New York: Farrar, Straus and Giroux, 1993.

Showalter, Elaine. *The Female Malady: Women, Madness, and English Culture, 1820–1980*. 1985. New York: Penguin, 1987.

Silver, Brenda R. "'Anon' and 'The Reader': Virginia Woolf's Last Essays." *Twentieth Century Literature* 25 (Fall/Winter 1979): 356–441.

Simpson, George. "Editor's Introduction: The Aetiology of Suicide." In *Suicide* by Emile Durkheim, translated by John A. Spaulding and George Simpson, 13–32. Glencoe, Ill.: Free Press,

Sinclair, May. *A Journal of Impressions in Belgium*. New York: Macmillan, 1915.

Skidelsky, Robert. *John Maynard Keynes*. Vol. 1: *Hopes Betrayed 1883–1920*. New York: Viking, 1986.

Smith, David C. *H. G. Wells: Desperately Mortal*. New Haven: Yale Univ. Press, 1986.

Sorley, Charles Hamilton. *Marlborough and Other Poems*. 4th ed. Cambridge, England: Univ. Press, 1919.

Spalding, Frances. *Vanessa Bell*. New Haven: Ticknor and Fields, 1983.

Spater, George, and Ian Parsons. *A Marriage of True Minds: An Intimate Portrait of Leonard and Virginia Woolf*. New York: Harcourt Brace Jovanovich, 1977.

Spearing, E. M. *From Cambridge to Camiers under the Red Cross*. Cambridge, England: W. Heffer and Sons, 1917.

Spotts, Frederic, ed. *Letters of Leonard Woolf*. San Diego: Harcourt Brace Jovanovich, 1989.

Squier, Susan Merrill. *Virginia Woolf and London: The Sexual Politics of the City*. Chapel Hill: Univ. of North Carolina Press, 1985.

Stansky, Peter, and William Abrahams. *Journey to the Frontier: Two Roads to the Spanish Civil War*. Chicago: Univ. of Chicago Press, 1966.

Stape, J. H. "Virginia Woolf's *Night and Day*: Dates of Composition." *Notes and Queries* 39 (June 1992): 193–94.

Statistics of the Military Effort of the British Empire During the Great War 1914–1920. London: His Majesty's Stationery Office, March 1922.

Stephen, Adrian. "The Tribunals." In *We Did Not Fight*, edited by Julian Bell, 377–92. London: Cobden-Sanderson, 1935.

Sternlicht, Sanford. *Siegfried Sassoon*. New York: Twayne, 1993.

Strachey, Lytton. *Emminent Victorians*. 1918. London: Penguin, 1986.

"Sugar Cards: Last Days for Making Application." *Times of London*, 3 Oct. 1917, 3.

[Tawney, R. H.] "Some Reflections of a Soldier." *Nation* 20 (21 Oct. 1916): 104–6.

Taylor, A. J. P. *English History 1914–1945*. New York: Oxford Univ. Press, 1970.

Tennent, R. J. *Red Herrings of 1918*. Tunbridge Wells, England: Midas Books, 1980.

Tennyson, Alfred. *The Poems of Tennyson*, edited by Christopher Ricks. 1969. Essex, England: Longman, 1987.

Terraine, John. *Impacts of War: 1914–1918*. London: Hutchinson, 1970.

Thomas, Sue. "Virginia Woolf's Septimus Smith and Contemporary Perceptions of Shell Shock." *English Language Notes* 25, no. 2 (Dec. 1987): 49–57.

Tomlinson, H. M. *All Our Yesterdays*. New York: Harper, 1930.

Tracey, Herbert, ed. *The British Press: A Survey, a Newspaper Directory, and a Who's Who in Journalism*. London: Europa [1929].

Tratner, Michael. "Figures in the Dark: Working Class Women in *To the Lighthouse*." *Virginia Woolf Miscellany* 40 (Spring 1993): 3–4.

———. *Modernism and Mass Politics: Joyce, Woolf, Eliot, Yeats*. Stanford: Stanford Univ. Press, 1995,

Trombley, Stephen. *All That Summer She Was Mad. Virginia Woolf: Female Victim of Male Medicine*. New York: Continuum, 1982.

Turner, E. S. *The Phoney War on the Home Front*. London: Michael Joseph, 1961.

Tylee, Claire M. *The Great War and Women's Consciousness: Images of Militarism and Womanhood in Women's Writing, 1914–1964*. Iowa City: Univ. of Iowa Press, 1990.

Usui, Masami. "The Female Victims of the War in *Mrs. Dalloway*." In *Virginia Woolf and War*, edited by Mark Hussey, 151–63. Syracuse: Syracuse Univ. Press, 1991.

———. "The German Raid on Scarborough in *Jacob's Room*." *Virginia Woolf Miscellany* 35 (Fall 1990): 7.

———. "A Portrait of Alexander [*sic*], Princess of Wales and Queen of England, in Virginia Woolf's *The Waves*." In *Virginia Woolf: Themes and Variations*, edited by Vara Neverow-Turk and Mark Hussey, 121–27. New York: Pace Univ. Press, 1993.

Virginia Woolf Manuscripts from the Monk's House Papers at the University of Sussex. Microfilm. 6 reels. London: Harvest Press Microfilm, 1985.

Walpole, Hugh. *The Dark Forest*. London: M. Secker, 1916.

———. *The Herries Chronicle*. London: Macmillan, 1939.

Walzer, Michael. *Just and Unjust Wars: A Moral Argument with Historical Illustrations*. 2d ed. New York: Basic Books, 1992.

Waugh, Alec. *The Loom of Youth*. With a Preface by Thomas Seccombe. 1917. London: Grant Richards, 1918.

Webb, Beatrice. *Diary of Beatrice Webb*. Vol. 4. Edited by Norman and Jeanne MacKenzie. Cambridge: Harvard Univ. Press, 1985.

———. *My Apprenticeship*. New York: Longmans, Green, 1926.

West, Anthony. *H. G. Wells: Aspects of a Life*. New York: Random House, 1984.

West, Rebecca. "Miss Sinclair's Genius." In *The Young Rebecca*, edited by Jane Marcus, 304–7. Bloomington: Indiana Univ. Press, 1982.

———. *The Return of the Soldier.* 1918, rev. 1980. New York: Carroll and Graf, 1990.

Wheal, Elizabeth-Anne, Stephen Pope, and James Taylor. *A Dictionary of the Second World War.* New York: Peter Bedrick, 1990.

Willis, J. H., Jr. *Leonard and Virginia Woolf as Publishers: Hogarth Press, 1917–41.* Charlottesville: Univ. Press of Virginia, 1992.

Winter, Jay (J. M.). "Britain's 'Lost Generation' of the First World War." *Population Studies* 31 (Nov. 1977): 449–66.

———. *The Great War and the British People.* London: Macmillan, 1986.

———. *Sites of Memory, Sites of Mourning: The Great War in European Cultural History.* Cambridge, England: Cambridge Univ. Press, 1995.

———. "Some Paradoxes of the First World War." In *The Upheaval of War: Family, Work, and Welfare in Europe, 1914–1918,* edited by Richard Wall and Jay Winter, 9–42. Cambridge, England: Cambridge Univ. Press, 1988.

Wohl, Robert. *The Generation of 1914.* Cambridge Mass.: Harvard Univ. Press, 1979.

———. "The Generation of 1914 and Modernism." *Modernism: Challenges and Perspectives,* edited by Monique Chefdor, Ricardo Quinones, and Albert Wachtel, 66–78. Urbana: Univ. of Illinois Press, 1986.

Woolf, C. N. Sidney. *Poems.* Richmond, England: Hogarth Press, 1918.

Woolf, Cecil. Letters to the author: 30 May 1991 and 20 Sept. 1995.

Woolf, Leonard. *Beginning Again: An Autobiography of the Years 1911 to 1918.* New York: Harcourt Brace Jovanovich, 1964.

———. *Downhill All the Way: An Autobiography of the Years 1919 to 1939.* New York: Harcourt Brace Jovanovich, 1967.

———. *The Journey Not the Arrival Matters: An Autobiography of the Years 1939 to 1969.* New York: Harcourt Brace Jovanovich, 1969.

———. *Letters of Leonard Woolf.* Edited by Frederic Spotts. (See "Spotts, Frederic, ed.)

Woolf, Virginia. "Art of Fiction." In *Collected Essays* 2: 51–55.

———. "The Artist and Politics." In *Collected Essays* 2: 230–32.

———. "'Before Midnight.'" In *Essays* 2: 87–88

———. *Between the Acts.* 1941. San Diego: Harcourt Brace Jovanovich, 1969.

———. "A Cambridge V.A.D." *Essays* 2: 112–14.

———. "The Cinema." *Collected Essays* 2: 268–72.

———. *Collected Essays,* edited by Leonard Woolf. 4 vols. New York: Harcourt, Brace and World, 1967.

———. *The Complete Shorter Fiction of Virginia Woolf,* edited by Susan Dick. San Diego: Harcourt Brace Jovanovich, 1985.

———. "A Death in the Newspaper." Jacob's Room Holograph 3: 61, 63. Henry W. and Albert A. Berg Collection, New York Public Library.

———. "De Quincey's Autobiography." In *Collected Essays* 4: 1–7.

———. *The Diary of Virginia Woolf.* Edited by Anne Olivier Bell. 5 vols. New York: Harcourt Brace Jovanovich, 1977–84.

———. "An Essay in Criticism." *Collected Essays* 2: 252–58.

———. *The Essays of Virginia Woolf,* edited by Andrew McNeillie. San Diego: Harcourt

Brace Jovanovich, 1986 (vol. 1, 1904–12); 1987 (vol. 2, 1912–18); 1988 (vol. 3, 1919–24).

——. *Freshwater: A Comedy.* Edited by Lucio Ruotolo. San Diego: Harcourt Brace Jovanovich, 1976.

——. "Heard on the Downs: The Genesis of Myth." In *Essays* 2: 40–42.

——. *Here and Now.* (See [The Years] Holograph. 8 vols.)

——. "The Historian and the Gibbon." In *Collected Essays* 1: 115–23.

——. "How Should One Read a Book?" In *Collected Essays* 2: 1–11.

——. "The Intellectual Imagination." In *Essays* 3: 134–36.

——. "Introductory Letter." In *Life as We Have Known It by Co-Operative Working Women,* edited by Margaret Llewelyn Davies. 1931. New York: W. W. Norton, 1975.

——. "Is This Poetry?" In *Essays* 3: 54–57.

——. *Jacob's Room.* 1922. San Diego: Harcourt Brace Jovanovich, 1950.

——. *Jacob's Room.* Edited by Sue Roe. London: Penguin, 1992.

——. Jacob's Room Holograph. 3 vols. Berg Collection. New York Public Library.

——. "Kew Gardens." In *Complete Shorter Fiction,* edited by Susan Dick, 84–89.

——. "The Leaning Tower." In *Collected Essays* 2: 162–81.

——. *The Letters of Virginia Woolf.* Edited by Nigel Nicolson and Joanne Trautmann [Banks]. 6 vols. New York: Harcourt Brace Jovanovich, 1975–80.

——. "The Mark on the Wall." In *Complete Shorter Fiction,* edited by Susan Dick, 77–83.

——. *Moments of Being.* 2d ed. Edited Jeanne Schulkind. San Diego: Harcourt Brace Jovanovich, 1985.

——. "Montaigne." In *Collected Essays* 3: 18–26.

——. "Mr. Bennett and Mrs. Brown." In *Collected Essays* 1: 319–37.

——. "Mr. Sassoon's Poems." In *Essays* 2: 119–22.

——. *Mrs. Dalloway.* 1925. San Diego: Harcourt Brace Jovanovich, 1953.

——. *Mrs. Dalloway.* New York: Modern Library, 1928.

——. "Mrs. Dalloway Manuscript." 3 vols. 1923–1925. MSS 51044–51046. British Library.

——. "Mrs. Dalloway on Bond Street." *Complete Shorter Fiction,* edited by Susan Dick, 146–53.

——. "The Narrow Bridge of Art." In *Collected Essays* 2: 218–29.

——. "The New Crusade." In *Essays* 2: 201–3.

——. *Night and Day.* 1920. New York: Harcourt Brace Jovanovich, 1948.

——. Notebook. Labeled "Book of scraps of J's R. and first version of The Hours [Mrs. Dalloway]." 6 Oct. 1922. Ms. Berg Collection, New York Public Library.

——. Notebook. Labeled "Choephori of Aeschylus." Jan. 1907. Ms. Berg Collection, New York Public Library.

——. Notebook. Labeled "Reviews 1924." Nov. 22, 1924. Ms. Berg Collection, New York Public Library.

——. "Notes on an Elizabethan Play." In *Collected Essays* 1: 54–61.

——. "The Novels of Turgenev." In *Collected Essays* 1: 247–53.

——. *The Pargiters: The Novel-Essay Portion of "The Years."* Edited by Mitchell Leaska. New York: Harcourt Brace Jovanovich, 1977.

——. "'The Park Wall.'" In *Essays* 2: 42–44.

——. *Pointz Hall: The Earlier and Later Typescripts of Between the Acts.* Edited by Mitchell A. Leaska. New York: Univ. Publications, 1983.

——. "Professions for Women." In *Collected Essays* 2: 284–89.

——. "Reminiscences." In *Moments of Being*, 28–59.

——. *Roger Fry: A Biography.* 1940. New York: Harcourt Brace Jovanovich, 1968.

——. *A Room of One's Own.* 1929. San Diego: Harcourt Brace Jovanovich, 1957.

——. "Rupert Brooke." In *Essays* 2: 277–84.

——. "A Sketch of the Past." In *Moments of Being*, 64–159.

——. "A Society." In *Complete Shorter Fiction*, edited by Susan Dick, 118–30.

——. "Sympathy." In *Complete Shorter Fiction*, edited by Susan Dick, 102–5.

——. "These Are the Plans." In *Essays* 3: 73–77.

——. "Thoughts on Peace in an Air Raid." *New Republic* 103 (21 Oct. 1940): 549–51.

——. "Thoughts on Peace in an Air Raid." In *Collected Essays* 4: 173–77.

——. *Three Guineas.* 1938. San Diego: Harcourt Brace Jovanovich, 1966.

——. *To the Lighthouse.* 1927. San Diego: Harcourt Brace Jovanovich, 1955.

——. *To the Lighthouse.* Edited by Susan Dick. Oxford, England: Blackwell, 1992.

——. *"To the Lighthouse": The Original Holograph Draft.* Edited by Susan Dick. Toronto: Univ. of Toronto Press, 1982.

——. "Two Soldier-Poets." In *Essays* 2: 269–72.

——. *The Voyage Out.* 1920. San Diego: Harcourt Brace Jovanovich, 1948.

——. "Walter Raleigh." In *Collected Essays* 1: 314–18.

——. "The War from the Street." In *Essays* 3: 3–4.

——. "War in the Village." In *Essays* 2: 291–93.

——. *The Waves.* 1931. San Diego: Harcourt Brace Jovanovich, 1959.

——. *"The Waves": The Two Holograph Drafts.* Edited by J. W. Graham. Toronto: Univ. of Toronto Press, 1976.

——. "Why?" In *Collected Essays* 2: 278–83.

——. "Why Art To-day Follows Politics." (See "The Artist and Politics.")

——. *The Years.* 1937. San Diego: Harcourt Brace Jovanovich, 1965.

——. [The Years] Holograph. 8 vols. Berg Collection. New York Public Library.

——, and Lytton Strachey. *Virginia Woolf and Lytton Strachey Letters.* Edited by Leonard Woolf and James Strachey. New York: Harcourt, Brace, 1956.

Wyllie, Robert E. *Orders, Decorations, and Insignia, Military and Civil with the History and Romance of Their Origin and a Full Description of Each.* New York: G.P. Putnam, 1921.

Zwerdling, Alex. *Virginia Woolf and the Real World.* Berkeley: Univ of California Press, 1986.

Index